DODECAPHONIC TONALITY

A New Tonal System For a New Century

JOSEPH M. KRUSH, PH.D.

© Copyright 2010, 2013, Joseph M. Krush, Ph.D.

All Rights Reserved.

No part of this book may be reproduced, stored in a retrieval system, or transmitted by any means,
electronic, mechanical, photocopying, recording,
or otherwise, without written permission
from Fideli Publishing Inc..

ISBN: 978-1-60414-675-2

This book is dedicated to Music Theorists and Composers everywhere. In particular, it is dedicated to the students of Music Theory and Composition, who will write the music of the future.

Surrey, British Columbia, Canada,
January 2013

Acknowledgements

The author wishes to acknowledge and to express great appreciation to his long-time musical friend, Claude McLean, A.R.C.T., B. Mus., M. Mus. for the dozens of hours that he spent on proofreading and making numerous suggestions for clarification.

He also wishes to express most sincere thanks to Dr. Keith Hamel, Professor of Music Theory and Composition, School of Music, University of British Columbia, for teaching him the use of his music-writing software, NoteAbility Pro, which was used for all the musical examples in this book.

Finally, he repeatedly thanks Robin Surface, President of Fideli Publishing Inc. for her patience with seemingly endless proofreading and revisions and corrections.

Table of Contents

PART ONE

CHAPTER ONE
Historical Perspective and Introduction 1

CHAPTER TWO
Musical Scales From the Middle Ages to the Present.. 6

CHAPTER THREE
The Harmonic-Melodic Octatonic Minor Scale and The Nonatonic Bi-Modal Uni-Tonal Scale
    and Their Key Signatures 19

CHAPTER FOUR
Triads and Seventh Chords and Their Analysis 28

CHAPTER FIVE
The European System of Harmonic Analysis 37

CHAPTER SIX
Mediants, Submediants, and Functionality... 45

CHAPTER SEVEN
The Fundamental Theory of Harmony 50

CHAPTER EIGHT
The Traditional Quintcircle, Related Keys, Modulation, and Change of Mode................................. 58

CHAPTER NINE
The Nonaphonic, Bi-modal Quintcircle, Related Keys, Modulation, and Semi-Modulation............ 64

CHAPTER TEN
Other Forms of Bi-Modalities 70

CHAPTER ELEVEN
More Historical Perspective and Summary 74

APPENDIX ONE
Theme and Variations — An Exercise in Nonaphonic Bi-Modality 79

APPENDIX TWO
List of Examples and Charts in Part One.. 81

APPENDIX THREE
References Cited... 84

PART TWO

CHAPTER TWELVE
The Overall Approach 87

CHAPTER THIRTEEN
Musical Acoustics and Set Theory 90

CHAPTER FOURTEEN
Rotating Quintcircles and Semi-Modulation 97

CHAPTER FIFTEEN
Compatibility of Keys 108

CHAPTER SIXTEEN
Nonaphonic, Tri-Tonal, Bi-Modal Systems 123

CHAPTER SEVENTEEN
Two Fundamental Decaphonic Bi-Modalities 129

CHAPTER EIGHTEEN
Other Decaphonic Bi-Modalities 146

CHAPTER NINETEEN
Hendecaphonic (Eleven-Tone) Systems 155

CHAPTER TWENTY
Dodecaphonic (Twelve-Tone) Systems 168

CHAPTER TWENTY-ONE
Dodecaphonic Tonality and Functionality 190

CHAPTER TWENTY-TWO
"Tonality, Atonality, Pantonality" by Rudolph Réti 197

CHAPTER TWENTY-THREE
"Twelve-Tone Tonality" by George Perle 201

CHAPTER TWENTY-FOUR
Composers of Bi-Modal Music and Psychology of Music 204

CHAPTER TWENTY-FIVE
Recapitulation and Coda 208

APPENDIX ONE
Theme and Variations — An exercise in Dodecaphonic Tonality 218

APPENDIX TWO
List of Examples and Charts in Part Two 221

APPENDIX THREE
References Cited 225

PART ONE

Uni-Tonal Nonaphonic Bi-Modality

CHAPTER ONE

Historical Perspective and Introduction

Almost all of Western Music is based on a system of heptatonic scales, that is, scales consisting of seven tones within each octave. Whether it be Church modes, or major or minor scales, one of these tones establishes itself as the tonal center, while another one assumes the position of being second in importance. We take this for granted, and do not give it a second thought. Exceptions to this are (among others) the chromatic scale, the whole-tone scale, and pentatonic scales. In all of the dodecaphonic music that has been written to date, no one tone or pair of tones ranks higher in importance than the others; hence, the music is atonal.

The oldest musical idea is to choose seven of the available twelve tones and to work within that framework. In the Middle Ages, the first heptatonic sets of notes, called modes, were established. All of these used what today are the white keys (on a keyboard) only. But they were all made different by varying the final (what we call the tonic), the ambitus (what we call the octave range) and the dominant, which was like a secondary tonal center. Over the centuries, all but two of the modes got phased out. The two that remained were the Ionian (what we call major) and the Aeolian (what we call natural minor). Since the Baroque period, the vast majority of Western Music has been written in either major or minor mode. The major scale has remained unambiguous to this day, but three forms of the minor scale have evolved: The original natural minor, the harmonic minor, and the melodic minor. When the melodic minor scale is incorporated, the fact is that nine of the twelve available tones are being used. If we were to write the melodic minor scale as shown in Example 1-1, then we could call it a nonatonic scale.

Ex. 1-1

However, that is not the way that we write this scale. In ascending form, we use the major scale, and change the third scale degree from a major third to a minor third. In descending form, we use the original Aeolian mode. So actually, we use one of two heptatonic sets, not one nonatonic set, of tones.

An invention occurs when an old idea and a new idea meet. The old idea was to choose seven of the twelve available tones. The new idea presented in this book is to invent a system in which nine of the twelve tones are used (hence, a nonaphonic system), and in which major and minor modes are combined to form bi-modality.

In Example 1-1, if we added the major third (e-natural), we would have bi-modality, but we would also have a decaphonic (ten-tone) system. This was, in fact, the original idea upon which this book was based. What happened then, though, was that ten tones turned out to be too many, because they yielded too many triads, too many seventh chords, and too many tonalities as subsets of the system. It turned out that the best number of tones to use to create the basic bi-modal system is nine.

We can derive the desired result in at least six different ways. The first way is to form a union of the major and harmonic minor scales, as shown in Example 1-2.

Ex. 1-2

The other five derivations are more interesting, and they serve to reinforce our confidence that we are doing the right thing. For this reason, Chapters Two and Three are devoted mostly to this topic.

The creation of a new nonaphonic bi-modal (major/minor) scale brings with it many challenges. A new, expanded tonal system must be constructed and defined. For one thing, we need new key signatures, and that is the topic of Chapter Three.

Right now we need to get started on the right track, and to do so we address three issues:

1. Why develop a nine-tone scale?
2. Why use bi-modality?
3. Why and how should we combine a nonaphonic system with bi-modality?

So first, why should we use 9 tones and not 8, 10, 11, or 12? The short answer to this question is that, for the basic system, eight tones are not enough, and ten tones are too many. A longer answer is that our task can be compared to that of an engineer selecting his structural materials. After all, Music Theory is, among other things, the engineering aspect of music. Scales, modes, keys, and key signatures are our raw building materials. The more thoughtfully and carefully these are selected, the finer our results will be. The ironic part is that more materials, or more "expensive" materials, do not automatically make a better choice than does a strategically chosen combination of various types of materials.

Our next question is "Why use bi-modality?" There are many excellent reasons to do so, and Music History (specifically the History of Music Theory) provides all of them. Common sense tells us that if throughout history as many as 14 different modes were used, and of these, major and (natural) minor turned out to be the only two survivors — and long-term survivors at that — it must mean that these two modes were by far the best of the lot. By "best" we mean most workable, most popular, most practical, most often used, and so on. But if we say that, then we better not dare to forget to add one stipulation: The natural minor was rarely fully satisfactory to people, and survived only because it took on enhanced, modified (harmonic and melodic) forms. This point is a very important one to us, because enhancement and modification are exactly the same two things that we are doing today.

There was no talk in the Middle Ages of relative (or tonic) major and minor keys. Not surprisingly, it was not until equal temperament was clearly established in the first half of the eighteenth century that pairing off of modes (one major and one minor) became standard practice. Due to the fact that they have the same key signature, the most common way of pairing these off has been that of a major key and its relative minor.

Still, many composers — including some of the greatest — liked, or even preferred, to pair off the Tonic Major with its own Tonic Minor. In spite of this, for some reason, something did NOT happen in Music History: NO key signatures for Tonic Major/minor were ever developed. We can speculate about possible reasons for this; here are two of them.

First, composers can — and do — use accidentals all they want. So one can write in C Major/minor (for example) and just indicate in each case whether b, e, and a are to be natural or flat. In the Middle Ages, there were no key signatures at all, and in the Renaissance, only partial key signatures were used. Only in the Baroque period did key signatures, as we know them today, evolve.

Another possible reason that bi-modal key signatures were never developed is that bi-modality was used in a specific way, namely, to determine the form of a piece. We see this in many of the works of Chopin, particularly in the short ones. Out of his 51 Mazurkas, seven are in a-minor. In all seven, the middle section is in A major, thus creating their A-B-A form. Opus 59, No. 3 is in f-sharp minor, with the middle section in F-sharp Major. And Opus 63, No. 3 is in c-sharp minor, with the middle section in D-flat Major. The same is true about his Waltz, Opus 64, No. 2. A posthumous waltz (marked "Vivace") is in e minor, with the middle section in E major.

Two other Waltzes are even more notable from the standpoint of bi-modality. Opus 34, No. 2 is in a-minor, but two sections are in A major, which gives it the form of: a-minor/A-Major/a-minor/A-major/a-minor. In the case of Opus 69, No. 2, in b-minor, the middle section is in B Major, but there is a bit more to it: While still in B major, Chopin cannot resist doing, in measures 82-94, as shown in Example 1-3.

Ex. 1-3

The seeds of bi-modality in the nineteenth and twentieth centuries, as well as the seeds from which this book grew, were sewn in works like these. Yet, for some reason, not one of Chopin's Mazurkas or Waltzes in a major key has a middle section in the tonic minor. He seemed to like to begin in "darkness" and to "turn on the lights" for the middle section only, but not to begin and end with the "lights on," and to "turn them off" only for the middle section. Nor are there any examples of A-B form in the sense of "Tonic minor-Tonic Major" or vice-versa.

So the answers to the question "Why use bi-modality?" are as follows:

1) For centuries, people have desired to pair up a major key with a minor key. By far, the most common method of doing this has been to link a major key with its relative minor. Some composers have paired up the major key with its tonic minor, but not nearly as much; others have not done so at all. There remains very much more that can be done by using bi-modality.

2) When a composer divides a piece into three (or more) sections in the form minor-Major-minor, but does not do something like Chopin did in the example above, this is not really bi-modality. It is alternating modality. The difference, of course, is that the "minor-Major-minor" form reflects the use of one mode OR the other, whereas simultaneous (or continuous) bi-modality is the use of one mode AND the other.

3) As mentioned above, the ascending form of the melodic minor scale is really the major scale with a minor (instead of major) third. This is already getting awfully close to bi-modality. Now, if we just use the Picardy Third in the last chord, the two modes become one. The potential for exploiting this partnership — much more than it has been — is tremendous.

4) We could produce a nonatonic system by adding together two major keys: A given key plus its double dominant, that is, V of V. For example, C+ plus D+ equals c-c#-d-e-f-f#-g-a-b-c. This, however, would produce tri-tonality, because it is impossible to add D+ without adding G+ as a subset in the process. Also, it is impossible to add two minor scales together and achieve a nonatonic total; at least ten tones are required, no matter what we do. This means that the only possible way to produce a nonaphonic system that is "bi-anything" is to combine a major and a minor key.

Our third and last question is: "Why and how should we combine a nonaphonic system with bi-modality?" Another way of asking this question is: "What are we doing and why are we doing it?"

What we are doing is taking two raw materials that are extremely compatible, and combining them.

Why we are doing so is because by doing so we can create an expanded — but still reasonably limited — system (or framework), that broadens our horizons, and one that we can see will enable us to create a new universe for tonal music.

The goal of this undertaking is to create, define, and present a new tonal system by pairing up a major key with its tonic minor key in a way that will enable us to write music in both these modes simultaneously. To do this, it is necessary to use a number of tones that is greater than seven. For a uni-tonal system, the number that works best is nine. This, of course, represents an expansion of heptatonic (or octatonic) scales and key signatures.

Some might ask what is considered to be of primary importance here — whether it is that the system is bi-modal or that it is nonaphonic. Other than saying that both are important, especially in combination, we can also say the following:

1) The saying "opposites attract" applies to major and minor modes. We know from reading the history of music in the Classical period that tonic and dominant were used as alternating, contrasting, keys. Of the hundreds of works written in Sonata-Allegro form, none are written by using two major keys (or two

minor keys) together. This in spite of the fact that it would have been very easy to create octatonic systems by combining tonic and dominant (for example c-d-e-f-f#-g-a-b) or tonic and subdominant (for example c-d-e-f-g-a-b♭-b), or all three, to form a tri-tonal, nonaphonic major system, as shown in Example 1-4.

Ex. 1-4

2) Once we have made up our minds that we want to create a bi-modal, uni-tonal system, what becomes important is to choose the number of tones that works best in order to achieve this. And here, something important needs to be said: "The more the better" is not true; in fact, "The less the better" is true.

In summary, the reason for creating nonaphonic bi-modality is: Because IT WORKS! It works as an expansion of tonal systems used in the entire history of music.

CHAPTER TWO

Musical Scales From the Middle Ages to the Present

Before we undertake to construct new scales, we had better take a look at the scales that already exist. The most complete list of musical scales appears to be on the Internet in Wikipedia, which devotes 51 pages to musical scales, and defines 37 of them.* These 37 are written out in Example 2-1 on the following pages, transposed (when necessary) to begin on c. They are presented in the following order:

      Pentatonic (or five-note) scales: 6 (Numbers 1-6),

      Hexatonic (or six-note) scales: 5 (Numbers 7-11),

      Heptatonic (or seven-note) scales: 19 (Numbers 12-30);
         of these 19, one is an Ancient Greek Chromatic
         Genus, and seven are Church modes,

      Octatonic (or eight-note) scales: 6 (Numbers 31-36),

      Dodecaphonic (or twelve-note) scale: 1 (Number 37).

Readers are requested now (before reading on) to take a good, long look at these. Sing them, or play them (or both), and make as many observations about them as come to mind. It is important to observe not just what is there, but also what is **not** there. The challenge here is to find the nonaphonic, bi-modal scale in the list. Hint: It is not there, as such, but it can be derived — in more ways than one. (Time out).

---

*Actually, more than 37 are described, but the rest are either not used in Western music or are otherwise not applicable to our study (for example, scales which result when the octave is divided into more than 12 parts).

Ex. 2-1 — page 1 of 6

Ex. 2-1 — page 3 of 6

Ex. 2-1 — page 4 of 6

Ex. 2-1 — page 5 of 6

1) Major Pentatonic, which equals black keys beginning on f#
2) Minor Pentatonic, which equals black keys beginning on e♭
3) Pentatonic, which equals black keys beginning on d♭
4) Pentatonic, which equals black keys beginning on a♭
5) Pentatonic, which equals black keys beginning on b♭
6) Iwato Japanese Pentatonic, which cannot be played on black keys only

7) Whole-Tone scale
8) Major Blues scale
9) Minor Blues scale
10) Augmented scale
11) Prometheus scale, which contains only and all the notes found in Scriabin's "Mystic Chord"

12) Ancient Greek Chromatic Genus
13) Ionian mode, which equals major scale
14) Dorian mode, which equals the white keys beginning on d
15) Phrygian mode, which equals the white keys beginning on e
16) Lydian mode, which equals the white keys beginning on f
17) Mixolydian mode, which equals the white keys beginning on g
18) Aeolian mode, which equals the natural minor scale
19) Locrian mode, which equals the white keys beginning on b
20) Harmonic minor scale
21) Melodic minor scale
22) Harmonic major scale
23) Major Locrian scale
24) Half-diminished scale, which equals Locrian sharp 2, which equals Aeolian flat 5

Ex. 2-1 — page 6 of 6

> 25) Gypsy Hungarian scale, which equals the Hungarian Minor scale
> 26) Gypsy Spanish scale, which equals the Phrygian Dominant scale
> 27) Acoustic scale, which equals the first seven different notes in the harmonic series
> 28) Altered scale
> 29) Arabic scale
> 30) Scala Enigmetica
>
> 31) Bebop dominant scale
> 32) Bebop Dorian scale
> 33) Bebop major scale
> 34) Bebop melodic minor scale
> 35) Octatonic scale, which equals the diminished scale beginning with "tone-semitone"
> 36) Octatonic scale, which equals the diminished scale beginning with "semitone-tone"
>
> 37) Dodecaphonic (Chromatic) scale

Very many observations can be made about these scales; so many, in fact, that this chapter would become extraordinarily long if we were to write up a detailed analysis. So only the most relevant features will be mentioned here.

In the pentatonic group, the first five scales are anhemitonic, meaning without semitones. The sixth one is hemitonic because it contains at least one (actually two) semitones. Because there are only five tones, two intervals of a major third result. These two factors combined make the scale sound uneven compared to other scales. Also, it sounds exotic (not to the Japanese, but to us).

In the hexatonic group (scales 7 to 11), scale 7 is the well-known whole-tone scale, which consists of every second note of the chromatic scale. It does not contain any perfect fifths or perfect fourths, but contains three tritones. Only augmented triads, and no seventh chords, can be formed using these six notes. So in a way, the whole-tone scale is a melodic and harmonic garbage can... Nevertheless, composers such as Debussy made beautiful use of it.

Scales 8 and 9 are jazz scales, in which d# and f# (respectively) are chromatic passing notes. If these are not used, the scales equal scales 1 and 2 respectively. Scale 10 is called the Augmented scale because it consists of two augmented triads. Scale 11 is really a list of the notes used by Scriabin to construct his quartal "Mystic Chord." The key signature is that of G Major plus F Major, even though the note g is missing.

The heptatonic group is by far the largest one, containing 19 of the 37 scales listed, so just over half. This is partly because it contains the oldest scale listed and the all-important original seven Medieval (or Ecclesiastical or Church) Modes. In scale 12, d-flat and a-flat are chromatic passing notes; if they are not used, then scale 3 results.

The seven Church Modes deserve special consideration, not just because of their historical significance, but also because we can easily establish key signatures for them, provided we indicate the tonic note, as shown in Example 2-2. (C Ionian has the key signature of C major; it is omitted here).

Incidentally, can any readers figure out the formulas used to derive the key signatures for any mode starting on any note? The answers are given at the end of this chapter.

Ex. 2-2

 14 = C Dorian, which has the key signature of the major key whose root is a major second below (B-flat major)

 15 = C Phrygian, which has the key signature of the major key whose root is a major third below (A-flat major)

 16 = C Lydian, which has the key signature of the Dominant major key, whose root is a perfect fourth below (G major)

 17 = C Mixolydian, which has the key signature of the Subdominant major key, whose root is a perfect fifth below (F major)

 18 = C Aeolian, which has the key signature of what we call its relative major key, whose root is a major sixth below (E-flat major)

 19 = C Locrian, which has the key signature of the major key whose root is a minor second above (D-flat major)

Scale 19 has to be the "perpetual disgrace" to the family of Church Modes. It contains a tritone instead of a perfect fifth above the tonic note, so the tonic triad is diminished. Also, the tonic note c clashes chromatically with the tonic note of the major key whose key signature it uses (D-flat Major). Because it has these characteristics, composers have found it extremely difficult to write a piece of music entirely in this mode.

The remaining eleven heptatonic scales are a mixture. Scales 20 and 21 are very common, but Number 22 is somewhat of a paradox. Its obvious feature is that with the sixth scale degree being lowered, the subdominant triad becomes minor and the supertonic triad becomes diminished; these, therefore, are borrowed chords. Scales 23 and 24 represent variations of scale 19. Number 23, without the f, equals number 7. Scales 25, 26, and 29 are three more examples of scales that sound exotic to us. Because they all contain augmented seconds, their steps sound uneven. Numbers 26 and 29 are the same, except for the seventh scale degree. This is not surprising if we recall the long Arabic (Moorish) occupation of Spain. Number 27 is more a list of notes than a scale. In number 28, every note, except the tonic, is flattened. Scale 30 is a "custom built" scale used by Verdi.

In the Octatonic group, scales 31 to 34 are jazz scales. Each one contains a chromatic passing note (b, e, g#, and g# respectively). If these are omitted, the resulting scales are 17, 14, 13, and 21 (ascending) respectively. Scales 35 and 36 are the octatonic scales which are sometimes called diminished scales, because if every second note is used, the result is a diminished seventh chord. These scales are the result of cross-pollination of the whole-tone scale with the chromatic scale (Number 37), in the sense that every second interval is a semitone and every other second interval is a whole tone. These three scales are all examples of symmetric scales. They also fall into the category of synthetic scales. Technically, almost any scale that a person dreams up (such as Number 30) is a synthetic scale. Scales such as these three (whole-tone, diminished, and chromatic) form a mathematical progression more than a musical one. Number 37 is really a list of all 12 available tones.

It is rather easy to make up such a scale. For example, we can readily construct a scale that proceeds in steps of 1-2-3-1-2-3 semitones, or 3-2-1-3-2-1 semitones, and call it the "1-2-3 scale," as shown in Example 2-3.

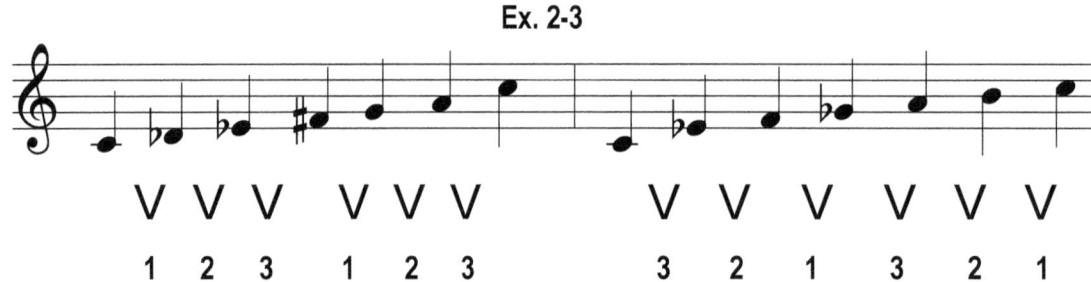

Ex. 2-3

Whether or not any composer can make practical use of this scale is another matter entirely.

Scales such as the "1-2-3 scale," the octatonic scales (Numbers 35 and 36), the whole-tone scale (Number 7), and the Locrian Mode (Number 19) suffer from many ailments. (We could really put them into an Intensive Care Unit of a Musical Hospital) … Here is why: First of all, scales that do not contain the perfect fifth, or at least the perfect fourth, (above the tonic note) make life very difficult for the composer of tonal music. Secondly, scales that contain the augmented fourth above the tonic, instead of the perfect fifth, make life doubly difficult. Thirdly, scales that proceed in augmented intervals are awkward to work with because of the gaps that these intervals create. For example, in Number 25, because e♭ is followed by f#, neither e-natural nor f-natural is available. To our Western ears, the steps of these scales sound uneven. But their exotic sound effect is wonderful.

On the other hand, in symmetrical scales, ascending or descending, the effect of finality is either poor or very poor. When the end of the scale is reached, it does not sound as if we landed (or reached a destination point). It sounds more as if someone cut off the rest of the melodic line with a pair of scissors. Incidentally, it is not what is on paper that counts; it is what the ear hears that truly counts. This is heard very clearly when we listen to the major scale and then to the whole-tone scale. In the former, the steps sound even, although they are not.* And in the latter, where the steps really are even, it does not sound like it. The interval between steps three and four sounds larger, and the whole thing sounds as if we suddenly switched keys at the half-way point.

So now, before we go on, did any readers find our nonaphonic, bi-modal scale in the list of 37? It is not there as such, but it is there three times — by derivation. The first time, it results from forming a union of scales 13 and 20, the same major and harmonic minor scales that we added in Chapter One. The second derivation comes from uniting scales 21 (ascending) and 22, that is, by combining the ascending melodic minor scale with the harmonic major scale. The third derivation is also a pairing, but it is a bit disguised, in that g# must be changed to a♭ when we add scales 33 and 34 (the Bebop major scale and the Bebop melodic minor scale). This is why it was suggested to sing or play these scales. If and when we do, it does not matter that the two g-sharps are chromatic passing notes and not written as a-flats; the resulting sound is the same. From the music theorist's viewpoint, though, spelling *does* matter; this will be discussed in the next chapter.

Now, with regard to the question of what is *not* there: Unless we combine scales as described above, there is no nonatonic scale. In fact, the only place where one can find a so-called nonatonic scale is on page 72 of the KGT (Klingon Galactic Traveler), where it says the following:

"Older Klingon music was based on a nonatonic scale — that is, one made of nine tones. Each tone has a specific name, comparable to the "do, re, mi" system used in describing music on Earth. The nine tone names are (the first and ninth, as with Earth's "do", being the same): 1. –yu 2. –blm 3. –'egh 4. –loS 5. –vagh 6. –jav 7. –Soch 8. –chorgh 9. –(yu)"

But this is **not** a nonatonic scale; it is octatonic. The Klingons don't know what they are talking about; the earth is safe! So there are really no nonatonic scales defined **yet** — on earth, or anywhere else.

There are no decatonic (ten-tone) or hendecatonic (eleven-tone) scales, either. Scale Number 37 (the chromatic scale) is dodecatonic (twelve-tone), but it is only a scale in theory. In practice, there are no key signatures for chromatic scales; nor does one write music in C-chromatic or G-chromatic, for example.

This brings us to the last point to be made about what is *not* there: Key signatures. It was shown earlier how key signatures could be defined for the seven Church modes. But what would happen if we tried to define key signatures to correspond with the other heptatonic scales? The results would be as shown in Example 2-4.

---

*This is why Julie Andrews was so successful in teaching the Von Trapp children how to sing.

16 • *Dodecaphonic Tonality*

Ex. 2-4

Some of these are fairly clear, but others are quite difficult to decipher. And these are only for C, with the tonic note indicated, at that. By the time we added transpositions, almost nobody could recognize what was what. Someone would have to compile a dictionary of key signatures.

The fact remains that scales and key signatures define the raw materials used in any piece of music. This is true even in atonal music — if we think of a tone row as the chromatic scale with its tones rearranged in a specific way. In the case of some of Bartók's unorthodox key signatures (for example, in the Mikrokosmos), these have a more practical look, such as one showing a-flat only.

Three common definitions of scales are the following:

1) The tonal material of music arranged in an order of rising pitches,

2) A related set of pitches that can be used as a compositional unit,

3) A group of musical tones that provides raw material for part or all of a musical work.

One definition of a key signature is: "A set of symbols, called sharps and flats, which define the set of tones being used in a piece of music, and hence, the key in which the piece of music is written." At least that is what a key signature is **supposed to do.** The reality is, that, in spite of the tremendous amount of music that has been written over the centuries, we have developed key signatures for only two modes: Major and Natural Minor. The key signature that is being used for Harmonic and Melodic Minor modes is actually borrowed (or stolen) from the corresponding Aeolian Mode. As Music Theorists living in 2013, we can certainly afford to create some new standardized key signatures. This is the topic of the next two chapters, and some later ones, for which the groundwork has now been laid.

Here is an afterthought for readers who noticed that the only scale of the 37 listed in Example 2-1 that is different descending than ascending is scale 21, the melodic minor scale. People can argue that the melodic minor scale had to be invented in order to avoid the presence of an augmented second. But we can also argue that it did not. There **is** a way around it, as shown in Example 2-5.

Ex. 2-5

There. No augmented second. Happy now?

* * *

You can figure out the key signature in your head for any mode starting on any note, if you memorize the following formula: First, consider the location of the white-key-only mode (having a blank key signature) compared to c. Then proceed the same interval in the **opposite** direction. The key signature is that of the major key of the note on which you landed. The point is, that everything always has to balance out evenly.

EXAMPLE:

1) The Dorian mode using white keys only begins on d, which is a major second **above** c. So the key signature for x Dorian is that of the major key whose root is a major second **below** x. So f# Dorian has the key signature of E major.

2) The Phrygian mode using white keys only begins on e, which is a major third **above** c. So the key signature for x Phrygian is that of the major key whose root is a major third **below** x. So b Phrygian has the key signature of G major.

3) The Lydian mode using white keys only begins on f, which is a perfect fourth **above** c. So the key signature for x Lydian is that of the major key whose root is a perfect fourth **below** x. So A-flat Lydian has the key signature of E-flat Major.

4) The Mixolydian mode using white keys only begins on g, which is a perfect fifth **above** c. So the key signature for x Mixolydian is that of the major key whose root is a perfect fifth **below** x. So E-flat Mixolydian has the key signature of A-flat Major.

5) The Locrian mode using white keys only begins on b, which is a minor second **below** c. So the key signature for x Locrian is that of the major key whose root is a minor second **above** x. So e Locrian has the key signature of F major.

CHAPTER THREE

The Harmonic-Melodic Octatonic Minor Scale and The Nonatonic Bi-Modal Uni-Tonal Scale and Their Key Signatures

The evolution of minor scales in music is well-known. Because the Medieval Aeolian mode was almost never completely satisfactory to people, due to its lack of a leading note, the harmonic minor scale was born. So the leading note was gained, but then the resulting augmented second between the sixth and seventh scale degrees was deemed to be unacceptable, so the melodic minor scale evolved. Ironically, its descending form reverted back to the Aeolian mode. Nevertheless, no matter which form of the minor scale is used, the same key signature (that of the relative major key) has been retained to this day.

In the meantime, again ironically, someone invented the Harmonic Major scale by lowering the sixth scale degree, thus creating the very same augmented second that poses a problem in the harmonic minor scale. Perhaps some people would describe this whole picture as craziness. But for us, trying to construct a bi-modal (and, for now, also uni-tonal) system, this is wonderful, because it proves that the major and minor modes have been swapping tones with each other for a very long time. All that we have to do now is to get the two of them to unite and to join forces.

Minor keys suffer from three ailments: 1) either the lack of a leading note or the presence of an augmented second, 2) alternating raised and lowered scale degrees, and 3) key signatures that do not strictly identify the set of tones being used, as do the key signatures of major keys. In this chapter, we start by presenting one possible method of achieving standardization of the minor scale and its key signature. It meets the objective, which is to design a key signature that differs from that of the relative major key, but still relates to it, while at the same time specifying the differences between the two.

If we use the key of c minor for examples, then, strictly speaking, the three flats of E-flat Major are valid only for c Natural Minor. If key signatures for minor keys were truly to reflect the set of tones being used, then the key signature of c harmonic minor would be b-natural, e-flat and a-flat, and that of c melodic minor would be b-flat/b-natural, e-flat, a-flat/a-natural, in which the slash would stand for "and/or," as in Mr./Mrs. Smith.

We know that E-flat Major, c Natural Minor, and c Harmonic Minor use a set of seven tones each (although not the same seven), and c Melodic Minor makes use of nine tones. But the fact is that it is possible to employ eight tones, and thus to produce a compromise between the harmonic and melodic minor scales. The key signature for c minor then becomes b-natural, e-flat, a-flat, and a-natural alternate, as indicated in Example 3-1 on the next page.

Ex. 3-1

c–

This is an example of musical shorthand that means:

> **"The b-flat of the relative major key is changed to b-natural in order to create the leading note; the e-flat and a-flat are retained, and a-natural (in brackets) is used as a substitute for a-flat, whenever it is needed in order to eliminate the augmented second."**

Readers are not requested to memorize much of the contents of this book, but the above *pattern* (which applies to all flat minor keys) *and its interpretation,* should be memorized.

Because the order of flats is carved in stone, since e-flat and a-flat are present, we must explain what happened to that b-flat and why! Also, we must indicate that a-flat is the norm and a-natural is the exception, and why. This is why it is very helpful to introduce natural signs and brackets into key signatures.

The scale that corresponds with this designation is an octatonic scale that includes the minor third, both major and minor sixths, but only the major (not minor) seventh, as shown in Example 3-2.

Ex. 3-2

It is also extremely easy to derive this scale from the octatonic scale that begins with a whole tone and proceeds in alternating whole tones and semitones, as shown in Example 3-3. All that we have to do is to change the tritone above the tonic to a perfect fifth.

Ex. 3-3

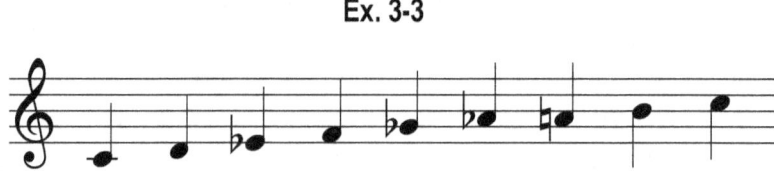

In minor keys whose key signatures contain sharps, these will have a slightly different appearance, but will still show the same three characteristics. For example, the key signature for f-sharp minor will look as shown in Example 3-4.

Ex. 3-4

f#–

This again is musical shorthand that means:

> "The key signature of the relative major key is retained. The minor sixth is the norm and the major sixth is shown (in brackets) because it is used as the alternative, when necessary, in order to eliminate the augmented second. The third remains minor because the mode is minor. The e-sharp is introduced as the leading note."

Here again, readers should memorize this *pattern and its interpretation*, because it is applicable to all sharp keys. The order of sharps is also carved in stone, so because e-sharp is present, we must account for the "a" that precedes it.

Two more observations can be made about this pattern. First, the relationship of the three sharps of the Relative Major (and of f# natural minor) to the six sharps of F-sharp Major is clearly visible, and this is a desirable feature. Second, one can easily tell that the scale is octatonic, and how it was made so, by the two d's indicated.

The key signatures for all 12 octatonic minor keys, plus one enharmonic key, are written out in Example 3-5. In both sharp and flat keys, the two sixths and the leading note are always spelled out in the key signature. In the sharp keys, the key signature of the Relative Major key comes first, and in the flat keys it is visible "in the background," so to speak. Perhaps adults do not need everything spelled out for them so blatantly, but most people learn key signatures as children, and children should be able to learn and to understand minor keys faster and better if this is explained to them.

Ex. 3-5

NOTE: In case any reader's head is spinning after reading this last one, the key signature for g# natural minor is five sharps, the same as that of B Major. But when we raise the seventh scale degree to form the leading note, f-sharp becomes f double-sharp. Once again, in traditional key signatures of minor keys, the leading note is never indicated; in these key signatures, it always is.

The melodic and harmonic consequences of standardization of minor scales and their key signatures by using the eight selected tones are fairly numerous, considerable, and beneficial, as listed in Example 3-6, this time using the key of a-minor.

Ex. 3-6 — Figure 1 of 2

Melodic

a) The augmented second disappears because f-sharp is placed between f-natural and g-sharp,

b) The scale is octatonic and, as such, it requires two forms of one scale degree, in this case, the sixth one,

c) It is not necessary to use g-natural, the minor seventh, at all,

d) The scale is both harmonic and melodic. It is harmonic because g-sharp is present. It is melodic because f-sharp is present, even though it follows f-natural,

e) The traditional descending melodic minor, which is the same as the descending Aeolian mode (or natural minor) is gone,

Ex. 3-6 — figure 2 of 2

a-:   i   ii°   ii°⁷   ii⁷   ii⁷   -   III⁺   iv   iv⁷   IV   -

C+:   vi   vii°   vii°⁷   -   -   ̸   -   ii   ii⁷   V   V⁷
                                              of V of V

a-:   -   -   V   V⁷$\begin{bmatrix}13\\11\\9\end{bmatrix}$ VI   -   -   -   -   vii°   vii°⁷   viiø⁷

C+:   ̸iii   ̸iii⁷   V   V⁷$\begin{bmatrix}13\\11\\9\end{bmatrix}$ IV   vii°   vii°⁷   ̸   ̸⁷   -   -   -
      of   of   of   of
      vi   vi   V   V

f) The first five notes of the scale remain unchanged. In the upper tetrachord, the presence of f-natural ensures that the sound is not totally major, and the absence of g-natural prevents it from being totally chromatic,

g) The steps of this scale sound perfectly even and equal.

Harmonic

a) Since g-natural is excluded, the following chords belonging to the relative major key are automatically excluded also: I, iii, iii^7, V, V^7 (crossed out in the example),

b) There is only one g, and it is g-sharp. As soon as it disappears and g-natural is introduced, the key changes to C Major,

c) There is no natural minor, so there is no minor dominant triad,

d) There are two different supertonic triads and two different supertonic seventh chords. The same is true of the subdominant, but when the minor seventh is added to the major subdominant triad, the resulting chord takes on a dominant function, as it becomes V^7 of V in the relative major, C,

e) Dominant sevenths, ninths, elevenths, and thirteenths remain unchanged, with one exception. The dominant major ninth is available, but should not be used in a minor key.

At this point, our job of constructing the nonatonic, bi-modal, uni-tonal scale is actually almost finished. Designing the standardized minor scale and its key signature was the longest part of the project. Now, all that is left for us to do is the obvious: We just add the major third of the major mode; all the other notes belonging to the major mode are already there. This is the fourth derivation of our nonatonic, bi-modal scale.

The twelve nonatonic bi-modal, uni-tonal scales, plus one enharmonic one, are written out in Example 3-7 on the next page.

24 • *Dodecaphonic Tonality*

Ex. 3-7

Now we have to write out the corresponding key signatures; this is done in Example 3-8 on the next page.

Ex. 3-8

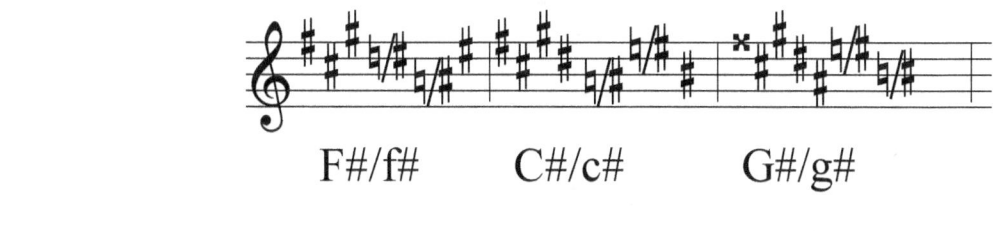

Readers should memorize this *pattern* also. Memorizing it should be easy, if the following comparisons to standardized octatonic minor key signatures are borne in mind:

1) **Octatonic minor scales contain the minor third only. They contain the minor sixth, as minor scales always have, plus the alternate major sixth (in brackets). Nonatonic bi-modal scales contain both major and minor thirds and both major and minor sixths.**

2) **Octatonic minor scales have the major sixth (in brackets) because it is an alternative to the minor sixth, not a passing note. Nonatonic bi-modal scales use the slash between the two thirds and between the two sixths. The slash means "and/or." All the notes are diatonic; none are passing notes.**

Because the order of sharps is opposite to the order of flats, and this order must always be retained, it is impossible to get all the key signatures to "look alike" in all respects. In print, we always write the major (upper-case) letter first, then the slash, followed by the minor (lower-case) letter, for example, C/c. In the key signatures, the appearance varies between flat and sharp keys. The most confusing are the first two, because they include both flats and sharps, which is something new. In D/d, the order looks reversed. In G/g, the leading note of both (and the key signature of G) appears last. In C/c, the key signature of C is indicated by the e-natural. In the next four cases, the order looks consistent.

In the sharp keys, the key signature for a-minor is indicated by the c-natural. In the rest of them, the key signature for the tonic minor key appears first. It has to be that way, because the extra three sharps needed for the tonic major key come "later." For example, for E+, we add c#, g#, and d# to the f# that is already present in e-. For C#+, we add the three sharps that follow the four sharps of c#-.

Our first four derivations of the Nonatonic bi-modal scale were all melodic, and were all achieved by addition. There is a fifth melodic derivation, and it is done by progressive addition, and one subtraction. If we begin with the Aeolian mode, we first add the leading note, and subtract the minor seventh. Then we add the major sixth, which gives us our standardized octatonic minor scale. Finally, we add the major third.

But there is also a harmonic derivation of the Nonatonic, bi-modal scale, and it is done all in one shot. We simply take the Tonic, Subdominant, and Dominant triads of both modes, and add up all the notes, as shown in Example 3-9. (Duplicates are indicated in quarter notes). This is our sixth derivation.

Ex. 3-9

* * *

Now that the task designated for this chapter has been completed, we can conclude our study of scales and key signatures by briefly considering a related subject.

Whether performers like it or not (and, unfortunately, many hate it)! music in print is a highly mathematical subject. It would not be unreasonable to offer at least one course, covering some specific aspects of Music Theory, in University Departments of Mathematics. In our study, it is most appropriate to touch upon the mathematical topic of Set Theory.

When reading Allen Forte's "The Structure of Atonal Music," we learn that he begins by defining sets of tones by using integers, beginning with zero. So if zero is c, then one is c# or d♭, two is d, three is d# or e♭, four is e, and so on. The set [0,3,7] equals c, e♭, g, and [0,4,7] equals c, e, g. This system suits serialists well, because it is appropriate to describe sets of atonal notes in this way, where the spelling of tones makes no difference. (The three notes b-sharp, d-double-sharp and f-double-sharp would also be designated as [0,4,7], and the three notes b-sharp, d-sharp, and g, would also be equal to [0,3,7]).

We have much to gain by applying principles of Set Theory to Tonal music as well, and we will use them to some extent in our study. After all, the 37 scales discussed in Chapter Two are all sets of tones, are they not? However, in the case of Tonal music, with its scales, keys, enharmonics, accidentals, key signatures, altered tones, blue notes, raised or lowered sixth and sevenths, relative major and minor keys, tonic major and minor keys, and so on, if we are to use Set Theory, then the system that we use has to be appropriate for Tonal music.

To serialists, enharmonics are not distinct objects; to us, they almost always are. So our rule is: Spelling IS important. To give just one example, g-sharp does not equal a-flat; the former is the leading note of A major and a-minor, and the latter is the diatonic sixth scale degree in c minor and a lowered sixth in C major. Readers can list (collectively) several dozen other examples of their own. The point is that the Bebop Melodic Minor scale (Number 34 in Chapter Two) may *sound* the same as our standardized octatonic minor scale, but it is not the same scale.

In Tonal music, we must "Write What We Mean, and Mean What We Write." Inaccuracies are unacceptable in Set Theory. And in computer language, there is no ambiguity, either, and our students are growing up in the age of computers. This is why the key signatures that we use should also be unambiguous, and should reflect exactly, 100% accurately, the set of tones that is being used. That is one of our goals in this chapter and beyond.

CHAPTER FOUR

Triads and Seventh Chords and Their Analysis

Let us begin by building diatonic triads on each scale degree and see what results in Example 4-1.

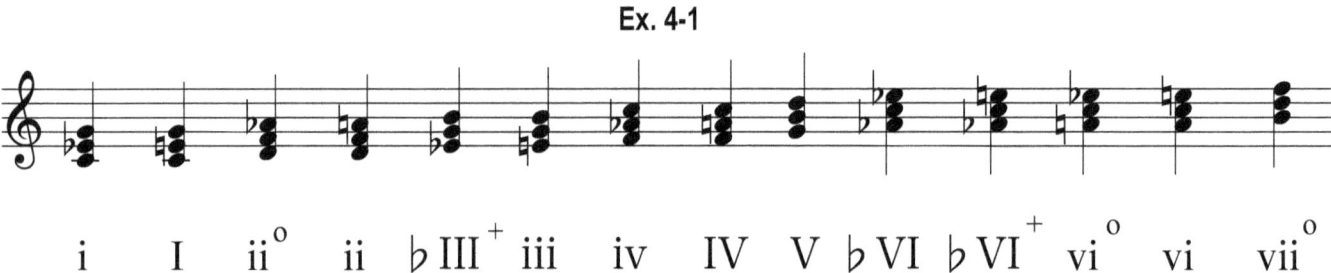

The total number of possible combinations is 14. The tonic and subdominant appear in major and minor forms. The supertonic appears also in two forms, but these are minor and diminished. The dominant and leading-note triads appear in only one form — major and diminished respectively. The vii° triad defines the key because b and f are both natural.

So far, we have eight triads. But now, we encounter two forms of the mediant triad (augmented and minor) and all four forms of the submediant triad (major, augmented, diminished, and minor). This is, comparatively speaking, a very large proportion — almost half — of the 14 triads. For this reason, these will have to be examined more closely later. First, however, let us build seventh chords on each scale degree and see what happens (in Example 4-2). It turns out that 17 different chords are possible. So now, the composer has 31 different triads and seventh chords from which to choose.

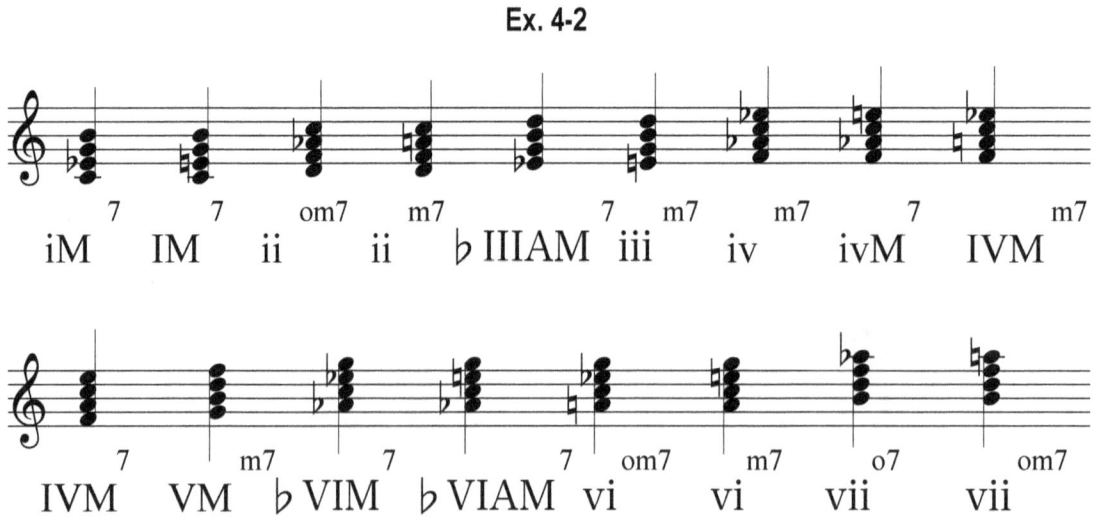

This is great in theory, in that it provides us with a greatly expanded harmonic vocabulary. However, from the point of view of functionality, practicality, and usefulness, it is not entirely so. We have some sorting to do, and one way to approach it is by functions.

Ex. 4-3: Tonic

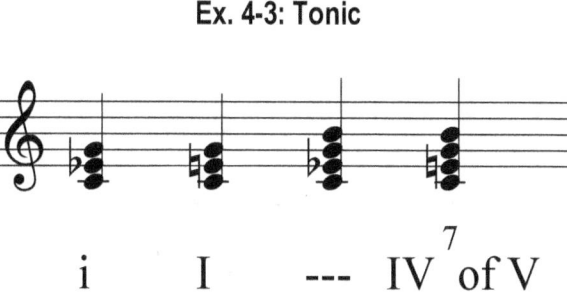

i   I   ---   IV^7 of V

The major and minor tonic triads are what make this system bi-modal. The first seventh chord does not work as a primary function of any kind, because there is no tonic, dominant, or subdominant chord that contains e-flat but no b-flat. The second seventh chord works as a subdominant function — of the dominant. This will be explained more clearly later.

Ex. 4-4: Dominant

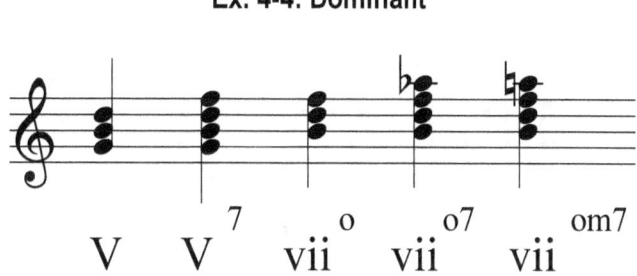

V   V^7 vii$^\circ$ vii$^{\circ 7}$ vii$^{\circ m7}$

All five dominant triads and seventh chords have a dominant function. The vii° triad is actually V^7 with the root omitted. The vii°^{7} and vii°^{m7} are dominant ninths (minor and major respectively) with the root omitted.

Ex. 4-5: Subdominant

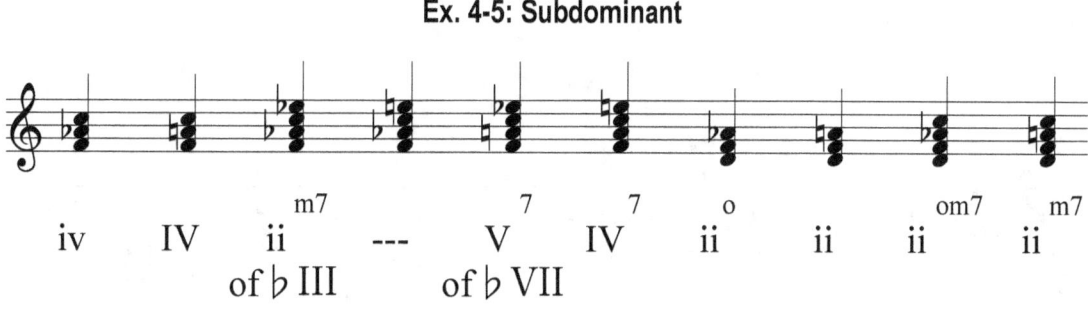

iv   IV   ii^{m7} of ♭III   ---   V^7 of ♭VII   IV^7 ii$^\circ$ ii   ii^{om7} ii^{m7}

All subdominant and supertonic triads have a subdominant function. Of the six seventh chords derived from these triads, five have functionality, but one (the second one) does not. Here again, there is no subdominant chord that contains a-flat but no e-flat. The third seventh chord shown is V^7 of B-flat major or minor. But there is no b-flat in the C major/minor nonatonic scale. So this chord will be used only in modulation.

30 • *Dodecaphonic Tonality*

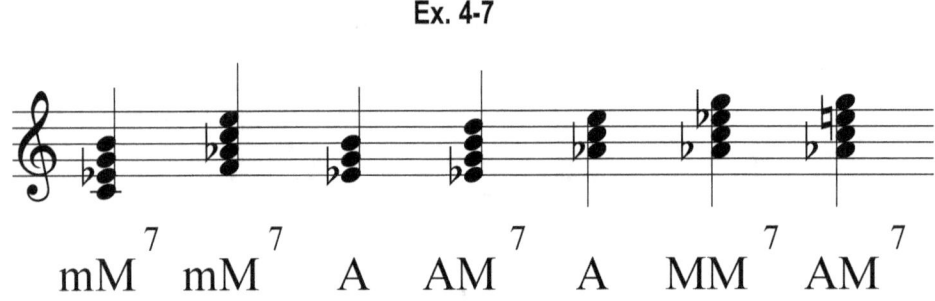

Ex. 4-6: Mediant and Submediant

Here, four of the triads have some kind of functionality, while two do not. Also, three of the seventh chords have some kind of functionality and three do not. Mediants, Submediants, and Functionality is the topic of Chapter Six.

ANALYSIS

Let us first take a look at Example 4-7, which shows all seven of the triads and seventh chords that were left without harmonic symbols.

Ex. 4-7

Both triads are augmented. Of the five seventh chords, two are mM⁷, one is MM⁷, and two are AM⁷. The two augmented triads can have a dominant function, but only in a specific inversion and used in a specific way. When the fourth scale degree is added, these are known as Dominant thirteenth chords. The thirteenth is resolved by skip down a third to the tonic note. In a four-voice setting, the fifth, ninth, and eleventh (above the root of V) are omitted, as shown in Example 4-8.

Ex. 4-8

Other than this, usefulness of these triads is mostly limited to imitating the sound of a choo-choo train ...

One very insightful way of examining the seventh chords is to put them in first inversion and analyze them. All of these are now in the form of a triad with an added sixth, as shown in Example 4-9.

Ex. 4-9

We see now that a minor second results in each case — and that is the number one problem. The number two problem is that in every case, except in the first two chords, the sixth is minor, and it sounds against a perfect fifth. The third problem is that in the first two chords, where the sixth is major, the triad is augmented.

The point is that secondary seventh chords are most useful when they are in first inversion, *and* the triad is either major or minor, *and* the sixth is a major sixth. All chords having this interval structure have subdominant functions.

The Nonaphonic system provides us with a large number of mediant and submediant chords that are useful by nature. But, in spite of that, if we ever became utterly desperate to use any of the five chords above, we could; all we would have to do is to cheat ... We could use the triads that are there for what they are, and call the fourth note a non-harmonic tone (nht). The five seventh chords would then become the following:

	c- = i	f- = iv	G+ = V	A♭+ = VI	C+ = I
nht:	b	e	e♭	g	a♭

Now let us consider the three MM^7 chords shown in Example 4-10.

Ex. 4-10

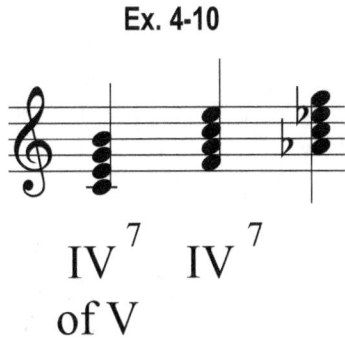

IV^7 IV^7
of V

We labeled the first two as shown, but dismissed the other one as non-functional. There is a point to be made here. In traditional harmony, I^7 and IV^7, both of which are MM sevenths, have always been available. IV^7 is used often, but I^7 is not, because it contains both the tonic note and leading note. Two ways of reading it are the tonic note and iii or the root and third of both I and V. So it would seem that if I^7 does not have a tonic function, then it should have a dominant function. In fact, it has neither. The only functional use of I^7 is as a subdominant seventh of V. It then resolves to V of V, which resolves to V.

It is not a good idea to label the third chord as IV^7 of IV of IV of IV. If we did things like that, then we would soon be calling some chord something like "iii of VI of V of ii of VII," which is nonsense. We could conceivably call it IV^7 of ♭III, but only if and when it behaves as such. In general, we can claim and show functionality of a chord if we can relate it as a function of a function of one scale degree (example V of V of VI). But if a chord is more remote than that, then it is no longer functional. (Some exceptions do occur, as in the case of a chain of bracket dominants, in which each chord is V of the chord following it).

Just before we get back to reviewing the functional chords, this is a good time to take a look at another unusual chord, the Dominant eleventh chord. Some authors dismiss it as being rather useless because it clashes the V^7 chord against the tonic note (just as I^7 clashes the leading note against the tonic note). This argument is made because we are used to the idea that the entire world sings in four voices, not more or fewer. So we take the V^{11} chord, which contains six tones, and (rightfully) eliminate the fifth and the ninth, ending up with the dreaded "V^7 against tonic note" sound, as shown in Example 4-11.

Ex. 4-11

$$V^{11}$$

However, if we write in six voices, as composers in the Renaissance did quite frequently, we end up with a good-quality chord and resolution, as shown in Example 4-12.

Ex. 4-12

IV   I
V

Instead of thinking of it as V^{11}, we can think of it as IV superimposed over V. This makes it a beautifully bi-functional chord. It also proves that the tonic can be approached by both the dominant and subdominant at the same time.

Now we can examine the 24 functional chords. Of these, two are tonic, five are dominant, ten are subdominant, and seven (two plus five) are mediant and submediant.

Ex. 4-13: Tonic

i   I

There are two tonic triads because this is a bi-modal, uni-tonal system.

Ex. 4-14: Dominant

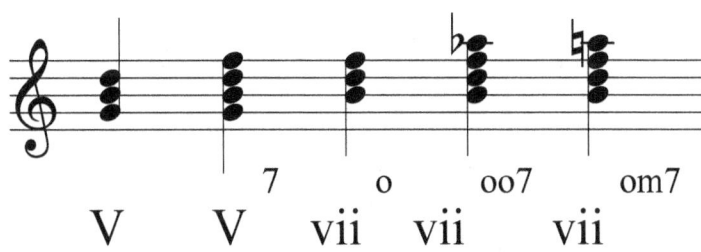

V   V^7 vii^o vii^{oo7} vii^{om7}

The dominant function of these chords was explained earlier. There is nothing new here because the dominant function is what binds the tonic major key together with its tonic minor.

Ex. 4-15: Subdominant

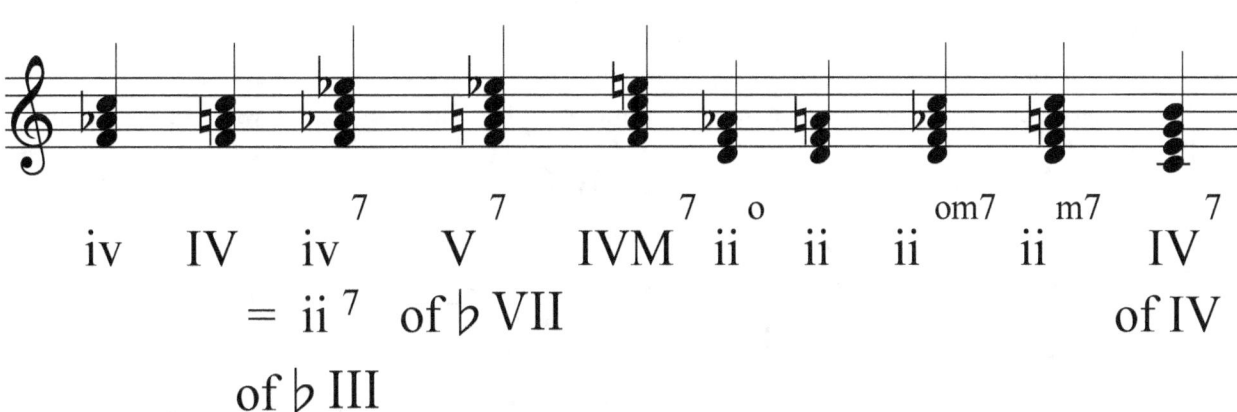

iv   IV   iv^7 V^7 IVM^7 ii^o ii   ii^{om7} ii^{m7} IV^7
= ii^7 of ♭VII   of IV
of ♭III

All these chords have a subdominant function, except for the fourth one, which has a dominant function. Once again, when secondary seventh chords have a subdominant function, it is a good idea to regard them in first inversion, as added-sixth chords. To the ear, the third takes over as the most important tone in the chord, while the root plays the role of the characteristic dissonance of the subdominant, the added (always major) sixth. This is true even if the seventh is absent.

In the twentieth century, composers sometimes gave this chord a tonic function, and ended many compositions with I or i with an added major sixth (especially in jazz music).

Two more observations can be made about these chords. First, the Nonaphonic system leans heavily in the direction of the subdominant. Chords that are traditionally subdominant (or supertonic) "borrowed" chords are no longer borrowed, because the key signature accommodates them.*

The second observation is that of the bi-functionality of some chords. This phenomenon appears here, but it will appear even more often when we analyze mediant and submediant chords.

To begin looking at bi-functionality, let us black out the key signature and consider the F-major triad followed by the C-major triad. We see in Example 4-16 that four different pairs of harmonic analyses are possible, depending on what the mysterious key signature is.

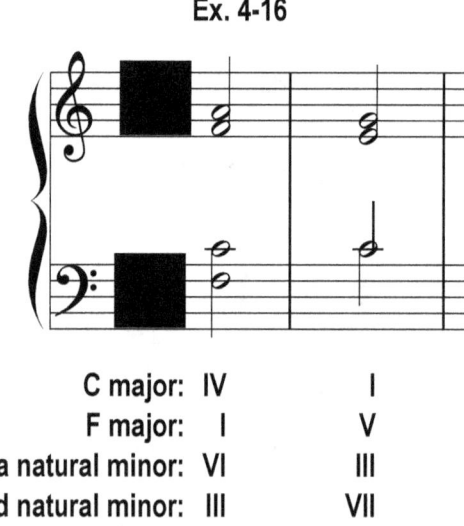

Ex. 4-16

C major:	IV	I
F major:	I	V
a natural minor:	VI	III
d natural minor:	III	VII

In fact, the mysterious key signature could be f#, that of G Major, in which case the chords would be ♭VII (or IV of IV), and IV. That gives us at least five different possible analyses, and proves that each of these two chords can have different functions at different times. The general conclusion is that when the two chords are placed in context, most likely one (or perhaps two) of the analyses will describe the progression most accurately, depending on which chords precede and follow.

Bi-functionality of chords is nothing new. In traditional harmony, the chord in Example 4-17 has a dominant function in C major and a subdominant function in a-minor simultaneously, especially when used as a pivot chord in modulation.

Ex. 4-17

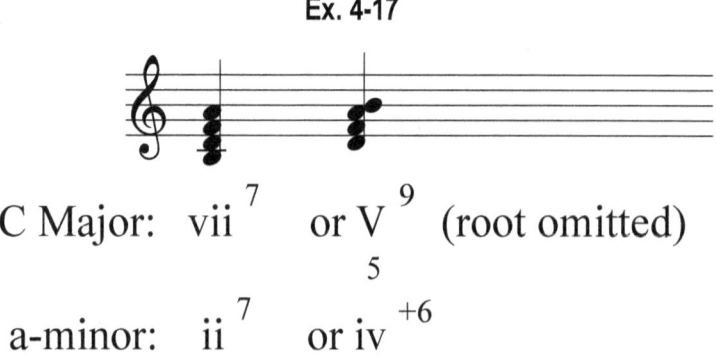

C Major: vii^7 or V$^9_5$ (root omitted)

a-minor: ii^7 or iv^{+6}

In modern music, it can also have a tonic function in d-minor, being i^{+6}.

---

*Since they are no longer borrowed chords, after using them, you no longer have to go to the music library to return them…

MEDIANT AND SUBMEDIANT

Because the Nonaphonic system combines the tonic major and minor modes, we ended up with a proportionally large number of mediant and submediant chords at our disposal. This can get confusing, so we need to do a bit more sorting and analysis in order to clarify how these chords fit into the whole picture.

First, we take a quick look at the three seventh chords in Example 4-18.

Ex. 4-18

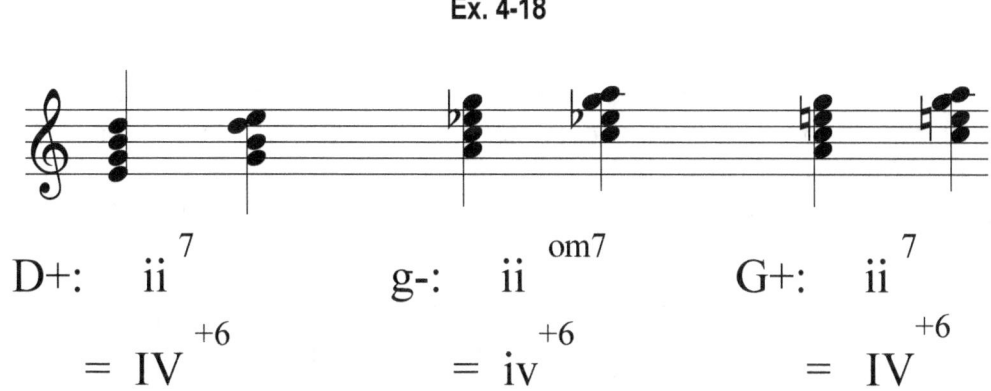

All three of these are subdominant added-sixth chords, but in three different keys (other than C major or minor). These will come in very useful in Part Two, when we get into Bi-Tonal Bi-Modality.

Right now, we should take a longer look at the four triads shown in Example 4-19.

Ex. 4-19

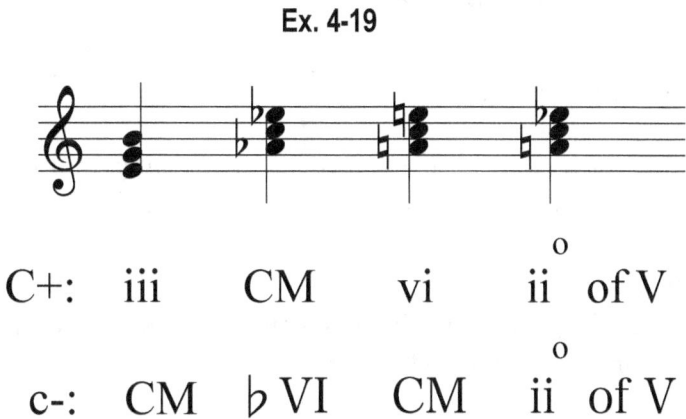

The last chord is ii° of V in both C+ and c-. But the first three have harmonic symbols in only one of these two keys; in the other key, they are Chromatic Mediants (CM).

When we speak of mediant relationships, the term "mediant" always entails the submediant also. Mediant relationships are all those that exist between two triads whose roots are a major or minor third apart. In traditional harmony, diatonic mediant relationships have two tones in common, and both chords belong to the key of the central triad. So for C Major, the two diatonic mediants are a-minor and e-minor, as shown in Example 4-20.

Ex. 4-20

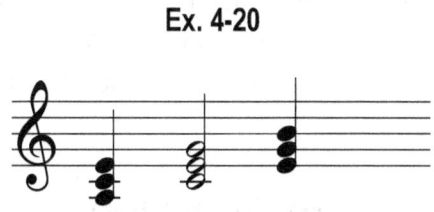

In a minor key there is one diatonic mediant triad a third below the tonic and two possible diatonic mediants a third above, as shown in Example 4-21.

Ex. 4-21

In traditional harmony, chromatic mediant relationships exist between two triads that have roots that are a third apart, and which have one tone in common. There are four such triads in both major and minor key, as shown in Example 4-22.

Ex. 4-22

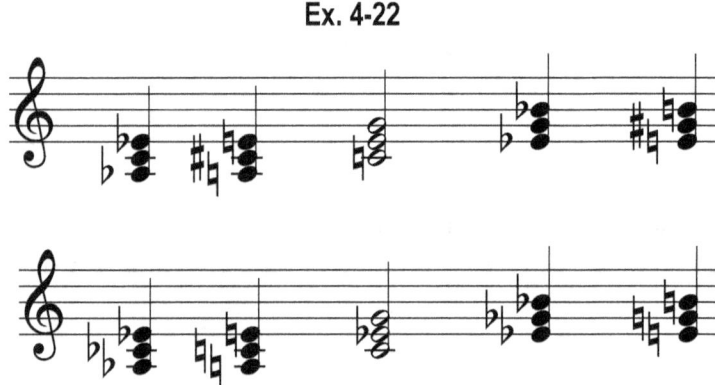

Chromatic mediant triads do not belong to the key of the central triad, so there are no harmonic symbols for them in that key.

It is possible to expand the concept of chromatic mediant relationships. If we do, then we add doubly chromatic mediants, which have no tones in common with the central triad. But to do so is to carry the concept of "relationship" a bit too far.

The relevant point for us is that we do have an explanation for why the Nonaphonic system contains so many mediant and submediant chords: Since the Nonaphonic system is bi-modal, all of these chords are either diatonic, or they are the chromatic mediants of traditional harmony.

SUMMARY

This has been an exhaustive (and perhaps exhausting) study of all the triads and seventh chords available in the basic Nonaphonic Bi-Modal, Uni-Tonal System. It was, however, necessary, because when the number of available tones increases from seven to nine, the number of available triads and seventh chords increases much more, as we have seen. So first, we have to be aware of their existence. Next, we have to know which ones are always functional, functional only sometimes, bi-functional (or even tri-functional), or without functional harmonic symbols. Even if we do not talk in terms of functions, we still have to know which chords are very useful, somewhat useful, rarely useful, and so on. Finally, we have to learn when and how to use all of them. The following chapters deal with these matters.

INTERMISSION

CHAPTER FIVE

The European System of Harmonic Analysis[*]

Continental Europeans do not use the Roman numeral system of harmonic analysis that is in use in Great Britain and North America. Instead, they use a functional system of chord symbolism. We in North America have very much insight to gain by studying even only the basics of their system, because functions are insufficiently discussed — or understood — here. Their system is a real eye-opener for people who are familiar with the Roman numeral system only. It requires a fair amount of study to understand it, but once a person catches on to it, it becomes most sensible.

The European system of harmonic analysis is a functional system, based on the presupposition that there are three (and only three) functions, and that each chord may be classified into (at least) one of these. Consequently, only functional symbols, and no Roman numerals, are used. The primary functions are Tonic, Dominant, and Subdominant (hereafter T, D, and S respectively), and these are the chords built on the first, fifth, and fourth scale degrees respectively, in both major and minor keys. Secondary chords are referred to as "parallel" chords, and always lay at a distance of a third away from one of T, D, or S. The third is diatonic (so that it may be major or minor), and the direction reverses with the mode. In a major mode, the parallel is always a third *below* its primary triad, and in a minor mode it is always a third *above* its primary triad. Thus, by comparison to Roman numeral notation, the system appears as shown in Example 5-1.

Ex. 5-1

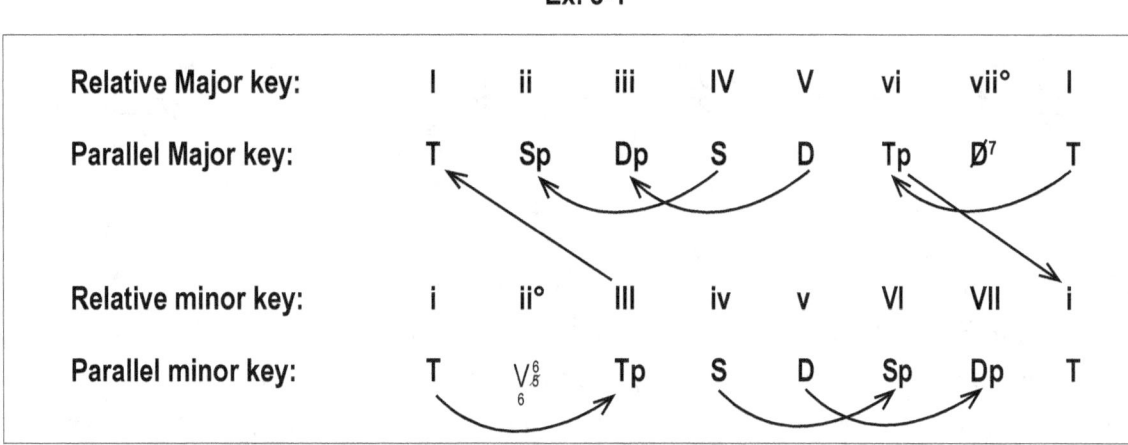

---

[*]This chapter consists partly of a reprint of pages 532-539 of the author's doctoral dissertation: "History of Harmony and Counterpoint, Volume II, The Renaissance" by Józef M. Chomiński: A Translation, Evaluation, and Critique (Doctoral Dissertations in Musicology, 1981).

The following are the most important features of this system:

1) "Parallel," which means "a third away," also refers to the key. The "parallel minor" is what North Americans call the "relative minor." (The North American "parallel minor" would be called the "tonic minor"). Since the Tp triad in a major key is the one built on the sixth scale degree, the parallel key is that which has this triad as the tonic. The same holds true (but in reverse) if one begins with the minor key: Since the Tp is the triad built on the third scale degree, the parallel (major) key is that which has this triad as the tonic.

2) All letters are upper case; the quality of a triad is never reflected in the symbol. It is understood that the dominant triad in a minor key is diatonically minor (because the key signature for parallel keys is always identical), and that it becomes major when one raises the seventh scale degree.

3) A secondary triad retains the function of its primary triad. This means that in a major mode, chord vi has a T function, but in a minor mode chord VI has a S function.

4) Diminished triads have no status of their own. In a major mode, the designation $\cancel{D}$ for vii° indicates that the dominant-seventh chord appears incomplete, that is, with its root missing. In a minor mode, the symbol for ii° is slightly more complex. To begin with, the symbol S^6_5 is never used as such. The S is understood, and S^6 means "subdominant added sixth" — this is Rameau's famous "sexte-ajoutée." Here, the 5 is included so that it may be crossed out, which specifies that it is to be omitted. Finally, the 6 is placed below the symbol to show that the added sixth is to be placed in the bass. These designations are illustrated in Example 5-2.

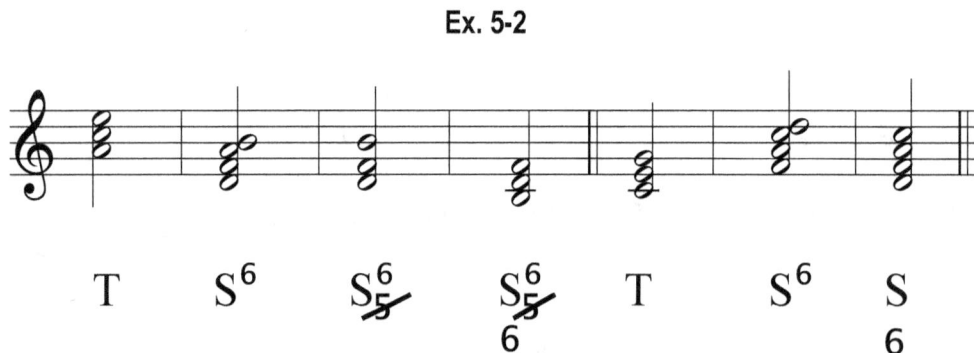

Ex. 5-2

From the above, it follows that S^6 has the same meaning in a major mode. The important point in all of this symbolism is that it emphasizes that the chord designated in Roman numeral analysis as ii^7 has a subdominant function, and that its acoustical root is *not* its written root, but the *fourth* scale degree. In fact, the written root becomes an added sixth and, as such, is considered to be the characteristic dissonance of the subdominant function (just as the seventh is the characteristic dissonance of the dominant function). The connection between the two becomes evident when one observes that these dissonances together form the characteristic tritone (of the key signature) found in both the D^7 of the major key and in the S^6 of the parallel minor, as shown in Example 5-3.

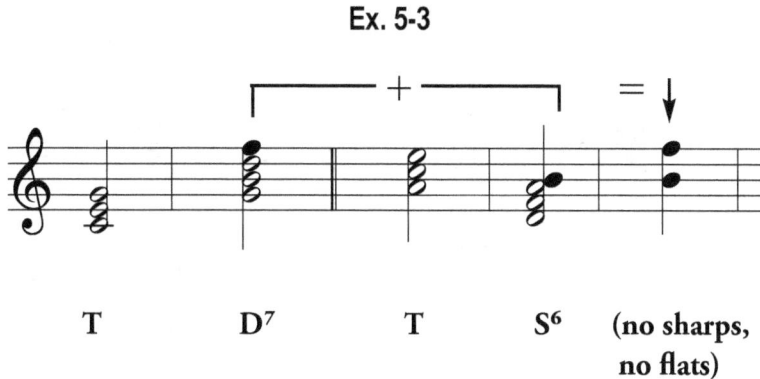

Ex. 5-3

T   D⁷   T   S⁶   (no sharps, no flats)

5) In addition to the fact that the Tp triad forms the tonic of the parallel key, the Dp and Sp triads form the dominant and subdominant, respectively, of the parallel key. This explains why the parallel direction reverses with the mode (see the arrows in Example 5-1 above) and why only diatonic forms of triads appear in that example.

The three most important features of this system may now be summarized. Firstly, it is very important to realize that this system is comprised of a *complex* of symbols, which are *inter-related* between parallel keys. This becomes clear when one realizes that the S⁶ shown above is actually identical to the incomplete dominant-ninth chord (with its fifth in the bass) of the parallel major key, as shown in Example 5-4. (The symbol 9< means major ninth).

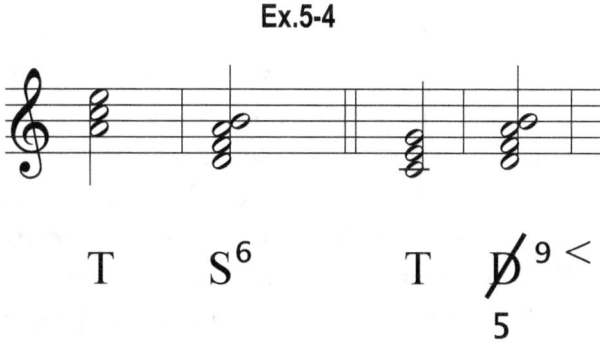

Ex.5-4

T   S⁶   T   D̸⁹<
                5

Secondly, it should be observed that virtually every chord thus far has been explained and symbolized in terms of T, D, and S. What is more, all other chords are also conceived in terms of these three basic functions, the most important of which are listed in Example 5-5.

NOTES: D̄ means double dominant; S̄ means double subdominant. When D or D⁷ is crossed out, it means that the root of that chord is omitted, but it still remains its acoustical root. 6> means minor sixth; 5> means flattened fifth; 9> means minor ninth; 13> means minor thirteenth.

Ex. 5-5

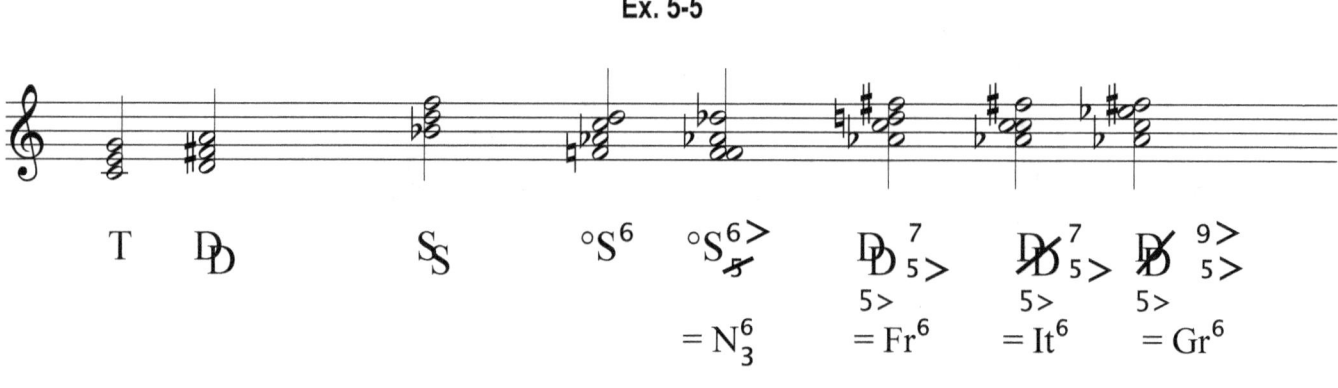

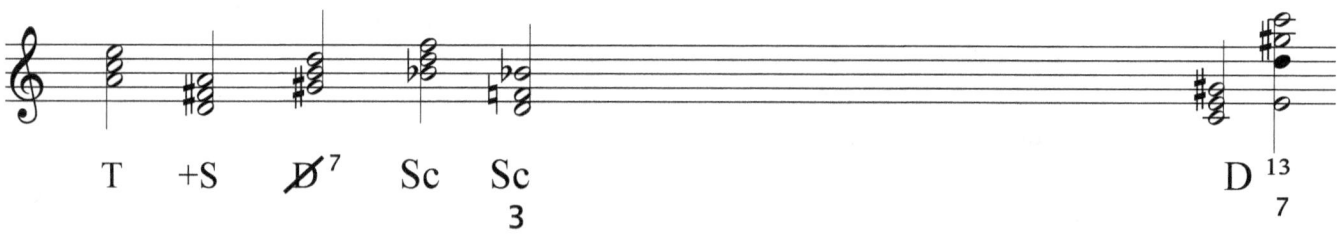

From the above, we see that the double dominant in a major key is equivalent to the major subdominant in the parallel minor. The triad whose root lays a major seventh above the tonic of the parallel minor is the incomplete dominant seventh chord in this key. The triad whose root lays a minor seventh above the tonic of the parallel major is the double subdominant. The double subdominant in a major key is equivalent to the subdominant contra-parallel (Sc) in the parallel minor. (It is so called because its root lays a third in the opposite direction from S as that of Sp). The subdominant contra-parallel in first inversion (in a minor key only) is commonly known as the Neapolitan Sixth. The parallel major key does not possess a subdominant contra-parallel. Here, the Neapolitan Sixth chord is derived from the borrowed S^6 chord: The added sixth is flattened and the fifth is omitted. Augmented Sixth chords are derived from the double dominant seventh and (minor) ninth. The fifth is always flattened and placed in the bass, and the root is omitted in the Italian and German Sixth. Only the German Sixth requires the addition of the minor ninth. In the parallel minor key, the augmented triad, which arises on the third scale degree (when the seventh scale degree is raised), has no status of its own. Most frequently it appears in first inversion with the fifth scale degree in the bass. Then the seventh above the fifth (i.e. the fourth scale degree) is added, and the result is the dominant-thirteenth chord.

Thirdly, it is necessary to be aware of the fact that in this system, the relationship between the root of a chord and its function is emphasized very strongly; such is not the case in the Roman numeral system. This is seen clearly in a comparison of ii^7 and II^7 with S^6_6 and $\mathit{D\!D}^7$. In the Roman numeral system, the quality of the triad is indicated in the symbol, but the function is not. Also, the root of both chords is considered to be the second scale degree. In the European functional system, on the other hand, the quality of the triad is not reflected in the symbol, but the function is the most conspicuous thing designated by it. More importantly, the root of each chord is stipulated by the symbols, which tell us that the difference between the two chords is much greater than a chromatic alteration of the fourth scale degree: Not only do the roots differ, but so do the functions, the derivations of the chords, and the dissonant tones.

A similar case may be made for the N^6_3 chord in a major key. In the symbol $°S^{6>}_{\cancel{5}}$ the S tells us that the chord has a subdominant function and that the fourth — and not the second — scale degree is its root. The ° symbol means that the triad is minor in quality, and that it is a borrowed chord (otherwise, the quality would not be indicated). The $^{6>}$ symbol indicates that the flattened sixth is added and that *it* is the dissonance. The $\cancel{5}$, of course, designates that the fifth of the (subdominant) triad is to be omitted. This symbol places the Neapolitan Sixth chord into its proper perspective: It explains why it is almost always used in first inversion and why the bass is normally doubled. It also establishes the fourth scale degree as the most important element of the chord, and recognizes the lowered second scale degree as the dissonance.

Finally, in the cases of Augmented Sixth chords and the augmented triad, it is the *acoustical* root of the chord, which determines its function, and, by the same token, its symbol. For example, the French Sixth is an altered double dominant seventh chord; its root is the second scale degree and *not* the lowered sixth (which actually is an altered fifth). The Italian and German Sixths are derived similarly, and all three function as dominants of the second classification. Similar Augmented Sixth chords may, of course, be built on the fifth scale degree as the acoustical root; these are dominant functions of the first classification. In the augmented triad, the acoustical root is again permitted to predominate, simply because the chord is otherwise rather useless from the functional point of view. When used in a logical manner, however, it assumes a dominant function.

Some European scholars stretch the interpretation of their functional system of harmonic analysis to the limit, and claim that every chord that does not have a tonic function has a dominant function *of some sort*. They consider the subdominant (or "lower dominant" as the Germans and Polish call it) as a type of dominant. So not only the dominant parallel, but also the subdominant parallel, and the subdominant contra-parallel are considered to be types of dominants. Seventh chords built on these triads also become types of dominants. And since the double dominant is a type of dominant, then so is the double subdominant. Dominant types can be major, minor, diminished, or augmented. There are primary and secondary dominants, and dominants of the first, second, and even third, classification.

Other musicologists argue that in functional tonality, it is not the tonic that is the most important function, but the dominant, because it is at the center of most of the activity, so it dominates, as its name implies. In North America, we are accustomed to recognizing the tonic as the most important function, the dominant second, and the subdominant third in importance. It is noteworthy that mediants and submediants, as such, are not a part of the picture at all. So in summary, the three different views of functional tonality that exist are shown in Example 5-6.

Ex. 5-6

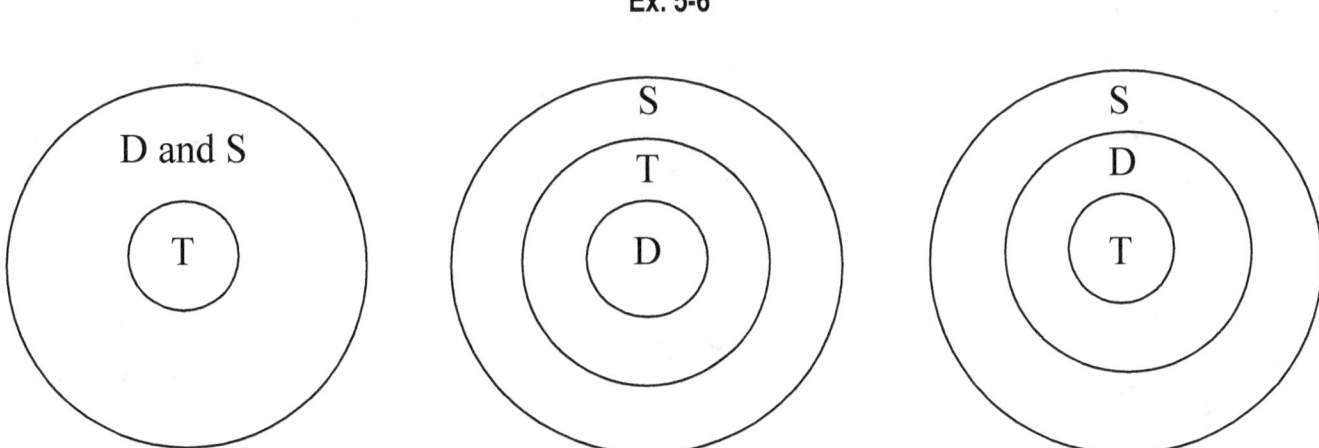

This concludes our basic overview of the European functional system of harmonic analysis. It should be emphasized that this system originated, and predominates, in Continental Europe. But then, is that not where almost all of the music of the common practice period that we study was written? …

In sharp contrast to that, it is astonishing that the British Theorist, C. H. Kitson, in his three-part textbook entitled "Elementary Harmony," does not mention functions even once. This is in spite of the fact that the subject being studied is functional harmony of the Baroque, Classical, and Romantic periods. So, ironically, it is possible to study functional harmony without learning about harmonic functions…

This author has been most fortunate to study systems of harmonic analysis with professors from Europe, Great Britain, and North America, both in Canada and in the U.S.A.. The overall picture is that in North America, since the Roman numeral system of harmonic analysis predominates, most people are not exposed to functional analysis very much, if at all. Consequently, the concept of harmonic functions becomes difficult to grasp, even though mathematical functions are well understood. Harmonic functions are thought of as elusive, mysterious, ambiguous, poorly defined, and so on. And this is a shame, because, for one thing, rather than drawing these complex diagrams consisting of seven Roman numerals and lines, curves, and arrows drawn all over the place, all we have to do is to draw two triangles, as shown in Example 5-7.

Ex. 5-7

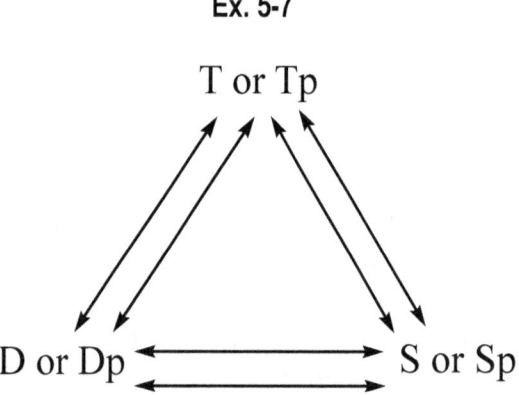

In common language, to perform a certain function means to do a certain thing, or to act or to behave in a certain way, or to perform a specific role or action or activity. This applies also to each of these three groups of chords, but there is more to it. They function only when they interrelate with each other, that is, by continuously changing juxtapositions, doing so by constant alternations and rotations, as shown in Ex. 5-7 above. Harmonic functions are discussed in greater detail in the next two chapters.

Right now, in order to summarize this topic of discussion to this point, and to help us sort out all the different chords that are available for our use, we can draw up a model of the structure of Functional Tonality. To begin, we write out the harmonized Major and relative minor scales, as well as the same triads with added diatonic sevenths. There are also three triads and four seventh chords that result when the natural minor scale is used. These seven chords are all duplicates of chords belonging to the relative Major key. All the chords so derived, together with their harmonic analyses, in both European Functional and North American Roman numeral symbols, are written out in Ex. 5-8.

Ex. 5-8

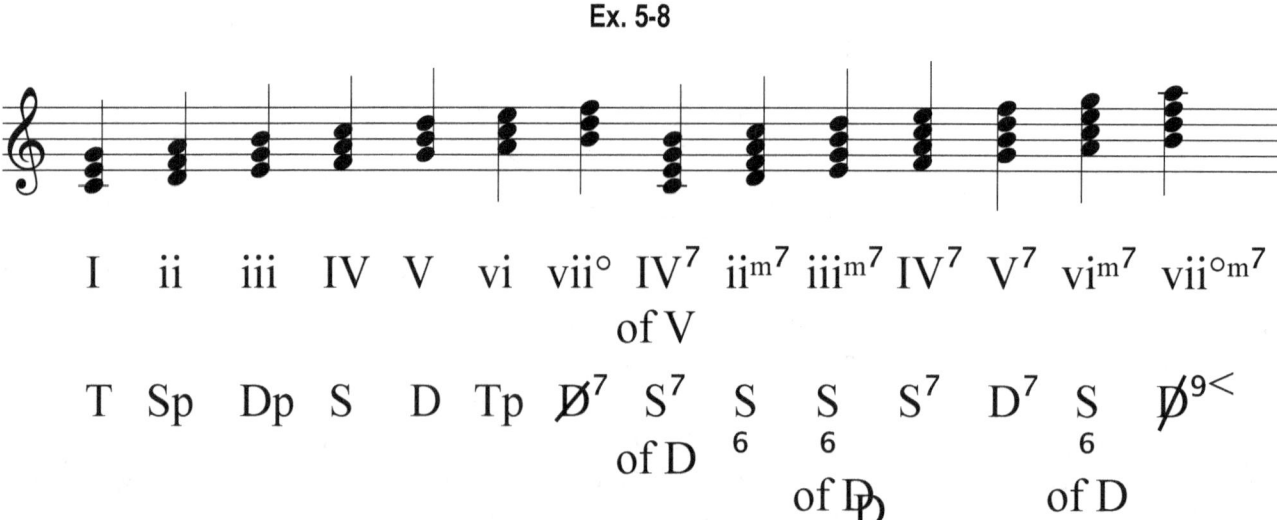

Ex. 5-8 Cont'd

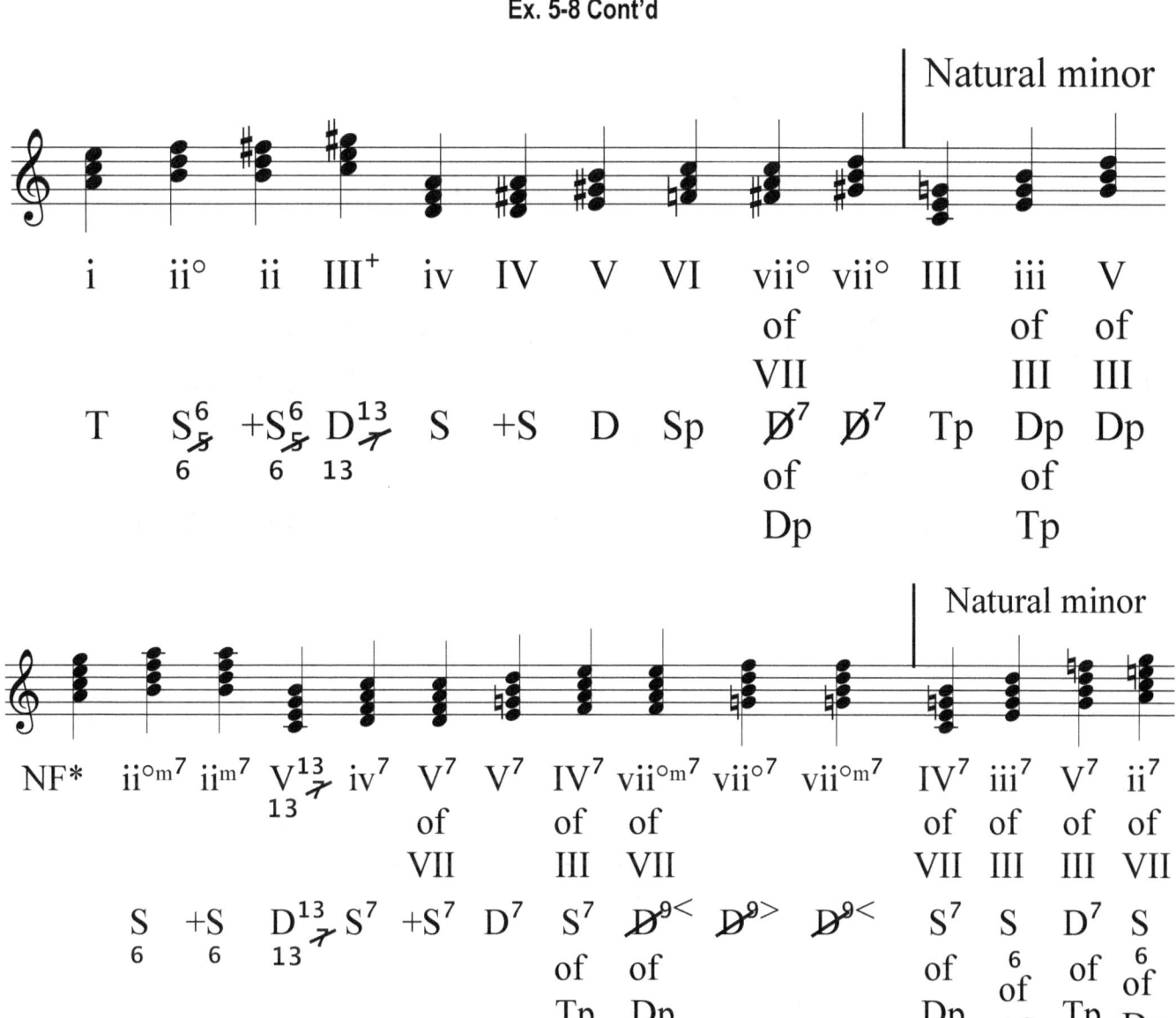

*NF = Non-Functional. In a minor key, the root and third of i, together with the root and third of V, do not comprise a chord that has a Tonic or Dominant or Subdominant function; it's a dud…

Now we enter all the Roman numeral harmonic symbols into the appropriate pillars in our model, which appears as Example 5-9 on the following page.

The total number of chords is 35, distributed as follows: Tonic: 4, Dominant: 15, Subdominant: 16. Of course, it is understood that there are very many other chords used in functional tonality that are not listed here. In the Subdominant group, there is ♭VII or IV of IV (the Double Subdominant), the Neapolitan Sixth chord, other secondary subdominants, and other secondary supertonic chords of various types. In the Dominant group, there is even more: All Augmented Sixth chords (built on various scale degrees) and numerous secondary Dominant triads and seventh chords. Then there are Dominant ninths, elevenths, and thirteenths. All of these contain at least one note that is chromatic, not diatonic.

If we were to list every chord that came to mind, we would end up constructing a house several stories high, and that is not the objective here. The objective is to construct all possible *diatonic* triads and seventh chords and to leave it at that, because 35 basic chords are plenty to enable us to compare this model to the Nonaphonic, Bi-Modal model, which we will draw up in the next chapter.

Ex. 5-9

FUNCTIONAL TONALITY

SUBDOMINANT GROUP	TONIC GROUP	DOMINANT GROUP
RELATIVE MAJOR KEY	**RELATIVE MAJOR KEY**	**RELATIVE MAJOR KEY**
ii, IV, IV^7 of V, ii^{m7}, iii^{m7}, IV^7, vi^{m7}	I vi	iii, V, $vii°$, V^7, $vii°^{m7}$
RELATIVE MINOR KEY	**RELATIVE MINOR KEY**	**RELATIVE MINOR KEY**
$ii°$, ii, iv, IV, VI, $ii°^{m7}$, ii^{m7}, iv^{m7}, IV^7 of III	i VI (in V-VI only)	III^+, V, $vii°$ of ♭VII, $vii°$, $V^{13}_{\,7}$, V^7 of ♭VII, V^7, $vii°^{m7}$ of ♭VII, $vii°^7$, $vii°^{m7}$
16	4	15

CHAPTER SIX

Mediants, Submediants, And Functionality

Following the model of the last chapter, we now have to build a house of Nonaphonic Bi-Modality. A new system beckons a new way of looking at things. The problem at hand is that the Nonaphonic, Bi-Modal system contains an unusually large number of mediants and submediants, and they all have to fit into the house somehow, somewhere. And when they do so, their functions have to be identified, defined, and explained.

There are two fundamental guidelines to follow in order to reach the goal of our model being a true reflection of reality: First, any chord that has — or can have — tonic, dominant, or subdominant functionality has to go into the appropriate pillar. Second, any chord that does not have tonic, dominant, or subdominant functionality cannot be forced into any of those pillars or "dropped off" there, just because we have nowhere else to put it.

But what are we to do when our mediants and submediants do not fall into either chord category? The only sensible solution is to construct Mediant and Submediant pillars. And in doing so, we must introduce the concept of Mediant (and Submediant) functions.

We have seen that Europeans have shown successfully that every chord in a major or a minor key can be categorized as having at least one of the three primary functions. Hugo Riemann declared this first — but that was in 1893. We can safely assume that he would not say the same thing today about dodecaphonic music, or other twentieth-century music, and most likely not about our Nonaphonic, Bi-Modal system, either. Not only that, if we tried to incorporate all chromatic mediants into the framework of the European functional system, we could not do it, because there is simply not enough room there for all of them to fit in.

In any event, all triads are considered to be either primary (I, IV, V, or i, iv, V) or secondary (ii, iii, vi, vii°, or ii°, III⁺, VI, vii°). Of the secondary triads, ii and ii° always have a subdominant function, and vii and vii° always have a dominant function. The mediants and submediants take on primary functions as substitutes — but not 100% of the time, especially not every time that sevenths (major, minor, or diminished) are added to them. And if we consider chromatic (and doubly chromatic) mediants, they rarely have primary functions, and, in some cases, almost never. For this reason, we must declare mediants and submediants to be *secondary functions,* and we must define and explain what that means.

A simple answer is just to say that whenever we cannot show that a chord has primary functionality, it has secondary functionality. This is better than saying that it is semi-functional. It does not happen often, but if there truly is no clear way to show (without being absurd about it) that a chord can play a tonic, dominant, or subdominant function, then we can call it non- functional.

A very important factor that comes into play is that in our Nonaphonic, Bi-Modal system, we have two sets of mediants and submediants: The major mode set, and the minor mode set. (In C Major/c minor Nonaphonic, we could call them the "natural set" and the "flat set"). So if a passage is in one of the two modes, it is not reasonable to expect the mediants and submediants that belong to the other set to have primary functionality in that passage. But we can still use them, just as we use chromatic mediants in traditional harmony.

Another factor that enters the picture is that some of our mediant and submediant chords will have primary functionality at certain times. This means that just as we will transfer the mediants and submediants that were in the primary pillars into the secondary pillars, we will have to do some transferring in the reverse direction as well. It follows that there is nothing wrong with a given chord being in two — or even three — different pillars.

Before we draw up our model, we need to write up a more detailed explanation of what the chords that appear in our new, secondary pillars do — or can do. Flexibility in role is the primary feature of these chords. They will not all behave in the same way, and any given chord will not behave the same way all the time.

Primary functions are set in their ways. The tonic is the alpha and omega. Music begins there, travels all over the place, and finally returns there. (That is not to say that it does not drop in at home once in a while and then venture off in another direction; it does). Dominants and subdominants are extremely popular points of destination. We go there, perhaps stay a while, and then continue on. Sometimes we go back and forth, and not necessarily just once.

In a way, tonality is tri-polar. If the tonic is the North Pole, then the dominant is the South Pole. The subdominant can be the East Pole (in Warsaw, of course) … What is missing is everything in between, and herein lays the answer we are seeking: MEDIAnts and subMEDIAnts play the role of interMEDIAry chords. That is precisely what a secondary function is and does.

Secondary functions cannot stand alone because, unlike primary functions, they are not vital. When no secondary functions are used, the harmony soon becomes boring. So they are introduced for the mutual enhancement of both. This in itself is not a new thing to music. What is new is that in the Nonaphonic, Bi-Modal system we have mediants and submediants that are functional sometimes and not at other times.

So far, we have answered the "w" questions of "what, where, when, and why". Now we need the answer to "how". Analysis provides this answer. Mediants and submediants as secondary functions can work in different ways. Here is a partial list; readers can add to it as they discover other instances and examples.

1) Pointing chords — towards or away from any of the primary chords,
2) Traveling or "in-transit" chords — neutral in directional force,
3) Linking chords,
4) Variety chords or interest chords,
5) Color chords — especially the chromatic ones,
6) Friction or tension chords.

We do not include substitute chords in this list, because in that role they become functional (as in the deceptive cadence, where vi is substituted for I, so its third is doubled).

The best way to figure out what a mediant or submediant chord does and how it works is to take note of how many tones it has in common with the chords that precede and follow it. This will be discussed in detail in the following chapter.

Right now, we can draw up our model of the structure of Nonaphonic Bi-Modality. We begin by re-writing all the triads and seventh chords that were discussed in Chapter Four. This is done in Example 6-1.

Just to recap, we started out with 14 triads and 17 seventh chords. Of these, at first we labeled all of the triads functional, except for the two augmented ones. We also labeled all the seventh chords functional, except for five: Two mM sevenths, one MM seventh, and two AM sevenths. Subsequently, we showed that the two augmented triads can have Dominant functionality, and that the MM seventh ($\flat$VIMM^7) can be labeled as IV^7 of $\flat$III, so we can show that it can have Subdominant functionality, if we want to "push it." So the final tally is: Functional Triads: All 14, Functional Seventh chords: 13, and Non-Functional Seventh Chords: 4. It is important to start keeping track of these things already now, because in Part Two, when we get into Bi-Tonal Bi-Modality, and the number of tones used will be greater than nine, then the number of resulting mediant and submediant triads and seventh chords will increase much more.

In Example 6-1 below, the first thing shown below each chord is its Roman numeral symbol. Immediately below that is the name of the pillar into which it will go. Then, if it is to go into another pillar, the alternate harmonic symbol is given, and below that, the name of the second pillar appears. Finally, in four cases (♭VI, vi°, vi°m7, and vim7), this happens a third time.

Ex. 6-1

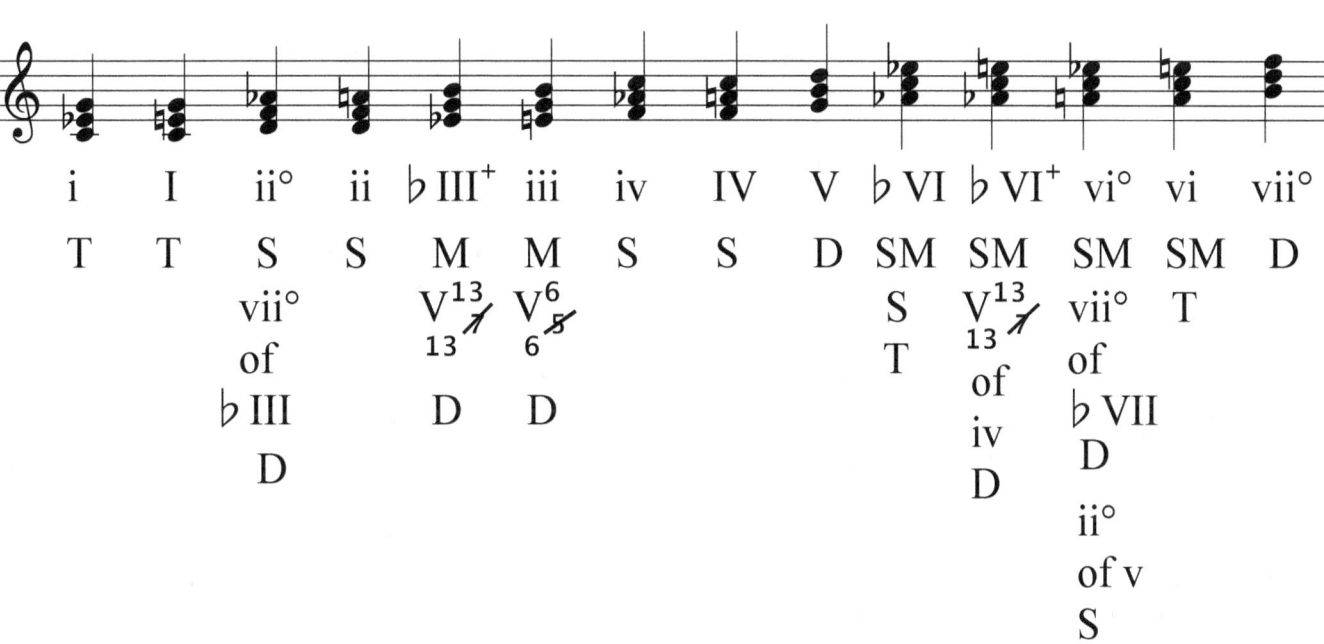

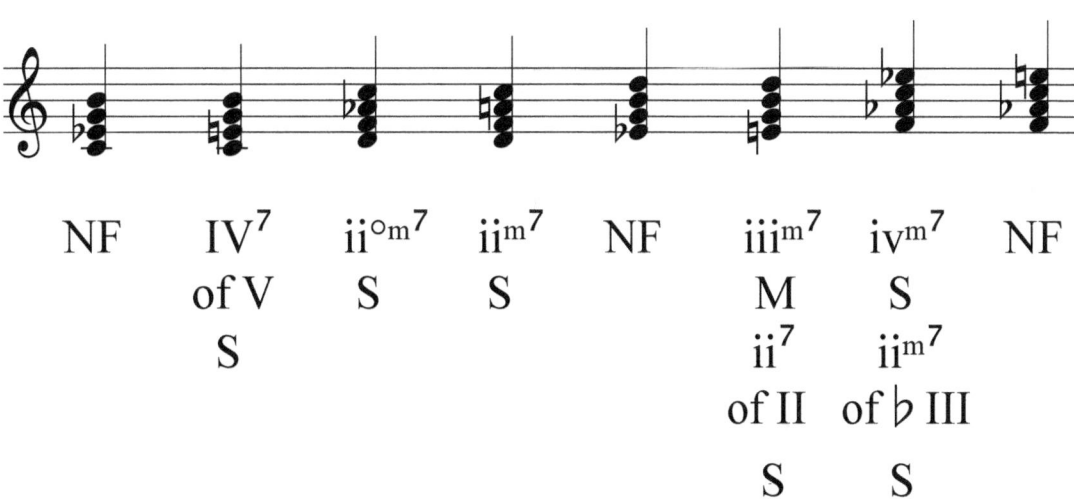

Ex. 6-1 Cont'd

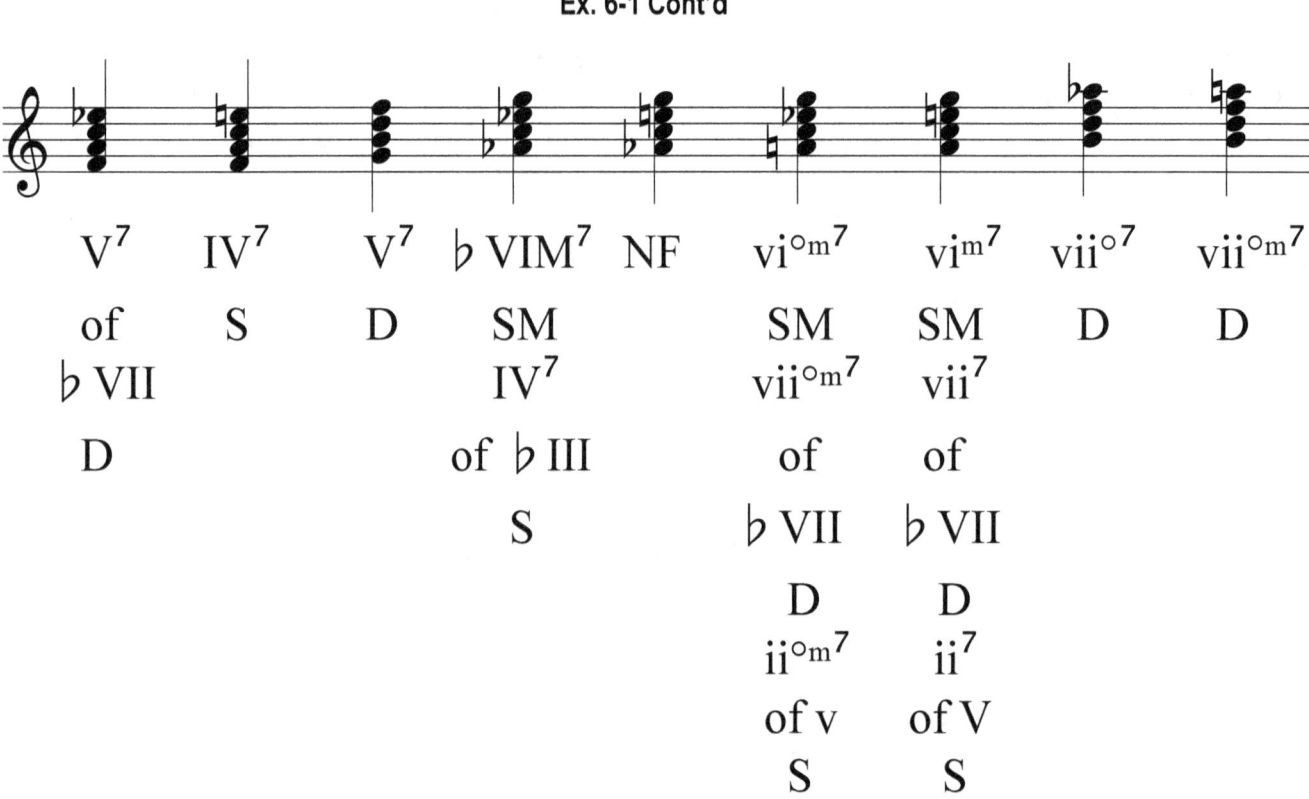

Finally, we draw up our model of Nonaphonic Bi-Modality by moving all the chords into the new "Century 21" House labeled Example 6-2. We can see clearly now what has happened: All Functional Mediants and Submediants have ended up in their own pillars plus at least one other one. The four Non-Functional seventh chords are excluded from the house.

The total number of chords, including duplicates, is 43, distributed as follows: Tonic: 4, Dominant: 13, Subdominant: 16, Mediant: 3, Submediant: 7. Fifteen chords have one function only, eight have two possible functions, and four have three possible functions. There are no chords here that can be called "new," because they have always existed, at least as borrowed chords or chromatic mediants. Some of these were rarely, or almost never, used in the opposite mode. But now they have moved into the house; they are all diatonic.

Ex. 6-2

NONAPHONIC BI-MODALITY

SUBDOMINANT GROUP	SUBMEDIANT GROUP	TONIC GROUP	MEDIANT GROUP	DOMINANT GROUP
ii°, ii,	♭VI, ♭VI+,	i,	♭III+,	vii° of ♭III,
iv, IV	vi°, vi,	I,	iii,	♭III+ = $V^{13}_{13\ 7}$,
♭VI,	♭VIM7,	♭VI,	iii^{m7}	
ii° of v,	vi°^{m7},	vi		iii = $V^{6}_{6\ 5}$,
IV7 of V,	vi^{m7}			
ii°^{m7}, ii^{m7},				V, vii°, V7,
ii7 of II,				$V^{13}_{13\ 7}$ of vi,
iv^{m7},				
ii^{m7} of ♭III,				vii° of ♭VII,
IV7,				
IV7 of ♭III,				V7 of ♭VII,
ii°^{m7} of v,				
ii7 of V				vii°^{m7} of ♭VII,
				vii7 of ♭VII,
				vii°7,
				vii°^{m7}
16	7	4	3	13

One final note should be added here about chords that have not been included in either house, although they could have been. It is no secret that all sorts of chords exist that are not triads, or seventh chords, or extended tertian chords. There are chords with added seconds, or added fourths, or chromatically altered tones; there are quartal chords, quintal chords, and so on, and so on. But we are not writing a complete dictionary of chords here. It is not a goal to list as many different chords as we can possibly think of, or to make this book as thick as possible ... Nonetheless, the doors to both houses remain open, both to new residents and to guests.

CHAPTER SEVEN

The Fundamental Theory of Harmony

There are dozens and dozens of harmony textbooks all over the world, and most of them contain numerous pages of rules, suggestions, advice, examples, theories, opinions, and even contradictions. One of the largest and most complex topics covered is that of chord progressions. In this study, we will address the topic, but we will not provide yet another version of that same information.

Suffice it to say that many of these "rule books," when addressing the subject of progressions, read something like this: "The progression of chord X to chord Y is good. Y to Z is not good. X to Z is sometimes good and sometimes bad. A to B is OK. C usually goes to D, but it can go to E or F. Normally, G goes down a third. H goes up a fifth. I goes up by step. J to K is a progression, but K to J is a retrogression. L to M is a progression, and M to L is also a progression," etc., etc. ..."

After a person reads all this, especially in two, three, or more different textbooks, it is enough to make him want to take half a bottle of Tylenol ... This is, in fact, a complex subject, and very difficult to master. The worst thing about it is that it can happen that one can follow all the rules, and the result may still not sound right. This means that one has either hit a dead end, or is in for a hit-and-miss experience of revision, or both.

There is, however, one general rule that is as foolproof as any rule ever gets. It is called The Fundamental Theory of Harmony, and again, we have the Europeans to thank for it.* This Theory is very simple to explain, to understand, to apply, and to use to check if any given harmonic solution is acceptable or not — without playing it or hearing it.

Observation One:

In major or minor tonalities, the root movement between two chords can be only by second, fifth, or third (up or down).

Observation Two:

When the root moves by second (up or down), the two chords have no tones in common. This is called a Very Strong (VS) progression.

---

*This author learned this Theory decades ago, not from any textbook, but from lectures given by his Icelandic professor of Theory and Composition, the late Dr. Hallgrimur Helgason (1914-1994). Dr. Helgason was a prolific composer, music theorist, historical musicologist, and performer. He knew at least six European languages: Icelandic, German, French, Italian, Spanish, and English. He studied first in Leipzig, and subsequently obtained his Doctorate in Music from the University of Zurich, where he was a pupil of Paul Hindemith (1895-1963).

Observation Three:

When the root moves by fifth (up or down), the two chords have one tone in common. This is called a Strong (S) progression.

Observation Four:

When the root moves by third down, the two chords have two tones in common. The root of the second chord IS NOT anticipated in the first chord. This is called a Weak (W) progression.

Observation Five:

When the root moves by third up, the two chords have two tones in common. The root of the second chord IS anticipated in the first chord. This is called a Very Weak (VW) progression.

THEORY OF HARMONY

A VS or S progression may be followed by any progression. A W progression should not be followed by another W progression, and must not be followed by a VW progression (except in extremely rare circumstances). Only VS or S are acceptable as the succeeding progression. A VW progression must almost always be followed by a VS progression. If this is not possible, it should be followed by a S progression. To follow it by a W progression is bad, and to follow it by another VW progression is almost always unacceptable.

There is a lot to be said for this Theory. First, it makes a tremendous amount of genuine, logical common sense. Second, it does not refer to the functions of chords. But if we look at it closely, we see that it is root movement by thirds that are being restricted: "Do not allow the root to move by thirds two (or more) times in a row" is another way of phrasing this commandment. And chords whose roots are a third apart are precisely the ones that are paired up in the European functional system as Tonic and Tonic Parallel, Dominant and Dominant Parallel, and Subdominant and Subdominant Parallel. So the goal of a resulting healthy mixture of functions is automatically — almost magically — achieved.

The third feature of this Theory is that it contains the secret — the "magic" — formula for writing harmonic progressions: *Always consider all chords three at a time.* This means that the thing to do when writing and checking your work is to consider together the first three chords, then chords 2, 3, and 4, then 3, 4, and 5, then 4, 5 and 6, then n, n + 1, n + 2, and so on, for every chord n, all the way to chords (L – 2), (L – 1), and L, where L is the last chord. If you make sure that every set of three consecutive chords follows the rules of the Theory, then you do not need to play them on a piano or to hear them.

Multiple examples could be considered here; Example 7-1 below is one of them.

Ex. 7-1

When the leading note moves to the tonic (in the soprano), we almost always use V to harmonize it. However, when the soprano line moves "do-ti-la," this is a very bad idea. We need to use iii in order to neutralize the natural tendency of the leading note to rise. But since I to iii is a VW progression, it must be followed by a VS progression, and when it is, the perfect solution results. The point is that I to iii is a VW progression, NOT a bad progression. "Bad" implies "Don't use it." In fact, in this case, it is the best choice that you can make.

So really, in spite of what people say, there is no such thing as a "bad" progression consisting of two chords. There are, however, bad progressions consisting of three or more chords, which occur when the rules of the Theory are not obeyed.

In the second example above, we can see that it is very easy to harmonize the first two chords and end up with only one tone in common. (The third is doubled in the last chord because we have actually written a deceptive cadence in a-minor).

The feature of this Theory that is the most relevant for us is that functions are not mentioned in the Theory. This means that it applies just as well to our Nonaphonic, Bi-modal system as it does to traditional harmony. This is a very fortunate thing because we do not have to write a whole new harmonic rulebook.

Because in the Nonaphonic, Bi-Modal system we have two sets of mediants and submediants, it is very easy to write root movements by thirds which have only one tone in common, and almost as easy to do so without anticipating the root of a chord in the chord preceding it (example c-minor to e-minor). So overall, we can end up with very few W and VW progressions, and therefore very few headaches. If anything, there is a danger of ending up with too few W and VW progressions, and therefore not enough variety in that respect. Common sense should come to the rescue here. We know that opposites are most effective when they are juxtaposed against each other: Dissonance vs. consonance, loud vs. soft, fast vs. slow, and so on. The same applies here. We obtain the best results when we employ a healthy proportional mixture of VS, S, W, and VW progressions.

This concludes our overview of the Fundamental Theory of Harmony. Generally speaking, it is quite certain that the most important progressions in a piece of music are the cadences. Some people call cadences punctuations; they can also be called resting points, turning points, destination points, form markers, and so on. Whatever their names, cadences are not all VS or even S progressions. Not only that, there are other cadences that we can use in addition to the standard four that are typically taught (V-I, I-V, IV-I, and V-vi, or V-i, i-V, iv-i and V-VI in a minor key). So in order to end this chapter, let us examine various strengths of progressions by looking at five less common, but still most useful, cadences.

The first is the final cadence of the Rachmaninoff Prelude in G Major, Op. 32, No. 5, shown in Example 7-2.

Ex. 7-2

One might hastily symbolize the second chord shown as I_4^6. But if we analyze these chords as $I - I_4^6 - I$, then why does the progression sound as if the harmony moves away from I and then back to it? Because the second chord does not have a tonic function; it has a dominant function, and the progression is really T-D-T. If we use Roman numerals, then we should symbolize it as:

$$V^{13}_{\cancel{7}}$$

The point is, that the acoustical root of this chord is not G, but D. Furthermore, if another note were to be added to this chord, it would be f#, not g. (We can prove this to ourselves by trying it on the piano.) Also, the d in the alto could then be changed to c (the dominant seventh). The reason that the composer wrote this chord as he did is that the texture of this particular Prelude is very light, and it would not have been right to thicken it for the second-last chord only, especially at the dynamic level "pp".

Our second example, Example 7-3, is the final cadence of a setting, in B♭+, of "Adoramus Te, Christe," which is a piece of Christian Church music, specifically, a motet.

Ex. 7-3

Now, even if we checked every harmony textbook in the world, we would probably not find a "vi-I Cadence" mentioned or described, let alone defined, anywhere. After all, this is a VW progression, so how can it possibly be a cadence? And yet, it *sounds* like a cadence, so it must be one.

This author does not mind admitting to his readers that it took him an extremely long time to figure out what is going on here. As it turns out, the acoustical root of the second-last chord is E♭, which is absent from the score. The chord is IV^7 with the root omitted, and the cadence is a Plagal (or Church) cadence. Again, we can show that this is so by playing it, preferably on an organ, with the E♭ a major tenth below the G, in the pedals. The conclusion here is that chord vi, the Submediant (or Tonic Parallel) comprises the third, fifth, and seventh of IV^7, just as the Subdominant triad comprises the third, fifth, and seventh of ii^7.

This is a very serene piece of music, sung slowly, reverently, and ending very softly. As was the case in the previous example, this is no place for a "sledge hammer" cadence; hence, the reason for the utmost subtlety of the final cadence.

The first two examples are ones of weak cadences; the next two are examples of strong cadences. In the third example, Example 7-4, we present a short melody, and ask readers to think of a rather rare cadence that works perfectly at the halfway point, marked X and Y.

Ex. 7-4

There is nothing wrong with using V-vi^6 there, or even V-I^6. However, the following solution, in Example 7-5, is much more imaginative and interesting.

Ex. 7-5

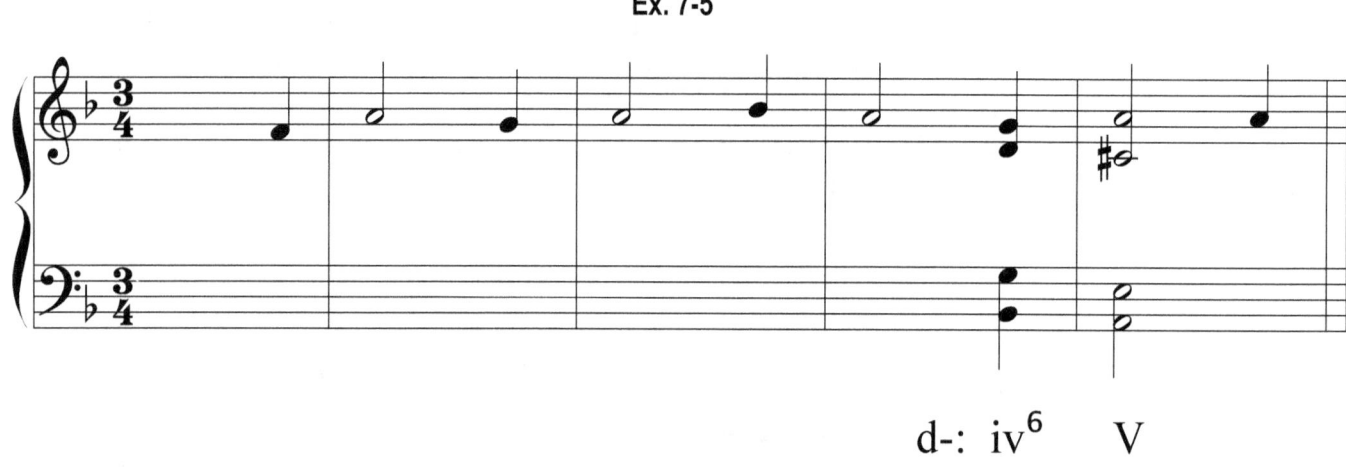

d-: iv^6 V

This is a Phrygian cadence in the relative minor key, so called because the bass moves downwards by minor second. The point here is that you can think of doing this *only* if you are thinking of b-flat as being the key signature of F+ **AND/OR d-!** This is Bi-Modal thinking, and we need to think this way full-time when using our new system. (Of course, that means "major and tonic minor," and not "major and relative minor").

The phenomenon of the bass moving down (or up) by semitone is an important one in the study of strengths of progressions. Root movement *or* bass movement by semitone creates a stronger progression than does similar movement by whole tone. That is why the Phrygian Cadence, as shown in Example 7-5 is special. It is also the reason that the Deceptive Cadence is stronger in a minor key than in a major key; the root moves by semitone in the former, and by whole tone in the latter.

We normally associate the term "leading note" with the seventh scale degree, which resolves by step upwards. But there are other leading notes, in the sense that any note that resolves by semitone (up or down) can be called a leading note. For example, with respect to the Dominant Seventh chord, Europeans call the seventh scale degree the authentic leading note and the fourth scale degree the plagal leading note. When these two leading notes are in the outer voices, as shown in Example 7-6, the resulting progression is especially strong, due to the tension and resolution created in the two voices that supply the "frame" of the harmony.

Ex. 7-6

$V^4_2 \quad I^6$

We can study that tritone in the Dominant Seventh chord even more closely. The tritone is the only interval that, when inverted, reproduces itself. In V^7 of C+/c-, b is the third of the chord, and f is the seventh. Now what happens if we reconstruct this chord in such a way so as to make the b the seventh degree and f the third? The result is that the chord changes from a Mm7th to an Augmented Sixth Chord, specifically, the German Sixth. This chord actually has four leading notes, and that is why parallel perfect fifths are permitted in order to effect its proper resolution, as shown in Example 7-7, which is our fourth cadence.

Ex. 7-7

C+: $Gr^6 \quad I$

It has been said that the strongest progression in music is V-I. That may be so, but which V? Is it V^7? V^9? V^{13}? Actually, because of its four leading notes, it is the German Sixth Chord, which is a version of V, at least according to the Continental Europeans. They analyze this chord as the "Incomplete (meaning with root omitted) dominant minor ninth with flattened fifth in the bass," as shown in Example 7-8.

56 • *Dodecaphonic Tonality*

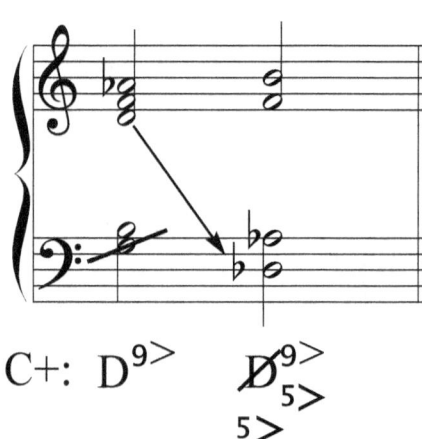

Ex. 7-8

Our fifth and last cadence is one used by Chopin in his Polonaise in e-flat minor, Op. 26, No. 2. The middle section of this work is in B Major; the last five measures of this section are shown in Example 7-9 below. If we listen to this passage *before* doing (or reading) the harmonic analysis of the last three chords, these sound like three different chords.

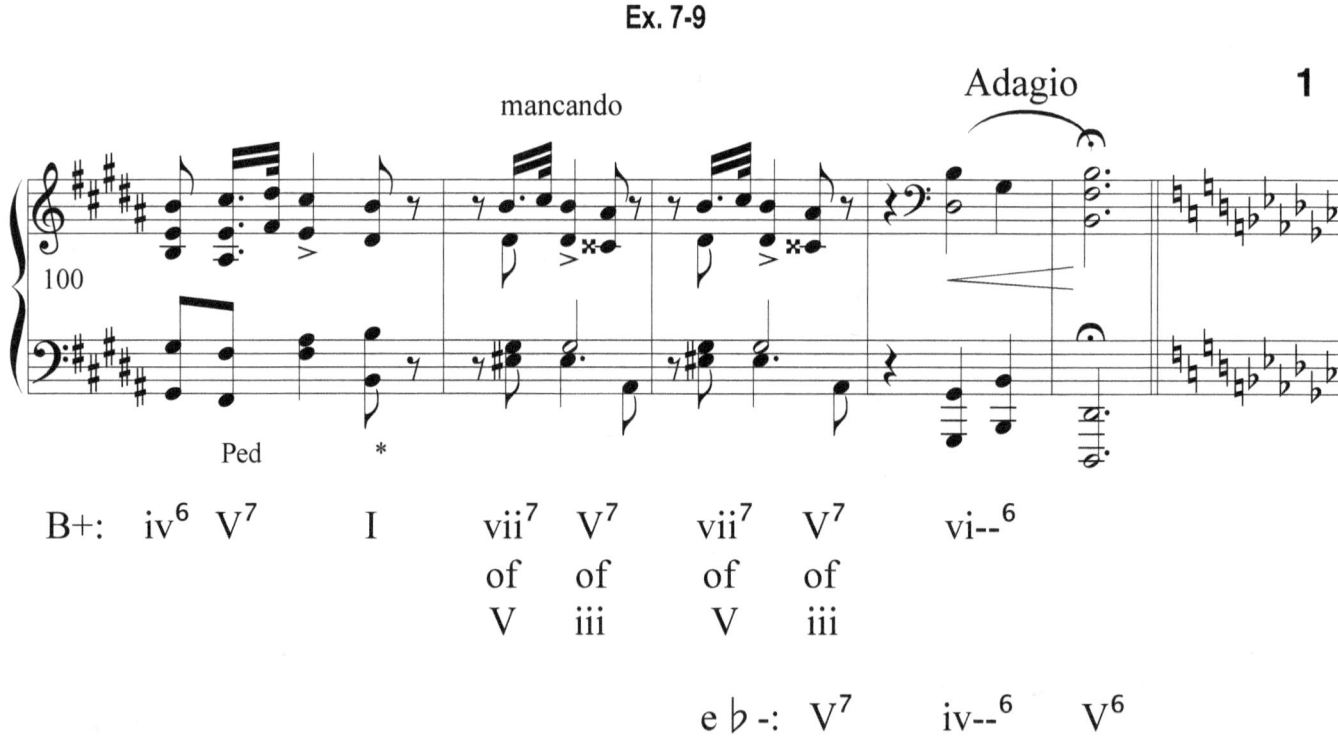

Ex. 7-9

Now, if we look at the harmonic analysis, we see that it shows that the second-last chord is just the first inversion of the third-last one. But that is not all there is to it. This chord is the pivot chord, and in the old key it has a tonic function, while in the new key, it has a subdominant function.

The point is, that here we have an example of something that is not mentioned in the Fundamental Theory of Harmony: A change of inversion of a chord, or a change of function of a chord, is actually a type of VW progression. It has to be, because it sounds like one. In fact, to some listeners, it may even sound like a S progression. What is more, Chopin could have easily written a Phrygian cadence here,* and resolved the second-last chord to V (in root position). But he chose to use V in first inversion instead. This emphasizes even more strongly the importance of inversions and of bass movement. **For us, the most important point of all this is that, in the bi-modal system, we can write diatonic progressions such as I^6 to i^6 or IV^6 to iv^6, which are most effective, yet not often used.**

These five cadences were presented here in order to demonstrate that we can elaborate on the Fundamental Theory of Harmony, and expand it, if we take into consideration additional factors, such as: Texture, acoustical roots of chords (which are omitted in the score), root and/or bass movements by semitone, the use of leading notes, and the use of inversions and bi-functional chords. We are not about to start labeling these as VVW (Very, Very Weak) or VVS (Very, Very Strong), but it is necessary to be aware that it is possible to create more than the basic four degrees of strength of progressions. Knowing this, we can also understand why a certain progression can sound weaker or stronger than it looks at first sight.

---

* He probably forgot to take it out of the *fridge in* time to use it…

CHAPTER EIGHT

The Traditional Quintcircle, Related Keys, Modulation, and Change of Mode

Whenever the traditional quintcircle (or circle of fifths) is presented, it is shown as a clock face, on which C major appears in the 12 o'clock position, together with a-minor, which has the same (blank) key signature. Keys with sharps in their key signatures go by perfect fifths clockwise, and keys with flats in their keys signatures go by perfect fourths counter-clockwise. They meet at the 6 o'clock position, which has both six sharps and six flats. Then, each goes on for one more "hour" in its own direction, so that the keys with sharps end at 7 o'clock with seven sharps, and the keys with flats end at 5 o'clock with seven flats.

Examples are provided using the 12 o'clock C major/a-minor position as the starting point. The group of six related keys is then C major and a-minor, G major and e minor, and F major and d minor. Any modulation that takes place from C major or a-minor to a key other than one of the related five is considered to be an "extraneous" modulation. "Extraneous" takes on the meaning "distant," so that we modulate either to a closely related key or to a distant key. It has become natural to think that the more "hours" away a key is from 12 o'clock, the more distant it is from C major and a-minor. This may be logical thinking, but, as will be shown later in this chapter, it is not entirely true. Example 8-1 on the next page shows the traditional quintcircle, but there is more. There is a "secret tunnel" that goes from C major to c minor and from a-minor to A major. (It must be secret, because almost nobody ever shows it)...

Ex. 8-1

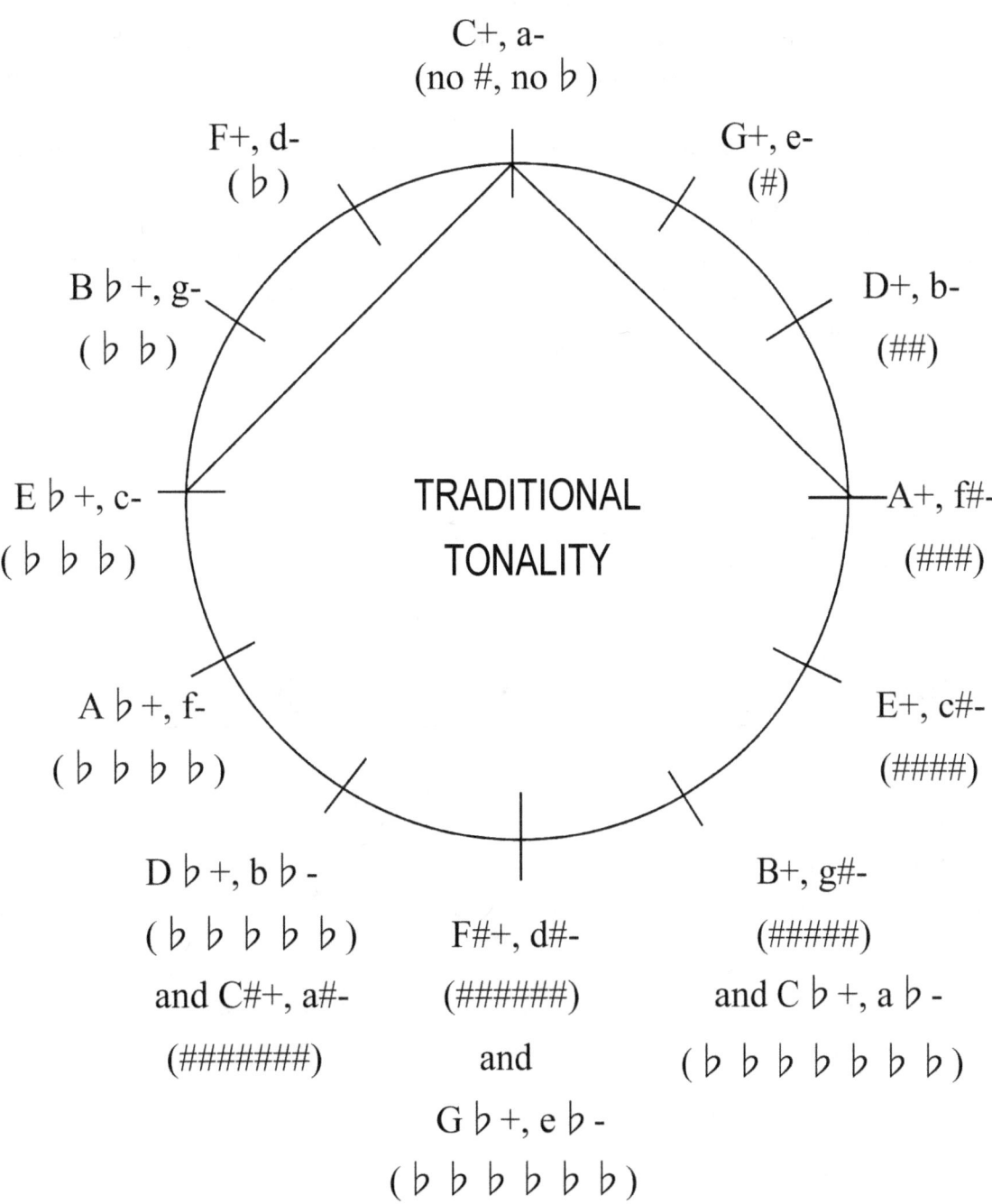

Anyone who takes this secret tunnel (and secret agents love it!) gets to travel non-stop, without detours, from 12 o'clock directly to 3 o'clock, or from 12 o'clock directly to 9 o'clock. There are many "trains" that travel through this secret tunnel. Some do not run as often as others, but here is a list of the most common ones: V, V^7, V^{-9}, V^{13}, vii°, and vii°^{m7}. Less common are: iv, ♭VII (= IV of IV), the three Augmented Sixths, and the Neapolitan Sixth.*

Chopin does not even take the secret tunnel; he flies and uses a parachute: He writes a double bar, changes the key signature to reflect the change of mode, and continues to compose. This proves an ironic fact: To achieve a change of mode, it is not even necessary to employ any modulatory techniques or procedures whatsoever. It is possible to "just do it."

There is a law of physics that states: "The angle of incidence equals the angle of reflection." This law can be applied here, at least for right angles. In the quintcircle with the secret tunnels, if we begin at 3 o'clock, we can aim for 12 o'clock, bounce off it, and deflect to 9 o'clock, using two "trains" and one "transfer," changing tracks at 12 o'clock, as shown in Example 8-2.

Ex. 8-2

It follows, by extension, that if we show all the secret tunnels, then within the quintcircle, a 12-pointed star appears, as shown in Example 8-3.

---

*Sundays and Holidays only

The Traditional Quintcircle, Related Keys, Modulation, and Change of Mode • 61

Ex. 8-3

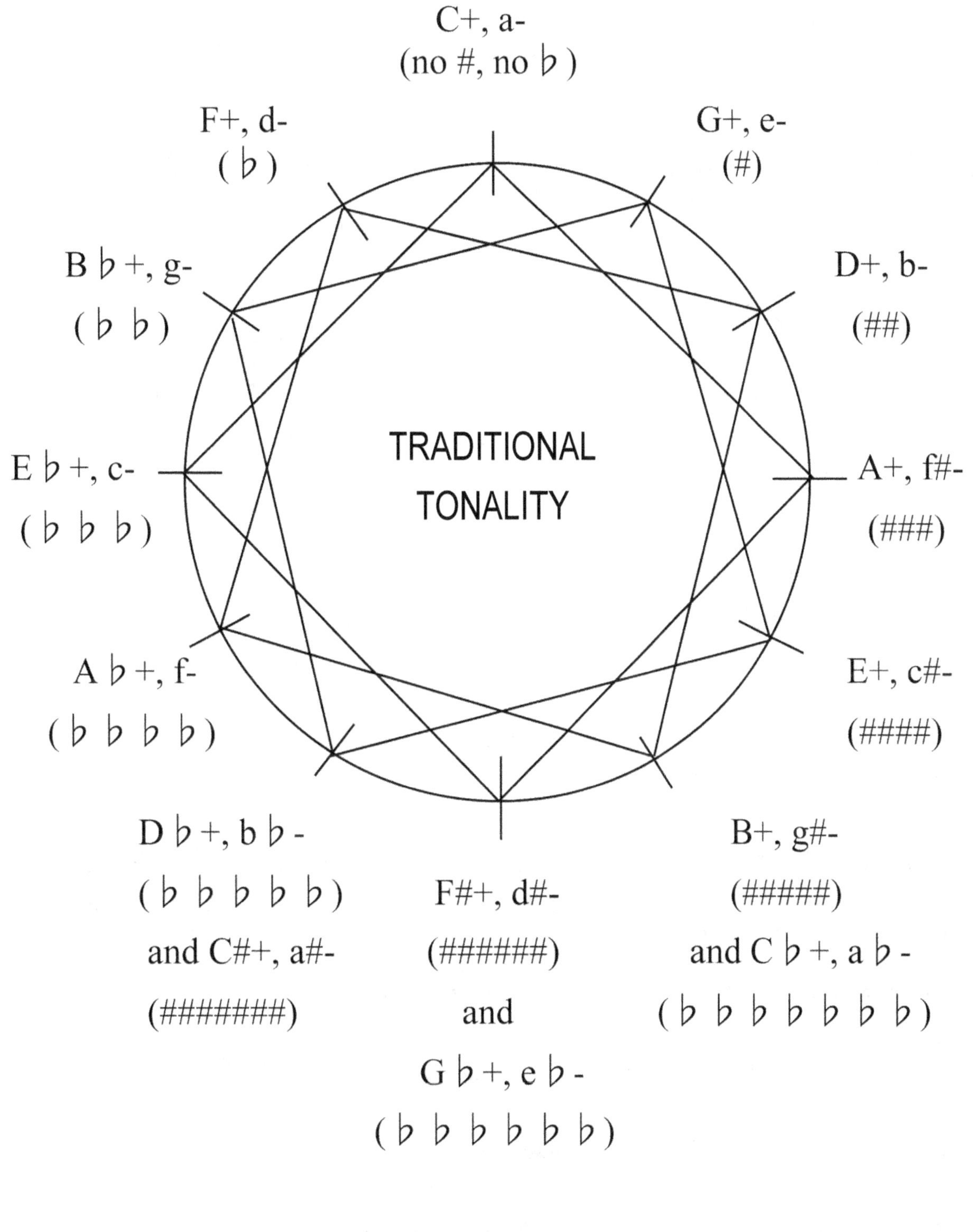

C+, a-
(no #, no ♭)

F+, d-
(♭)

G+, e-
(#)

B♭+, g-
(♭♭)

D+, b-
(##)

E♭+, c-
(♭♭♭)

TRADITIONAL
TONALITY

A+, f#-
(###)

A♭+, f-
(♭♭♭♭)

E+, c#-
(####)

D♭+, b♭-
(♭♭♭♭♭)
and C#+, a#-
(#######)

F#+, d#-
(######)
and
G♭+, e♭-
(♭♭♭♭♭♭)

B+, g#-
(#####)
and C♭+, a♭-
(♭♭♭♭♭♭)

We can now see that there is more to the quintcircle than just a circle. With the 12-pointed star in place, there are two clear categories of "extraneous" keys: Those that can be reached in two steps and those that require three steps to reach. No keys require more than three steps to reach, as the table below shows. In this table, "C" stands for a step taken by following the circle, and "ST" stands for a step taken by the secret tunnel.

Modulation from 12 o'clock to:	Number of steps required
1 o'clock	1: C
2 o'clock	2: 2C or ST + C
3 o'clock	1: ST
4 o'clock	2: ST + C or C + ST
5 o'clock	3: 2ST + C or 2C + ST
6 o'clock	2: 2ST
7 o'clock	3: 2ST + C or 2C + ST
8 o'clock	2: ST + C or C + ST
9 o'clock	1: ST
10 o'clock	2: 2C or ST + C
11 o'clock	1: C

NOTE: It only makes sense that the following pairs of lines duplicate each other: 1 and 11, 2 and 10, 3 and 9, 4 and 8, 5 and 7.

With apologies to those readers who dislike analogies or figurative terminology, there is a reason for all this talk of secret tunnels and the twelve-pointed star. Without these, the quintcircle alone leads people to jump to conclusions, some of them true, some false:

a) The farther away a key is, the more steps it must require to modulate to it.

False

b) Keys that are two stations apart are more closely related than keys that are three stations apart.

False

c) Keys that are three stations apart are more closely related than keys that are four stations apart.

True

d) Keys that are four stations apart are more closely related than keys that are five stations apart.

True

e) Keys that are five stations apart are more closely related than keys that are six stations apart.

False

f) Keys that are six stations apart are more closely related than keys that are seven stations apart.

True

Here is the explanation for the True and False statements: If we follow the quintcircle, bass movement is either up a perfect fifth, down a perfect fourth, again up a perfect fifth and down a perfect fourth, etc. ..., OR it is down a perfect fifth, up a perfect fourth, again down a perfect fifth and up a perfect fourth, etc. ... These are both good to do as exercises and for learning purposes, but composers just do not do that when composing a new piece of music. The only way to measure the true degree of extraneousness of keys is to take the shortest distance possible between all pairs of keys and to compare these distances. And that is exactly what the table above illustrates. Four keys (and their relatives) are one step apart. Five keys (and their relatives) are two steps apart. Two keys (and their relatives) are three steps apart, for a total of 22 keys. It just does not matter that a change of mode is called that (and not a modulation), because the term for what has occurred does not change the fact that the process has taken us to a point that is three stations away from where we started.

Let us take this a step further, and consider the square that joins 12 o'clock to 3 o'clock, 6 o'clock, and 9 o'clock. Suppose that we think of the circumference of the circle as a bus route. Starting at 12 o'clock station, there is nothing wrong with taking the bus for six stops to reach 6 o'clock station. But if the square is the subway system, most people would prefer to take it and stop only at 3 o'clock (or 9 o'clock) along their way. Since subway trains travel a lot faster than do buses, it takes about as long to travel two subway stops as it does to travel two bus stops, but the subway passenger gets a lot farther in about the same time.

Finally, we can think of the square as a baseball diamond. If the batter aims to score a home run, he runs as quickly and efficiently around the diamond as he can. This means that he barely touches each base with his foot, turns 90 degrees, and keeps running. We can do that also, using the *same* diminished seventh chord between bases. All we have to do is to change the spelling of the enharmonics involved in the transition, as shown in Example 8-4.

Once again, analogies are made here for a reason. A musical passage *is* a trip, and it is good to think of it as one. We always start at home, go somewhere, either stay there for a while, or keep going, possibly to another resting point, and so on, until we eventually return home to stay.

The following, then, is a summary of which keys are one, two, and three steps away from C major and a-minor:

One step away are: G+, e-, F+, d-, A+, f#-, E♭+, and c-.

Two steps away are: D+, b-, B♭+, g-, E+, c#-, A♭+, f-, F#+, and d#- (or G♭+ and e♭-).

Three steps away are: B+, g#-, D♭+, and b♭- (and their enharmonic duplicates, C♭+, a♭-, C#+, and a#-).

We will compare this summary to our findings in the next chapter, which covers the same topics in the context of the Nonaphonic Quintcircle.

CHAPTER NINE

The Nonaphonic, Bi-Modal Quintcircle, Related Keys, Modulation, and Semi-Modulation

Before we begin, can any readers figure out what Semi-Modulation is, while reading this chapter? The answer is given on its last page.

In the previous chapter, we saw how the tonic major and minor keys can be regarded as being just as closely related to each other (one step apart) as are keys that have one sharp (or one flat) more (or less) than the original key.

Because the Nonaphonic system is Bi-Modal, its quintcircle (circle of fifths) contains only 12 keys, as shown in Example 9-2 on the next page. Once again, we use 12 o'clock, which is now C+/c- Nonaphonic Bi-Modal, as the starting point, and take a look around. In doing so, it is helpful to refer to the Nonaphonic scales and key signatures written out in Examples 3-7 and 3-8 in Chapter Three. In addition to those, in Example 9-2, we use D♭+/d♭- because doing so makes it easier to analyze key relationships. The D♭/d♭ Nonaphonic Bi-Modal key signature and scale are shown in Example 9-1 below.

Ex. 9-1

D♭/d♭

Ex. 9-2

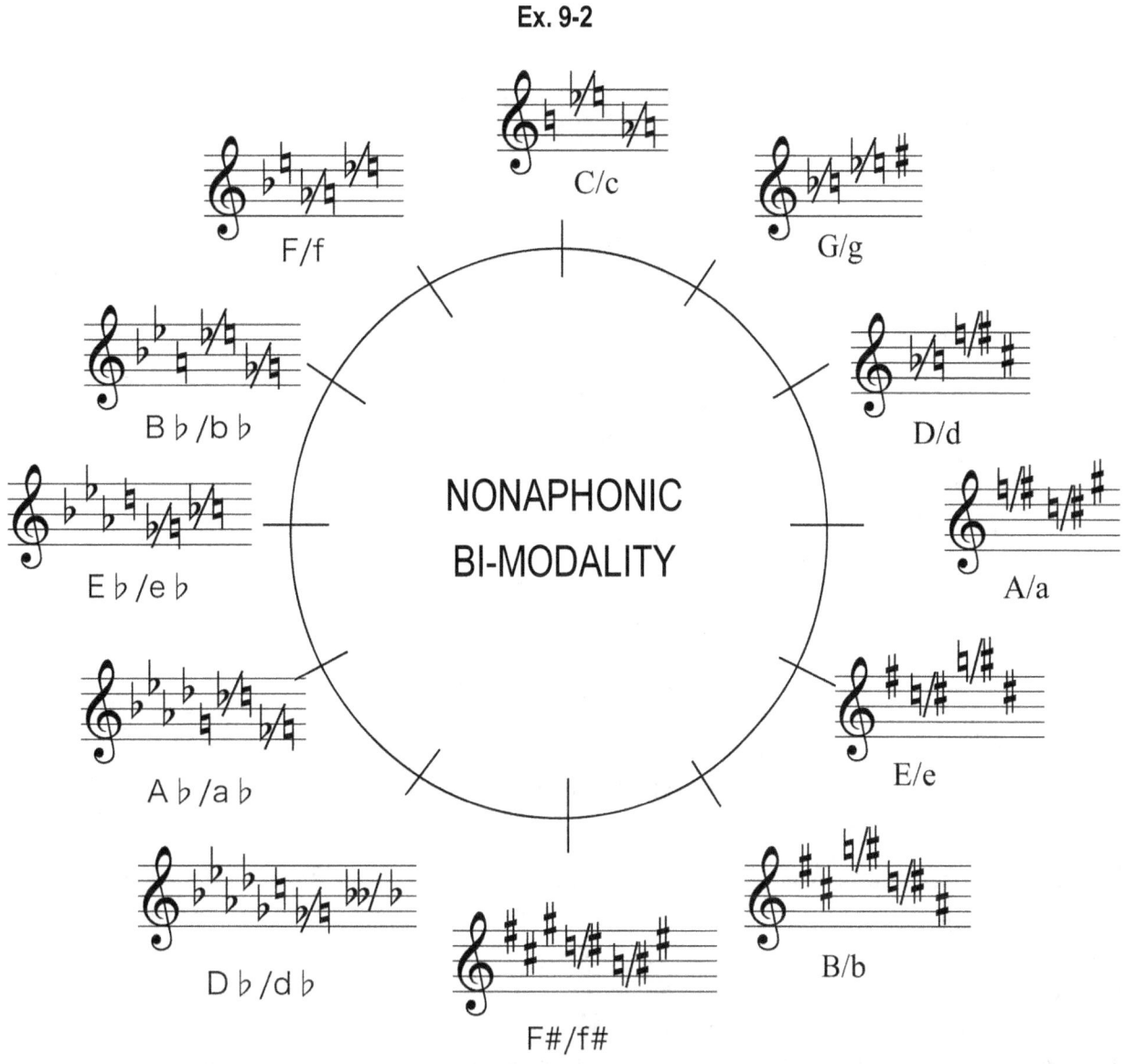

NOTE: These key signatures reflect Nonaphonic Bi-Modality most accurately, and that is precisely what key signatures are supposed to do. However, repeated use of accidentals within the score is unavoidable. Therefore, it would be appropriate to start a new trend, and to state the key signature only once, at the beginning of a composition, as we traditionally do with the time signature.

Because this system is different from the traditional one, there is a different way (which works better) to analyze how closely keys are related to each other. That way is to examine how many tones a given key has in common with the other eleven keys. So if the given key is C+/c-, the relationships are as shown in Chart 9-1. If we assign one proximity point for each tone in common, and half a proximity point for each enharmonic tone in common, then the total number of proximity points for each key becomes as shown in the third column.

Chart 9-1

KEY	NUMBER OF TONES IN COMMON WITH C+/c-	NUMBER OF PROXIMITY POINTS
G+/g-	7	7
F+/f-	7	7
D+/d-	6	6
B♭+/b♭-	6	6
A+/a-	6 plus 1 enharmonic	6.5
E♭+/e♭-	6 plus 1 enharmonic	6.5
E+/e-	5 plus 2 enharmonics	6
A♭+/a♭-	5 plus 2 enharmonics	6
B+/b-	4 plus 2 enharmonics	5
D♭+/d♭-	4 plus 2 enharmonics	5
C#+/c#-	2 plus 4 enharmonics	4
F#+/f#-	3 plus 3 enharmonics	4.5
G♭+/g♭-	3 plus 3 enharmonics	4.5

A couple of questions arise here. First, should enharmonics count? They do not always count, but when we are on the topic of modulation, they should. Second, are these proximity points appropriate? Well, it does not seem fair to consider an enharmonic equivalent to be every bit as good as the identical note. So this is one way to approximate the value of an enharmonic equivalent.

One reason that the comparative relationships of keys turned out as they did is that every key in this system contains two thirds and two sixths (major and minor). Because of this, a noteworthy result is that the two keys that are three stations away from the given key actually ended up with more proximity points than did the two keys that are two stations away from it. Even if we do not want to use proximity points, we can just use the statistics shown in the second column, and our general conclusion is about the same, namely, that the most closely related keys are the two next-door neighbors, as in the traditional quintcircle. But then there is a set of six keys that are almost as closely related. Finally, the last three keys, that really are extraneous, are again the same three keys that are the least closely related in traditional tonality.

Chart 9-2 shows a comparison of key relationships in traditional tonality, with C-Major and c-Harmonic Minor being used as the given keys.

Chart 9-2

KEY	NUMBER OF TONES IN COMMON WITH C+	KEY	NUMBER OF TONES IN COMMON WITH c-
G+	6	g-	4
F+	6	f-	4
D+	5	d-	3
B♭+	5	b♭-	3
A+	4	a-	4 plus 1 enharmonic
E♭+	4	e♭-	4 plus 1 enharmonic
E+	3	e-	3 plus 1 enharmonic
A♭+	3	a♭-	3 plus 1 enharmonic
B+	2	b-	3
D♭+	2	d♭-	3
F#+	1 plus 1 enharmonic	f#-	2 plus 2 enharmonics
G♭+	1 plus 1 enharmonic	g♭-	2 plus 2 enharmonics

The major key set came out as expected, but the harmonic minor set just does not have similar consistency. So next, in order to make another comparison, we draw up Chart 9-3 for key relationships between octatonic minor scales, using c- as the given key.

Chart 9-3

KEY	NUMBER OF TONES IN COMMON WITH c-	NUMBER OF PROXIMITY POINTS
g-	5	5
f-	5	5
d-	5	5
b♭-	5	5
a-	5 plus 1 enharmonic	5.5
e♭-	5 plus 1 enharmonic	5.5
e-	4 plus 1 enharmonic	4.5
a♭-	4 plus 1 enharmonic	4.5
b-	3 plus 1 enharmonic	3.5
d♭-	3 plus 1 enharmonic	3.5
f#-	3 plus 3 enharmonics	4.5
g♭-	3 plus 3 enharmonics	4.5

Indeed, these results are much different, because the number of common tones does not proceed in a steady decrease at all. And if we had decided to allot a full point for enharmonics, the results would have been even stranger, because the totals would then have been (top-down): 5, 5, 5, 5, 6, 6, 5, 5, 4, 4, 6, and 6. So, as the saying goes, "Go figure …"

Next, we draw up Chart 9-4 for key relationships between traditional melodic minor keys. These, of course, are nine-tone scales, but they contain two sixths and two sevenths (rather than two thirds). Again, we use c- as the given key. (The same results are obtained if we use a melodic minor key plus its relative major).

Chart 9-4

KEY	NUMBER OF TONES IN COMMON WITH c-	NUMBER OF PROXIMITY POINTS
g-	7	7
f-	7	7
d-	7	7
b♭-	7	7
a-	6 + 1 enharmonic	6.5
e♭-	6 + 1 enharmonic	6.5
e-	5 + 1 enharmonic	5.5
a♭-	5 + 1 enharmonic	5.5
b-	4 + 2 enharmonics	5
d♭-	4 + 2 enharmonics	5
f#	3 + 3 enharmonics	4.5
g♭-	3 + 3 enharmonics	4.5

These results just go to prove that two different sets of nine-tone scales do not yield identical results in commonality of tones, although 8 out of 12 are identical, and the remaining 4 are close.

In fact, it is a good idea, at this point, to summarize the five charts into one Proximity Points Comparison Chart. We do so in Chart 9-5, which appears below. In it, "En" stands for "Enharmonic." When reading the numbers in this chart, we must remember that major and harmonic minor scales are heptatonic, and the melodic minor scale is nonatonic. (We could, of course, calculate all the percentages of common tones and draw up converted charts using these).

Chart 9-5

GIVEN KEY	MAJOR C+	HARMONIC MINOR c-	OCTATONIC c-	MELODIC MINOR c-	NONAPHONIC BI-MODAL C+/c-
PROXIMITY POINTS TO:					
G+/g-	6	4	5	7	7
F+/f-	6	4	5	7	7
D+/d-	5	3	5	7	6
B♭+/b♭-	5	3	5	7	6
A+/a-	4	4 + 1 En	5 + 1 En	6 + 1 En	6 + 1 En
E♭+/e♭-	4	4 + 1 En	5 + 1 En	6 + 1 En	6 + 1 En
E+/e-	3	3 + 1 En	4 + 1 En	5 + 1 En	5 + 2 En
A♭+/a♭-	3	3 + 1 En	4 + 1 En	5 + 1 En	5 + 2 En
B+/b-	2	3	3 + 1 En	4 + 2 En	4 + 2 En
D♭+/d♭-	2	3	3 + 1 En	4 + 2 En	4 + 2 En
F#+/f#-	1 + 1 En	2 + 2 En	3 + 3 En	3 + 3 En	3 + 3 En
G♭+/g♭-	1 + 1 En	2 + 2 En	3 + 3 En	3 + 3 En	3 + 3 En

Readers can crunch the numbers in all these charts for themselves, and make numerous observations about them. For one thing, we can observe immediately that the mutual relationships between keys in our octatonic and nonaphonic, bi-modal systems are generally closer than they are in traditional modalities. It is clear that the octatonic and nonatonic, bi-modal scales and key signatures open up a new can of ... tonalities.

There are no changes of mode, in the traditional sense, in this system, because both modes are inherent in each key by its nature to begin with; bi-modality is the "name of the game" here. But a modulation in this system will mean, for example, a switch from C+/c- to G+/g-, or to D+/d-, etc..

What happens, though, if we perform a switch such as from C+/c- to C+/g-, or from C+/c- to B♭+/c-? These are definitely possible, as are many other key changes of this type. For these, we must introduce a new concept, that of **Semi-Modulation,** which simply means that one half of the original bi-modality stays the same, while the other half changes. When this happens, the result is bi-tonal, or even tri-tonal, bi-modality. That is the subject of Part Two of this study, entitled: Bi-Tonal, Tri-Tonal, and Polytonal Bi-Modalities Using 9 to 12 Tones.

CHAPTER TEN

Other Forms of Bi-Modalities

This chapter is optional, but it is included, because the information herein will provide us with a more complete picture of bi-modalities in general. It is natural for us to think in terms of major and minor modes only. However, we know that in the Middle Ages, there were seven basic Church modes; the Ionian, plus the six shown in Example 2-2. These can be divided into two groups: those containing the major third (above the root), and those containing the minor third. So the first group consists of the Ionian, Lydian, and Mixolydian modes, while the second group consists of the Dorian, Phrygian, Aeolian, and Locrian modes.

This means that we can construct bi-modalities of the Major/minor form in twelve different ways, as shown in Example 10-1 below. In this example, we will call the Ionian mode "Major," and the Aeolian mode "Minor."

Ex. 10-1

1) Major/Dorian
2) Major/Phrygian
3) Major/Minor
4) Major/Locrian
5) Lydian/Dorian
6) Lydian/Phrygian
7) Lydian/Minor
8) Lydian/Locrian
9) Mixolydian/Dorian
10) Mixolydian/Phrygian
11) Mixolydian/Minor
12) Mixolydian/Locrian

Now we can draw up Example 10-2, which shows the 12 resulting combinations, using c as the root. To make sure that there are no errors, we can refer back to the key signatures shown in Example 2-2. Example 10-2 appears on the following two pages.

Next, we examine the resulting sets. As it happens, purely by chance, the very first one is by far the best of the lot. Why this is so will become very clear as soon as we have studied 10-tone sets in Part Two. That is where we will be examining set 3 (Major/minor), a ten-tone set, in great detail. For now, we can look ahead a bit, and make an important observation, which will help to explain what is meant by "best of the lot."

Our fundamental nonaphonic set contains two thirds and two sixths (and the leading note). Set 3 contains two thirds, two sixths, and two sevenths. And set 1 is, so to speak, half-way in between, because it contains two thirds and two sevenths. So, as nonaphonic sets go, this one is a gem. Just as two sixths make both the major and minor subdominant triads diatonic, in the same way, two sevenths make both the major and minor dominant triads diatonic. We recall here that in the original, natural minor mode, the dominant triad is minor. In the case of the Major/Dorian combination, we get the best of both (dominant) worlds.

It follows from the above that this set can be derived in another way. For the moment, let us forget about modes entirely, and go back to the point at which we had the major scale plus the minor third, so eight tones. We decided that the next tone that we will add will be the minor sixth. But some might argue that the next tone that should be added should be the minor seventh (and not the minor sixth). However, these people may not be aware that, in doing so, they are actually proposing a combination of the major and Dorian modes. In any event, we have one derivation by combination, and another one by addition.

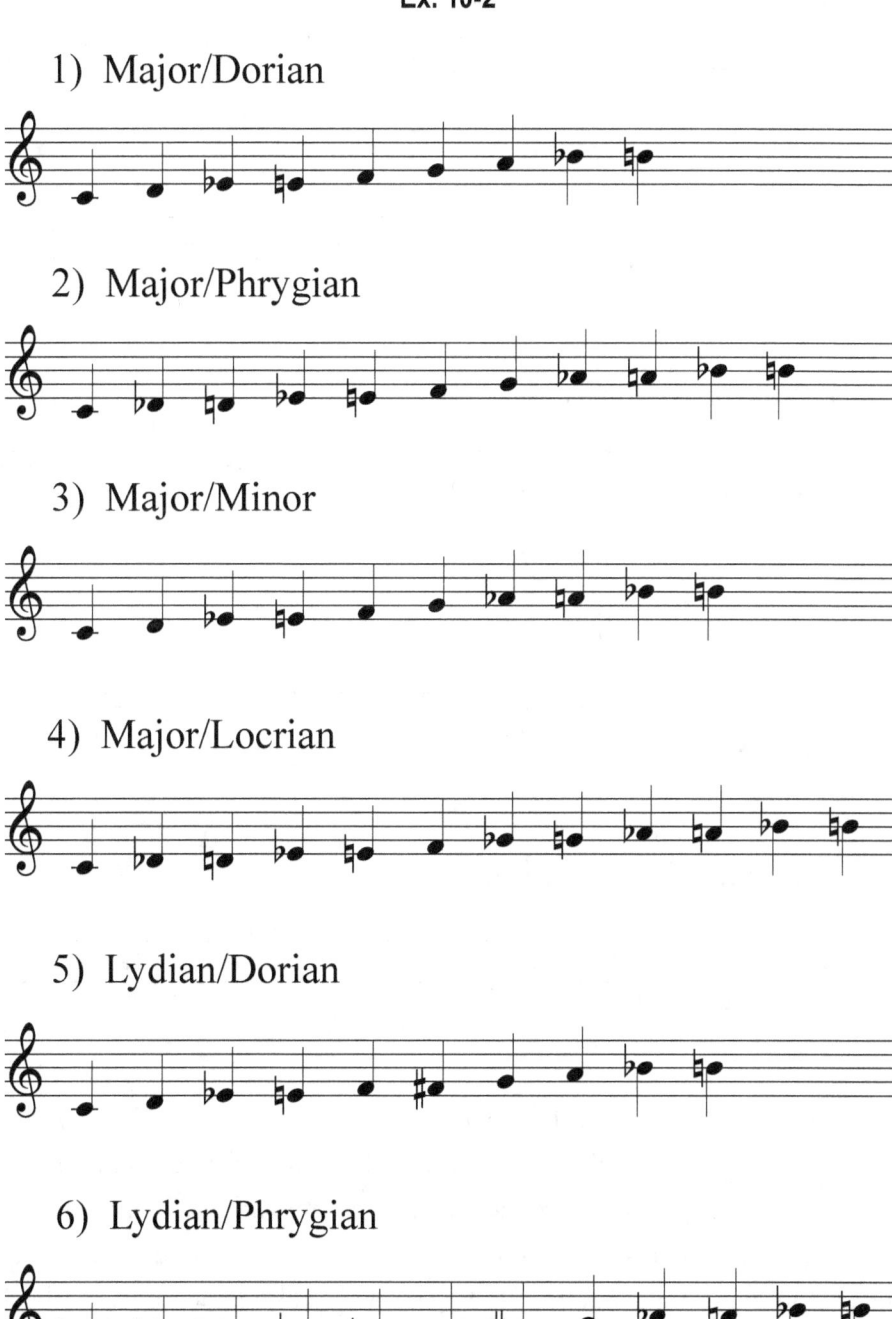

Ex. 10-2 Cont'd

7) Lydian/Minor

8) Lydian/Locrian

9) Mixolydian/Dorian

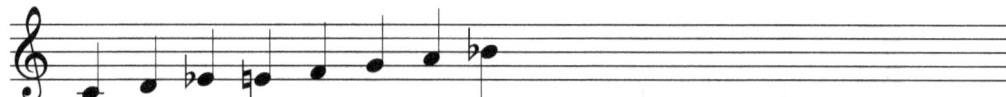

10) Mixolydian/Dorian

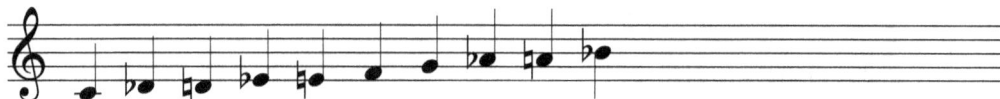

11) Mixolydian/Minor

12) Mixolydian/Locrian

There is only one other nonaphonic set in Example 10-2, and that is set 11, the Mixolydian/Minor. It bears a very close resemblance to our fundamental nonaphonic set, the only difference being that the minor seventh is present, while the major seventh is not. But since the major seventh is the leading note, its absence is a flaw. The history of the minor key has shown that we cannot live for long without the leading note … (The same problem exists in set 9, the only 8-tone set in the example). However, if we read the notes of set 11 beginning on f, we find that they are a transposition of set 1 up a perfect fifth. So sets 1 and 11 are actually the same set.

Finally, we recall that, at the end of Chapter One, we said "the less notes the better." So for all of these reasons, set 1, the Major/Dorian, is the best of the sets shown in Example 10-2.

Sets consisting of more than nine tones are all discussed in Part Two. There, set 3, the Major/minor set, will take centre stage. But if we examine sets 3, 5, and 10 more closely, we can look ahead, and observe something very interesting. Set 5, the Lydian/Dorian set, is actually the same as set 3, if beginning on the g of set 5. It is set 3 transposed up a perfect fifth.

When we first look at set 10, Mixolydian/Phrygian (the only remaining 10-tone set in the example), it does not look as good as set 3. It contains the minor second, instead of the leading note, which makes it a poorly structured set. However, if we take a closer look at it, then we observe that it is actually a transposition of set 3 up a perfect fourth. So sets 3, 5, and 10 are actually the same set, if starting on the f of set 10.

For the record, the remaining six sets (numbers 2, 4, 6, 7, 8, and 12) are of no particular practical value when regarded as combinations of modes. In Part Two, we will see that only very specific eleven-tone sets are useful as stepping stones between 10- and 12-tone sets. Finally, 12-tone tonal sets will form the culminating point of our study. But these will not be regarded either as chromatic scales, or as combinations of modes.

CHAPTER ELEVEN

More Historical Perspective and Summary

We began this study by examining many scales, the earliest of which were the Medieval Church Modes, and the latest of which were jazz scales. Now we should briefly mention tonal and atonal systems of the twentieth century, and put things into perspective.

The twentieth century was the first one in music history that was not dominated or defined by any one particular style or trait. Composers tried anything and everything. Stravinsky invented the white-against-black Petrushka chord. Prokofiev and Charles Ives also tried bitonality, and even polytonality. Other composers experimented with quarter-tones, dividing the octave into 24 parts. Still others even tried sixth-tones. Debussy and Ravel became musical impressionist painters. Bartók used unorthodox key signatures. And about 100 years ago, Schoenberg invented Dodecaphonic Atonality.

The rise of expressionism, and other developments, such as electronic music and musique concrète, placed a subconscious, **although perhaps unintended,** message into people's heads: The era of writing tonal music is over; everything worthwhile that can be written in tonal systems has already been written; we must move on to something else — anything else. On the other hand, the neoclassical movement was born, and it led to the legacies of composers such as Stravinsky, Bartók, and Hindemith.

For us, the most relevant developments were that tonality evolved into Wagnerian chromaticism, and was followed by atonality, the Second Viennese School, and experimentation with bitonality and polytonality, which turned out to be largely atonal also. Does it not seem that along the way a leap was made and a gap was left? Following tonal writing (no matter how chromatic), if composers were going to write in more than one key at a time, or to use sets of more than seven notes, why did they not first try uni-tonal, bi-tonal, or tri-tonal bi-modality using nine or more notes? Why did they skip from heptatonic tonal systems all the way to dodecaphonic atonality?

In fact, some famous Romantic composers did write bi-modal compositions. Many of the works of Schubert, among others, can be considered bi-modal. One excellent example of bi-modality can be found in the last of the "Lieder eines fahrenden Gesellen" by Gustav Mahler, of which measures 17 to 36 are reproduced on the next two pages, in Example 11-1. We can clearly see there the use of both major and minor thirds and sixths. Still, bi-modal tonal systems, using any number of tones, have never been defined.

More Historical Perspective and Summary

Ex. 11-1

Ex. 11-1 Cont'd

Presently, in the second decade of the twenty-first century, it is still safe to say that tonal music is not yet a thing of the past. The problem is, of course, that the more centuries pass, the harder and harder it becomes to write tonal music that both sounds good **and** that has not yet been written. Just this fact alone justifies the search for alternate tonal systems, such as bi-modality using at least one tonal center, and perhaps two or three.

In this chapter, we answer three questions: 1) Where have we been? 2) Where are we at this point? 3) Where are we headed?

So first, we started by noting that the pairing of a major key with a minor key has tremendous potential in tonal music. We noted that the most common such combination is major with relative minor, but that the combination of tonic major and minor could be exploited much more than it has been. So we constructed and defined a uni-tonal, bi-modal system, and in the process discovered that the best number of tones with which to do this is nine. To this end, we defined the standardized, octatonic minor scale, then added the major third to it, and thus came up with the nonatonic, bi-modal scale, which we crowned with its very own original, unambiguous key signature. This, then, led to the construction of the Nonaphonic, Bi-Modal Quintcircle.

With regard to question two, at this point, we have the Nonaphonic, Bi-Modal system, which consists of twelve keys of the form X+/x-. When we start to examine related keys and modulation, though, we find that these subjects open up a whole new world for us, for two reasons: 1) key relationships in this system are quite different that those of traditional tonality, and 2) If we ever retain half of a bi-modality and change the other half, then we must introduce the concept of Semi-Modulation.

From the mathematical standpoint, there are eleven possible modulations. They are from I/i to: II/ii, III/iii, IV/iv, V/v, VI/vi, VII/vii, #I/#i (= ♭II/♭ii), #II/#ii (= ♭III/♭iii), #IV/#iv (= ♭V/♭v), #V/#v (= ♭VI/♭vi), and #VI/#vi (= ♭VII/♭vii). We have not yet examined these, but when we do so in Part Two, we will find that in practice, it will not make sense to perform all eleven.

When it comes to Semi-Modulations, there are too many (22) mathematical possibilities to list here, just for the sake of listing them. Some examples are: I/i to II/i, (example C/c to D/c), I/i to I/ii, (example C/c to C/d), I/i to I/iii, (example C/c to C/e), I/i to III/i, (example C/c to E/c), and so on. All 22 of these will be dealt with in detail in Part Two.

And this brings us to the answer to question three: Since it is possible to construct and define Uni-Tonal Bi-Modality, it should also be possible to do so for Bi-Tonal, and even Tri-Tonal Bi-Modalities, through the use of Semi-Modulations and Rotating Quintcircles. Indeed, it is possible to do this, but not by using only nine tones. For different combinations of keys, ten, or eleven, or all twelve, tones will have to be used.

We got off easy constructing octatonic and nonatonic scales and key signatures, because they were done by addition, that is, we began with 7 notes, then added one, and then added another one. With 10- and 11- and 12-note scales, keys, and key signatures, making the correct choices becomes more difficult, because it is not unmistakably obvious which of the remaining notes should be added, and in what order. Approaching this task by addition again is fine, but we will also have to approach it in other ways. One way will be by subtraction, that is, we will begin with 12 tones, and decide which tone(s) should be the first to go, *and why.* For alternate solutions, we will turn to musical acoustics for answers.

In further study, we will also make more extensive use of Set Theory. The higher the number of tones being used, the more helpful set theory becomes. In particular, we will show that in 12-tone systems, there are many more than 12 notes — almost twice as many. Consequently, it is possible to form many different 12-tone sets. Those sets that are chosen randomly or haphazardly are not likely to be usable tonal sets. However, it is possible to find more than one 12-tone set that comprises a tonal system — if the choices of notes are made strategically.

Other possibilities that will be examined are combinations of one major key with two minor keys, and one minor key with two major keys. This will require us to venture into unfamiliar territory, that of Compatibility of Keys. We have already seen that in this new system, the overall picture of proximities of keys with respect to each other looks quite different than it does in traditional tonality. So the next thing that we will do will be to examine which pairings (and which three- or four-key combinations) are compatible, and which are not. Keys that are closely related are not necessarily compatible, and compatible keys are not necessarily closely related. "Compatible" means that the two keys being combined complement each other; they "get along," and bring out the best in each other; they fill in each other's gaps to form a complete whole. Some pairings of keys simply are not compatible, because they are too similar. In most cases, though, incompatible keys either constantly get in each other's way, or they repeatedly clash with each other, or, worse still, endlessly fight with each other for supremacy and domination. In order to sort all of this out, we will introduce the novel concept of "Sensitive/Assertive Tones," or "SATs." In general, when SATs keep meeting, and forming chromatic clashes with each other, then the result fails the harmonic analysis test for tonality. ("Failing the test" means that no three consecutive chords can be analyzed harmonically in any one key). This situation makes for a challenging study for us to undertake.

This whole business of combining modes and keys and examining the results becomes more and more fascinating as we keep going. Some combinations, which one expects would prove to create something workable, do not. Fortunately, others, which do not look promising, turn out to be excellent. Be that as it may, as we keep working on it, we do, indeed, end up constructing more than one system of **Dodecaphonic Tonality.**

APPENDIX ONE

Theme and Variations — An Exercise in Nonaphonic Bi-Modality

The Nonaphonic Bi-modal system was dreamed up fairly recently, on August 27, 2007 (at 4:00 a.m., Pacific time, to be exact!), so not too much music has yet been written using it. But now that we have worked our way through eleven chapters of text, we should have some fun, and compose a nonaphonic, bi-modal piece of music together. The "Theme and Variations" form is a good one to choose for our first composition, because it is an ideal one for combining unity with variety, and that is just what we need here.

The key for this exercise is G+/g-, and the theme consists of six notes: The B-A-C-♭ notes (b-flat, a, c, and b-natural) plus g as the tonic and f# as its leading note, which altogether comprise a bi-modal set. There are plenty of thirds, but no sixths. Since the predominant features of the nonatonic scale are the two thirds and the two sixths, for Variation One (starting in measure 10), we can introduce the two sixths by transposing the theme into the Subdominant. This works out perfectly, because the thirds of the Subdominant are the sixths of the Tonic. We can employ two-voice counterpoint, because this theme is most conducive to imitation. (The f can be sharp or natural). For Variation Two (starting in measure 17), we can combine the theme with Variation One, and add a third voice in Renaissance fauxbourdon style. The theme, plus the first two variations, are given below.

A countless number of further variations can be written. Readers can feel free to try writing a few of their own. The primary goal, of course, is to make everything sound bi-modal. Persons who wish to do so are invited to send their variations by e-mail to the author at:

Nonaphonic_Bi-Modality@shaw.ca

80 • *Dodecaphonic Tonality*

Theme and Variations

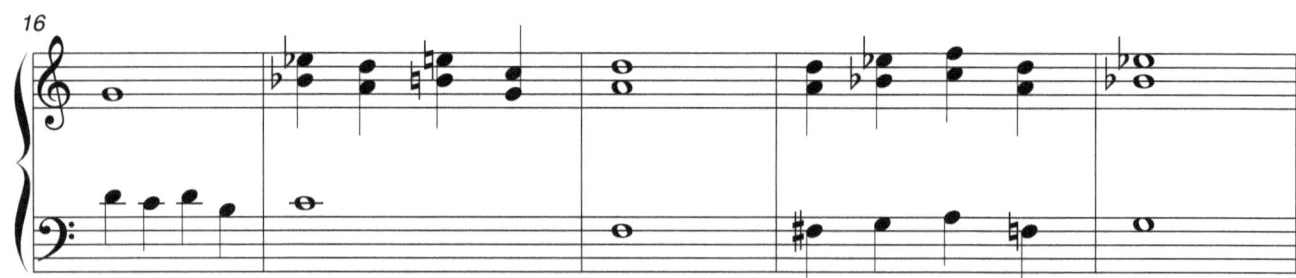

APPENDIX TWO

List of Examples and Charts in Part One

Ex. 1-1	9-tone melodic minor scale	1
Ex. 1-2	Union of major and harmonic minor scales	2
Ex. 1-3	Measures 82-94 of Chopin Waltz Op. 69, No. 2	3
Ex. 1-4	Tri-tonal nonaphonic scale (C+ plus F+ plus G+)	5
Ex. 2-1	List and musical examples of 37 different scales	7-12
Ex. 2-2	Six Church Modes (excl. Ionian) beginning on C	13
Ex. 2-3	"1-2-3" and "3-2-1" scales	14
Ex. 2-4	Undefined key signatures of 11 heptatonic scales	16
Ex. 2-5	Harmonic minor scale without augmented second	17
Ex. 3-1	Key signature for c octatonic minor	20
Ex. 3-2	c octatonic minor scale	20
Ex. 3-3	Octatonic (tone + semitone pattern) scale on C	20
Ex. 3-4	Key signature for f# octatonic minor	20
Ex. 3-5	13 key signatures for octatonic minor keys	21
Ex. 3-6	Melodic, harmonic consequences of octatonic scale	22
Ex. 3-7	13 nonatonic bi-modal, uni-tonal scales	24
Ex. 3-8	13 nonatonic bi-modal, uni-tonal key signatures	25
Ex. 3-9	Harmonic derivation of nonatonic, bi-modal scale	26
Ex. 4-1	Harmonized nonatonic bi-modal scale (all triads)	28
Ex. 4-2	Harmonized nonatonic bi-modal scale (all 7ths)	28
Ex. 4-3	Tonic functions (2 triads, 1 7th)	29
Ex. 4-4	Dominant functions (2 triads, 3 7ths)	29
Ex. 4-5	Subdominant functions (4 triads, 5 7ths)	29
Ex. 4-6	Mediant and Submediant functions (4 triads, 3 7ths)	30
Ex. 4-7	Chords without harmonic symbols (2 triads, 5 7ths)	30
Ex. 4-8	Dominant thirteenth chords	30
Ex. 4-9	5 7th chords in 1st inv. without harmonic symbols	31
Ex. 4-10	3 MM7th chords	31

Ex. 4-11	Dominant eleventh chord in 4 voices	32
Ex. 4-12	Dominant eleventh chord in 6 voices	32
Ex. 4-13	Tonic functions (2 triads)	33
Ex. 4-14	Dominant functions (2 triads, 3 7ths)	33
Ex. 4-15	Subdominant functions (4 triads, 6 7ths)	33
Ex. 4-16	5 harmonic analyses of F+ to C+ progression	34
Ex. 4-17	2 harmonic analyses of b dim-min7th chord	34
Ex. 4-18	Mediant and Submediant functions (3 7ths)	35
Ex. 4-19	Mediant and Submediant functions (4 triads)	35
Ex. 4-20	Diatonic mediants in a Major key	35
Ex. 4-21	Diatonic mediants in a minor key	36
Ex. 4-22	Chromatic mediants in Major and minor keys	36
Ex. 5-1	Roman Numeral and Functional Systems compared	37
Ex. 5-2	Subdominant added-sixth chord	38
Ex. 5-3	Characteristic tritone of blank key signature	39
Ex. 5-4	Subdominant and dominant functions compared	39
Ex. 5-5	Additional chords having D and S functions	40
Ex. 5-6	Diagrams of 3 different views of functional tonality	41
Ex. 5-7	Two "Magic" triangles of harmonic progressions	42
Ex. 5-8	Harmonized Major and relative minor scales	42-43
Ex. 5-9	Model of Functional Tonality	44
Ex. 6-1	Roman Numeral and functional symbols of chords	47-48
Ex. 6-2	Model of Nonaphonic Bi-Modality	49
Ex. 7-1	"Do-ti-la" harmonized	52
Ex. 7-2	Final cadence of Rachmaninoff Prelude	53
Ex. 7-3	Final cadence of "Adoramus Te, Christe"	53
Ex. 7-4	Melody without cadence at halfway point	54
Ex. 7-5	Melody with Phrygian cadence at halfway point	54
Ex. 7-6	Dominant 7th chord in 3rd inv. with its resolution	55
Ex. 7-7	German sixth chord with its resolution	55
Ex. 7-8	European functional analysis of German sixth chord	56
Ex. 7-9	Measures 100-104 of Chopin Polonaise in e♭-	56
Ex. 8-1	The traditional quintcircle with "secret tunnel"	59
Ex. 8-2	Progression from A+ to c- via "secret tunnel"	60

List of Examples and Charts in Part One

Ex. 8-3	The traditional quintcircle with 12-pointed star	61
Ex. 8-4	Progression around "baseball diamond"	63
Ex. 9-1	D♭+/d♭- nonatonic key signature and scale	64
Ex. 9-2	Quintcircle of Nonaphonic Bi-Modality	65
Chart 9-1	Proximity point chart for Nonaphonic Bi-Modality	66
Chart 9-2	Proximity point chart for Major and minor keys	65
Chart 9-3	Proximity point chart for Octatonic minor keys	67
Chart 9-4	Proximity point chart for melodic minor keys	68
Chart 9-5	Proximity points comparison chart	69
Ex. 10-1	List of Twelve Bi-Modal Combinations	70
Ex. 10-2	Twelve Bi-Modal Combinations in Notation	71-72
Ex. 11-1	Excerpt from "Lieder eines fahrenden Gesellen" by Gustav Mahler	75-76
	Theme and Variations	80

APPENDIX THREE

References Cited

Chapter One — Chopin Waltzes and Mazurkas

Chapter Two — Wikipedia: Musical scales, Klingon music

Chapter Five: — Krush, Joseph M., "History of Harmony and Counterpoint, Volume II, The Renaissance" by Józef M. Chomiński: A Translation, Evaluation, and Critique (Doctoral Dissertations in Musicology, 1981).

Chapter Seven — Lectures of Dr. Hallgrimur Helgason, Rachmaninoff Preludes, Adoramus Te, Christe (anonymous), Chopin Polonaises

Chapter Eleven: — Lieder of Gustav Mahler

PART TWO

Bi-Tonal, Tri-Tonal, and Polytonal Bi-Modalities Using 9 to 12 Tones

CHAPTER TWELVE

The Overall Approach

This volume is a continuation of "Nonaphonic Bi-Modality," which introduced a Uni-Tonal, Nine-Tone, Bi-Modal system. Readers should not expect to understand Part Two without first understanding Part One. Our task now is to keep going by building upon what we have done so far, and expanding it. This entire project begins with a "back to basics" approach. Having 12 tones at their disposal, composers have traditionally chosen seven of these as their basic working set, and used one, two, three, four, or all five of the remaining tones as extras, but by no means sparingly. In fact, in the nineteenth century, it came to the point where so many accidentals were being used, that the key signature itself lost most of its meaning.

In Part One, we saw what workable possibilities exist if we begin instead with an octatonic or nonatonic basic set. Now, we will use the Nonatonic, Bi-Modal set to develop 10-, 11-, and 12-tone tonal sets, and see what happens when we do.

In this regard, our approach can also be described as "one thing leads to another." If we can begin with seven tones and add one, and then add one more, then we can certainly add another one, and then another, and finally use all twelve. But that may not be the best approach. Using all twelve tones to form dodecatonic tonal sets will be a project in itself. It will be unique, because there will be no excluded tones, but our choices of enharmonics will cause us to create various sets. However, when it comes to forming 10- and 11-note sets, we might be better off to begin with all twelve tones, and then, carefully and strategically, decide which one or two of them to subtract. Whatever we do, we will have to pay close attention to the various consequences of choosing to eliminate any specific tone or pair of tones.

The description "one thing leads to another" applies also to tonalities. We will always use both modes, because using only one mode just does not present us with nearly as many possibilities for expansion. However, we will build bi-tonal systems that will not be confined to relative major—relative minor relationships. The two most obvious ones to examine will be a major key together with its relative and tonic minors (example C+ with a- and c-), and a minor key with its relative and tonic majors (example c- with E♭+ and C+).

In the above examples, the modalities are not balanced, because one outnumbers the other by a ratio of 2:1. This is fine in these two cases, but, in addition, we definitely will need to find combinations in which the number of major and minor modes is equal (for example two major and two minor). And for that, it will be necessary to explore Tri-Tonal Bi-Modalities.

Suppose, for example, that we choose C, E, and G as our three tonal centres. Which of the following six possible combinations should we pick?

C+, c-, e-, G+	C+, E+, e-, g-	C+, e-, G+, g-
C+, c-, E+, g-	c-, E+, e-, G+	c-, E+, G+, g-

What about six more combinations, using E♭+ instead of E+ and e♭- instead of e-? Fortunately, we are not at a total loss as to how to figure this out. A lot of the groundwork for finding the answers was already done in Chapter Six, which was devoted to Mediants, Submediants, and Functionality.

Another approach that we take in this project is from the standpoint of the history of music theory. It is not a goal here to repeat information presented in books devoted to that subject, but it is necessary to have an overall knowledge of pertinent aspects of that material. To this end, in Part One, we listed and examined as many scales used throughout music history as we could find. Also to this end, we did a study of key signatures.

There is a tremendous amount of musicological study being done worldwide, some of which is in the area of the history of music theory. However, even after years of such study, very few musicologists or music theorists ever turn their attention to what did *not* happen in Music History, although it could have, and perhaps even *should* have, happened!

Now, if we begin with our "back to basics" approach, add to it our "one thing leads to another" approach, and use these within the context of the history of music theory, we can construct a very basic time line, as shown in Example 12-1.

Ex. 12-1

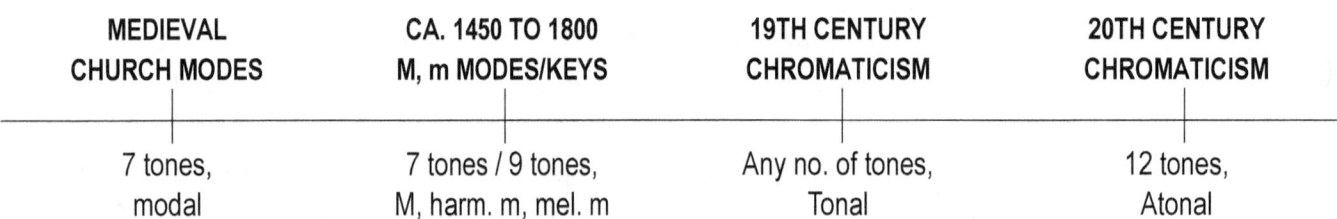

We can describe succinctly what happened before the nineteenth century: In the Middle Ages, seven-note Church modes were used. In the Renaissance, all but the Ionian and Aeolian modes were gradually phased out. In the Baroque period, twelve major and twelve minor keys became firmly established. In Classicism, these were used to the fullest. The Ionian mode became the Major mode, but the Aeolian (natural minor) was replaced by harmonic and melodic minor.

When we come to the nineteenth century, though, we better consider not just what happened, but what did *not* happen. This most curious phenomenon called "nineteenth-century chromaticism" took place. Was the music still tonal? Compared to what preceded, no, but compared to what followed, yes. Were major and minor keys and their key signatures used? Yes. Were seven-note sets used? No, because so many accidentals were used, that it is a wonder that they were not all used up to extinction ... Chromaticism spread like wildfire, so that 8, 9, 10, 11, or all 12 tones were used in almost every piece of music. But were 8-, 9-, 10-, 11-, or 12-tone tonal sets defined and assigned key signatures? No. When all twelve tones were used, was the music atonal, with serial techniques being used? No. Readers can add their own questions (and "yes" or "no" answers) to these, bearing in mind what did — and did not — happen. We do know what happened about 100 years ago: Schoenberg appeared and, rather abruptly, abandoned tonality and created the 12-tone serial music system.

All of this leads us to the focal point of our study, historically speaking: between nineteenth-century chromaticism and twentieth-century atonality, a huge gap was left. No bi-modal system, as such, was ever created. No 8-, 9-, 10-, 11-, or 12-tone tonal sets or keys were ever defined, nor were key signatures for such sets ever developed.* Instead, composers skipped directly to bi-tonality and polytonality, and used two (or more) traditional key signatures simultaneously.

---

*Even though the melodic minor uses nine tones, we do not consider it to be nonatonic, but consisting of two different seven-note sets. It would be truly nonatonic only if all nine tones were used in both ascending and descending forms, and its key signature reflected that.

In Part One, we developed an **octatonic minor** scale and key signature by adding the major sixth to the harmonic minor key set. Then we added the major third to create and define the nonaphonic, bi-modal scale and key signature. But bi-modality itself is nothing new. The nineteenth-century composers who wrote bi-modal music did, in fact, fill in a portion of the so-called "gap." And those who consistently used 10, 11, or all 12 tones filled it in a bit more. The point is, that they did so while maintaining use of traditional key signatures, which became essentially meaningless, since their music hardly remained in X-Major or y-minor for any significant length of time, if indeed at all. And composers did not write in defined keys of the form X-Major/x-minor, let alone X-Major/y-minor.

There is a fundamental difference between nineteenth-century chromaticism and what we are doing here. That phenomenon was not called "nineteenth-century diatonicism." Our system is based on the principle of **expanded diatonicism;** in fact, it is exactly that. By successive addition of tones and of the chords that result when we use these added tones, we expand our arsenal of **diatonic** melodic and harmonic resources.

Whenever it is possible to do so, it is to our great advantage to approach a problem, or to try to find answers to our questions, in more than one way. This is a type of two-directional (or multi-directional) approach, which was used in Part One. When we find the same answer in more than one way, we are happy. If we find two or more different answers, then we probably have some head scratching (further study and analysis) to do.

In Part One, it was rather easy to derive useable 8- and 9-tone sets, because the choices we made — by addition — were so sensible and logical. However, at this point, it is not obvious which of the remaining three tones we should choose to be our tenth tone, and then which of the remaining two should be our choice for tone eleven. "Hit and miss" is not a good approach to take. Instead, we turn to our fourth approach to this project: through the intriguing worlds of musical acoustics and set theory, where we can find answers. These are the subjects of Chapter Thirteen.

CHAPTER THIRTEEN

Musical Acoustics and Set Theory

The field of musical acoustics is one of this author's all-time favorite subjects, going back over 30 years. When music, mathematics, and physics are studied together, some very fascinating learning takes place. In the present situation, the question that we want to answer is: If we pick c as the tonic note, which two of the remaining eleven notes are the farthest related to it? Acousticians do not usually answer a question such as this directly, but indirectly, the answer is there. Volumes and volumes have been written over the centuries on consonance and dissonance, intervals, the monochord, vibration and vibrating strings, frequency and vibrating length and pitch, harmonics and overtones, open and closed pipes, mathematical calculation of intervals, intonation, scales, equal and unequal temperament, and so on, and so on. All of these are discussed in the Harvard Dictionary of Music, from which some of the material below is paraphrased. Out of everything that has been written on the subject of musical acoustics, we actually need to extract only a small amount in order to find the answer to our question.

Ironically, we do *not* find the answer in the equal-tempered system, because mathematically, it is *too* complex to give us the answer. Here is the problem: Equal temperament divides the octave into twelve exactly equal semitones. The frequency ratio of the octave is two (or 2:1). And this 2 is the only rational number in the entire system.

The keyboard (i.e. the chromatic scale) is a logarithmic scale. This means that whenever we go up by an octave, which is a linear unit of distance, the frequency of the new pitch is double that of the original one, therefore a multiple of two. For example, a', the "a" that is a major sixth above middle c (c') vibrates at 440 Hz ("Hertz" means cycles per second). The "a" that is a minor third below middle c vibrates at 220 Hz. The line graph of Example 13-1 shows all the a's on the piano and their corresponding Hz.

Ex. 13-1

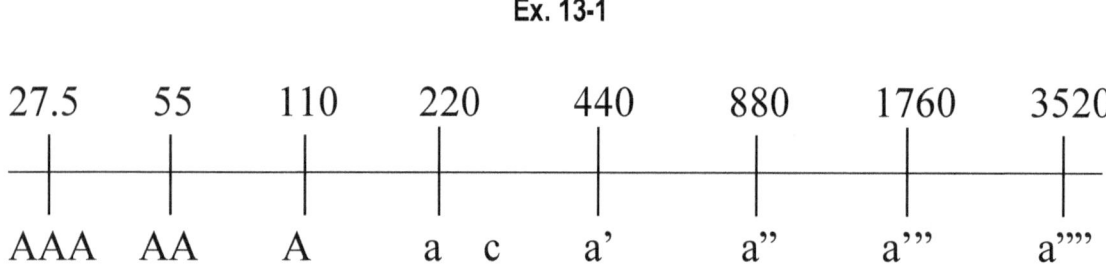

And this is where the simplicity ends. To divide the logarithmic octave (which all octaves are) into 12 exactly equal parts, we need to use the irrational number $\sqrt[12]{2}$ (the twelfth root of two), which equals approximately 1.05946 … So we let c = 1 and find the frequency ratios (to c) of the other eleven tones as shown in Example 13-2.

Ex. 13-2 Frequency ratios in the equal-tempered chromatic scale

c	=	1	=	1.00000...
c# = d♭	=	$1 \times (\sqrt[12]{2})^1$	=	1.05946...
d	=	$1 \times (\sqrt[12]{2})^2$	=	1.12246...
d# = e♭	=	$1 \times (\sqrt[12]{2})^3$	=	1.18921...
e	=	$1 \times (\sqrt[12]{2})^4$	=	1.25992...
f	=	$1 \times (\sqrt[12]{2})^5$	=	1.33484...
f# = g♭	=	$1 \times (\sqrt[12]{2})^6$	=	1.41421...
g	=	$1 \times (\sqrt[12]{2})^7$	=	1.49830...
g# = a♭	=	$1 \times (\sqrt[12]{2})^8$	=	1.58739...
a	=	$1 \times (\sqrt[12]{2})^9$	=	1.68178...
a# = b♭	=	$1 \times (\sqrt[12]{2})^{10}$	=	1.78178...
b	=	$1 \times (\sqrt[12]{2})^{11}$	=	1.88772...
c'	=	$1 \times (\sqrt[12]{2})^{12}$	=	2.00000...

There is no way on earth to tell from this list which tones are most or least closely related to c, so we cannot even guess at the answer to our question.

We must turn to a system of unequal temperament, called the just scale, which was used prior to the introduction of equal temperament. The just scale is based on three principles, the first of which is the same as that of equal temperament: the note that is an octave above the primary note vibrates at double its frequency. The second principle states that the note that lays a perfect fifth above the primary note vibrates at one and one-half (= 3/2) times its frequency. Finally, the note that lays a major third above the primary note vibrates at one and one fourth (= 5/4) times its frequency.

We can play with these numbers all we want, as long as we proceed with caution, and remember that the just scale is not equal-tempered. This means that some operations work, while others do not. Since we multiply to go up, we divide to go down. This always works. For example, since multiplying by 3/2 yields the perfect fifth up, dividing by 3/2 gives us the perfect fifth down. The same applies to perfect fourths. A perfect fifth plus a perfect fourth equals 3/2 times 4/3 = 2 = an octave. Since a major third plus a minor sixth equals an octave, then 5/4 times 8/5 = 2 = an octave also. A minor seventh (16/9) times a major second (9/8) also equals 2, and so on, and so on. What does not work is taking the augmented triad route. Three successive major thirds = $(5/4)^3$ = 125/64 = approximately 1.95, which is not equal to 2. Also, if we go up by a major second 12 times, that is $(9/8)^{12}$, the result is approximately = 4.11, and not 4.0, even though we ended up exactly two octaves higher. Even at that, this discrepancy is not large.

The big advantage of this system is that by using the three principles stated above we can derive ratios of vibration for all 12 tones, as shown in Example 13-3.

Ex. 13-3 Frequency ratios in the just chromatic scale

Note		Calculation		Ratio	
c	=			1 : 1	(starting point)
d♭ (after a♭ is derived)	=	8/5 ÷ 3/2	=	16 : 15	
d	=	3/2 x 3/2	=	9 : 8	
e♭ (after a is derived)	=	2 ÷ 5/3	=	6 : 5	
e	=			5 : 4	(given)
f	=	2 ÷ 3/2	=	4 : 3	
f#	=	5/4 x 9/8	=	45 : 32	
g	=			3 : 2	(given)
a♭	=	2 ÷ 5/4	=	8 : 5	
a	=	4/3 x 5/4	=	5 : 3	
b♭	=	8/5 x 9/8	=	9 : 5	
b	=	5/4 x 3/2	=	15 : 8	
c'	=			2 : 1	(given)

This list provides us with the answer to our question: the tones most closely related to c are the ones whose frequency ratio is composed of relatively small digits. In ordinary language, the simpler, or cleaner, or neater, or more basic the ratio looks, the closer it is related to the primary note. So really, in any system of temperament, the only antiseptically clean interval is the octave. After that, intervals can be arranged in order from the most consonant to less consonant, to dissonant, and to most dissonant. This order is as shown in Example 13-4.

Ex. 13-4 Intervals in order from most consonant to most dissonant*

1   2   3/2   4/3   5/4   5/3   6/5   8/5   9/8   9/5   15/8   16/15   45/32

There is no question that the two tones most distantly related to c are f-sharp and d-flat. This is the answer that we were looking for. Mathematical and acoustical proof of something that is not even visible, just audible, convinces us beyond any doubt that we have found the two tones that are the most distant "cousins" of c.

While we have this ordered hierarchy of tones in front of us, we might as well make some observations about the first ten tones, also. No-one should be surprised that the dominant follows the tonic and is followed by the subdominant. Even the fact that the third and sixth degrees of the major scale come next is not surprising. However, these are followed by their complementary intervals, (which are the third and sixth scale degrees of the minor scale), and not by the other two natural notes, d and b. The second scale degree comes next, but the minor seventh

---

*Ref. Tone: A Study in Musical Acoustics, Second Edition, by Siegmund Levarie and Ernst Levy, Kent State University Press, 1968, p. 201.

precedes the leading note. So the leading note is actually preceded by the first three flats! Such are the wonders of musical acoustics.

One question remains: why are we applying conclusions reached by use of just temperament when we use equal temperament? For one thing, irrational numbers cannot be ranked. No irrational number can be said to be more or less irrational than any other one, because there is no such concept. Rational numbers can be — and are — ranked according to various rules, theorems, observations, properties of prime numbers, factoring, and so on, and so on. At this point, we can compare the numbers of the two systems and see what observations can be made. These are shown in Example 13-5 below.

Herein lays another reason that we are justified in using the just scale to prove relative closeness or remoteness of the other eleven tones to the primary note: when we consider only one key, the discrepancies are relatively small. The smallest discrepancy is .151% (that of the perfect fourth), and the largest is 5.12% (that of the major sixth). In particular, the two tones that interest us (the last two) have discrepancies of about .7% and .8%. With accuracy like that, we can be certain that the conclusions we derive by using the just scale apply to the equal-tempered scale as well.

Ex. 13-5 Comparison of frequency ratios in scales

INTERVAL	FREQUENCY RATIO IN EQUAL TEMPERAMENT	FREQUENCY RATIO IN JUST SCALE	DIFFERENCE
Unison	1.00000	1/1	0.00000
Octave	2.00000	2/1	0.00000
Perfect fifth	1.49830...	3/2 = 1.5	- .00170
Perfect fourth	1.33484...	4/3 = 1.33333...	.00151
Major third	1.25992...	5/4 = 1.25	.00992
Major sixth	1.68178...	5/3 = 1.66666...	.05120
Minor third	1.18921...	6/5 = 1.2	- .01079
Minor sixth	1.58739...	8/5 = 1.6	- .01261
Major second	1.12246...	9/8 = 1.125	- .00254
Minor seventh	1.78178...	9/5 = 1.8	- .01822
Major seventh	1.88772...	15/8 = 1.875	.01272
Minor second	1.05946...	16/15 = 1.06666...	- .00720
Tritone	1.41421...	45/32 = 1.40625	.00796

Since we have found the answer to our question, we could stop at this point. However, with all these numbers in front of us, it is a good idea to make more use of the information, and to examine the tritone and the minor second more closely.

Over the centuries, some music scholars have called the tritone "the devil in music," while others have said that using it is "not necessarily a deadly sin." From the acoustical standpoint, we can play advocate of the devil in music. In equal temperament, the ratio of the tritone is $(^{12}\sqrt{2})^6$, which equals $\sqrt{2}$, which equals approximately 1.4142 ... But ($\sqrt{2}x$) is the ratio of the diagonal of a square (measuring x by x units) to its side, as shown in Ex. 13-6.

Ex. 13-6

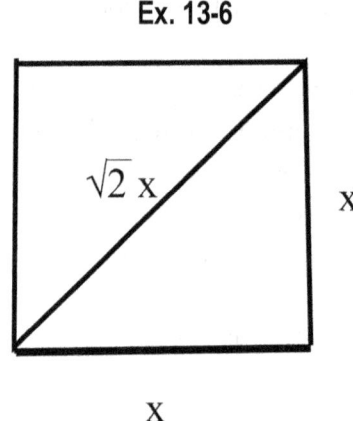

So in fact, in the physical world, √2 is an extremely common and useful number.

In the just scale, the frequency ratio of the tritone is 45:32. That is extremely close to the frequency ratio of the perfect fifth, which is 45:30 (= 3/2). This explains why dominant-seventh chords are so useful and so common. It also explains why the vertical tritone is completely acceptable in two-voice writing, as shown in Example 13-7.

Ex. 13-7

Now let us take a look at the minor second. Suppose that we set out to construct an eleven-tone scale. With c as the tonic, which tone should we omit? Most people would say f-sharp, and justifiably cite the supportive argument that the tritone is the devil in music, so f-sharp must be the first to go.

But it is possible to form a "dump the d-flat" camp of supporters also, and use the numbers presented in this chapter as supportive arguments. F-sharp is the first sharp, while d-flat is the fourth flat, so we need the former more than we need the latter. From that point of view, f-sharp is a closer relative of the c family, because we need it in order to modulate to the dominant. Even without modulating (or writing a transition), we need it to write the closing progression "V of V - V - I," which is an excellent one. By comparison, we need d-flat only for constructing the Neapolitan Sixth and Augmented Sixth chords derived from the dominant minor ninth chord. Other than that, it is almost completely useless. In fact, it is so extremely unrelated to the tonic, that we do not even try to construct a tonic minor ninth chord. What this means is that if we were allowed to exclude only one tone, it would *not* be nonsense to exclude the d-flat and retain the f-sharp instead. We would then use the supportive argument that the ratio 16:15 is not really significantly less awkward to work with than is 45:32.

In any event, we know that, from the acoustical standpoint, two different sensible hendecaphonic (11-tone) systems can be constructed. We also know that in developing a decaphonic (10-tone) system, we should exclude the *two* "devils" that provide the least support for the tonic. It is, however, arguable that it is not particularly sensible to aim deliberately at deriving hendecaphonic systems at all; more will be said about that in later chapters. For now, we turn our attention away from acoustics and towards a brief introduction to Set Theory.

* * *

Set Theory is a branch of mathematics, and a thick one at that. However, for our purposes, we will have all the information that we need if we only scratch the surface, so that is all that we will do. A **set** is a collection of things, each of which is called an **element** of the set. If a second set contains at least one, and at most all, of the elements of the first set, and that is all it contains, then the second set is a **subset** of the first set, and the first set is a **superset** of the second one.

For example, suppose Set A consists of the numbers {0, 1, 2, 3, 4, 5, 6, 7} and Set B consists of the numbers {4, 5, 6, 7, 8, 9, 10, 11}. The set {0, 1, 2, 3, 4} is a subset of Set A, but not of Set B. The set {4} is one subset of both Set A and Set B. In Set Theory, the **Universe** is the class that contains all of the elements and sets that one wishes to use in a given situation.

In addition, the concepts of **union** and **intersection** are defined as follows: the **union** of two sets is the combination of all of the elements of both sets. So the union of Sets A and B above is the set {0, 1, 2, 3, 4, 5, 6, 7, 8, 9, 10, 11}. (We need not state the 4, 5, 6, and 7 twice). The **intersection** of two sets is the set of elements that appear in both sets, or that the sets have in common. These are exactly the same elements about which we just said "need not be stated twice" when we write out the union. In the case above, they are the set {4, 5, 6, 7}. Of course, it is possible that the intersection of two sets is the empty set, designated as { }. For example, if Set C consists of the elements {1, 2, 3}, and Set D consists of the elements {4, 5, 6}, then the intersection of Sets C and D is { }, while the union of these two sets is {1, 2, 3, 4, 5, 6}. The **cardinality** of a set is the number of elements in the set. So the cardinalities of the sets shown above are as shown in Ex. 13-8 below.

Ex. 13-8 Cardinalities of various sets

SET	CARDINALITY
A	8
B	8
{0, 1, 2, 3, 4}	5
{4}	1
Union of Sets A and B	12
Intersection of Sets A and B	4
{ } = Empty Set	0
C	3
D	3
Union of Sets C and D	6
Intersection of Sets C and D	0

In 1973, Allen Forte, one of America's greatest music theorists, shed about a billion foot-candles of light on **The Structure of Atonal Music**, when he published his book bearing that title. He did it by applying set theory to music theory, specifically by regarding tone rows as sets, and fragments of them as subsets. He began with the set shown above as the union of sets A and B, where he let 0 = c, 1 = c# or d♭, 2 = d, 3 = d# or e♭, 4 = e, and so on, up to 11 = b. With that being his point of departure, he succeeded in showing, over and over again, how serial composers structured their music by using fragments (subsets) of their tone rows, whether it was horizontally, vertically, or by any other means. To achieve everything that Forte did, it was necessary for him to define and list an extremely large number of subsets, ranging in cardinality from two to twelve.

The above is, of course, only a small, very much abbreviated, sample of all the discoveries that Forte made about atonal music, and his book is a "must read" for any musician who wishes to understand … the structure of atonal music.

In this study, we, too, will apply set theory to music theory, in particular by working with our own sets and subsets. However, we cannot, and, even if we could, we should not use Forte's system. We cannot use it, because in his system, enharmonics are not treated as distinct objects, and in our system, they must be. We should not use it, even in modified form, because in its own way, it is unnecessarily too complicated for our needs. Not only that, we will not be fragmenting scales, because we are working with tonal, not atonal, music, and scales are not tone rows. The cardinalities of our sets and subsets will almost always be 7, 8, 9, 10, 11, or 12.

For us, it is by no means necessary to assign numbers to tones or to notes; in fact, if we did so, we would be causing ourselves problems by complicating the symbolism for no reason. For example, if we adopted a variation of Forte's system, and set c = 0, then we would either have to set c-sharp = 1 and d-flat = 2, or else do something such as: let c-sharp = 1.1 or 1(1) and d-flat = 1.2 or 1(2). So instead, we will just keep things simple, and use the following as a starting point:

C Major	= {c, d, e, f, g, a, b}
c Natural minor	= {c, d, e♭, f, g, a♭, b♭}
c Melodic minor	= {c, d, e♭, f, g, a♭, a, b♭, b}
c Harmonic minor	= {c, d, e♭, f, g, a♭, b}
c Octatonic minor	= {c, d, e♭, f, g, a♭, a, b}
C Nonatonic Bi-Modal	= the union of C+ and c Harmonic minor
	OR the union of C+ and c Octatonic minor, which = {c, d, e♭, e, f, g, a♭, a, b}.

We now have all the basic information and raw materials that we need in order to continue on from where we left off in Part One.

CHAPTER FOURTEEN

Rotating Quintcircles and Semi-Modulation

For this study, we begin by constructing two concentric quintcircles, with the major keys spelled out on the outside, and the Octatonic minor keys, also spelled out, on the inside. The home position for these is the one in which, for every key X, X-Major is aligned with x-minor, along the same radius, as shown in Example 14-1 on the next page. This is our model for uni-tonal, nonaphonic bi-modality, in which C+/c- is symbolized as I/i. It should be noted that I/i is one of several cases in which we could just as well use the harmonic form of i, since the major sixth scale degree is included in I, anyway.

Now, we keep the major-key quintcircle anchored in place as it is, cut out the minor-key circle, and start rotating it. We perform the eleven possible rotations, and examine the results. In each case, we need only to examine the 12 o'clock position, so that C+ is always I, while its minor-key partner changes. Each of these occurrences is called a semi-modulation*, because one-half of the bi-modality remains the same, while the other does not. The eleven results are summarized in Example 14-2 below. In column one, c = clockwise, and c-c = counter-clockwise. In columns three and four, En = Enharmonic.

---

*Since when? Since Tues., March 4, 2008, shortly after 2:00 a. m.

98 • Dodecaphonic Tonality

Ex. 14-1 Rotating Quintcircles; Majors and Octatonic Minors Original Position

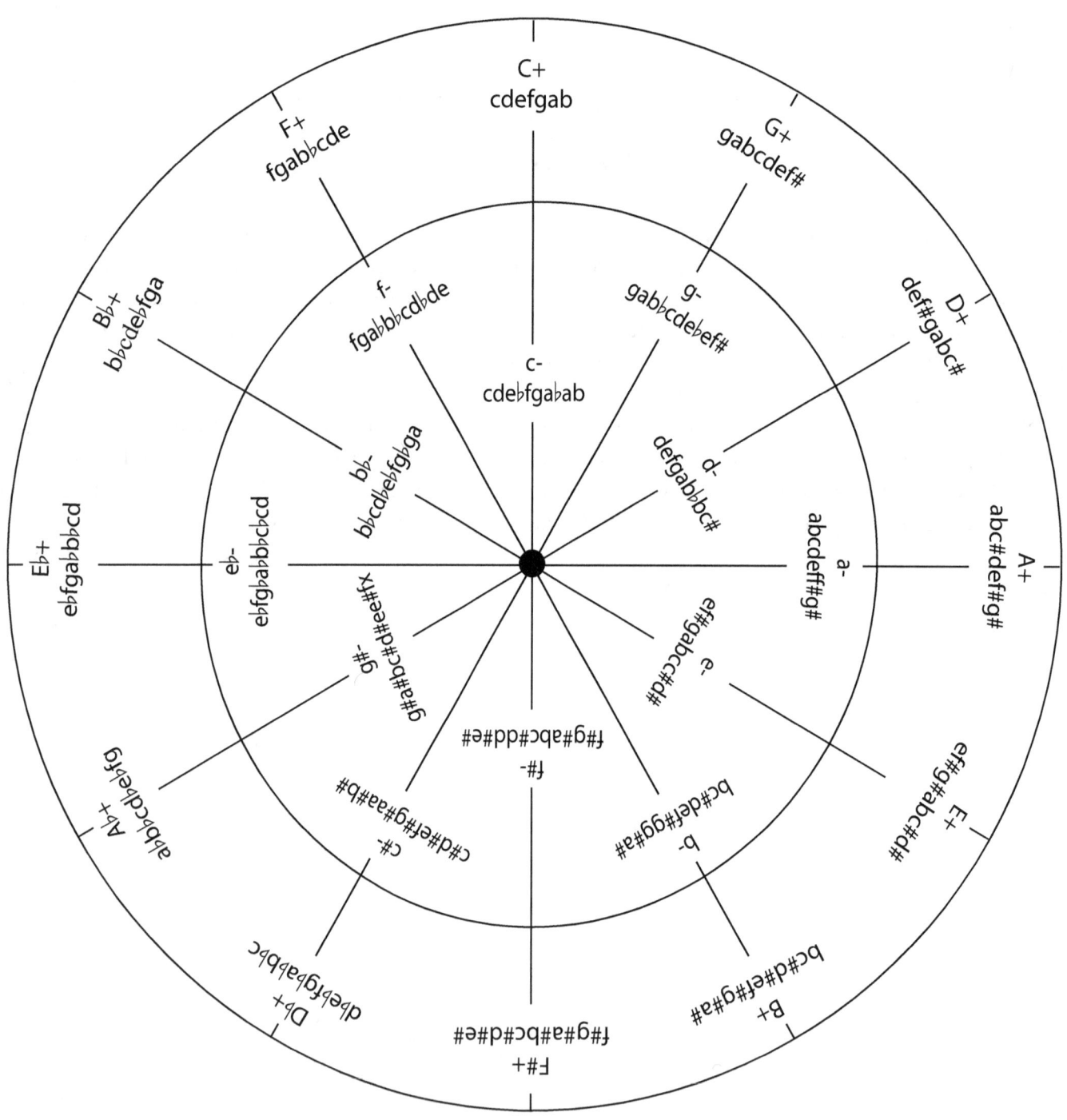

Turn to the back of the book for do-it-yourself Quintcircles pages.
Remove pages printed with individual circles, cut out and join circles.

Ex. 14-2 Semi-Modulations of the form I/x where C+ = I

ROTATION	RESULT	TOTAL NO. OF TONES	COMMON TONES
1) none	C/c = I/i	9	6
2) 1 hr c	C/f = I/iv	10	5
3) 1 hr c-c	C/g = I/v	10	6
4) 2 hrs c	C/b♭ = I/♭vii	11	4
5) 2 hrs c-c	C/d = I/ii	9	6
6) 3 hrs c	C/e♭ = I/♭iii	11 + 1 En	3 + 1 En
7) 3 hrs c-c	C/a = I/vi	9	6
8) 4 hrs c	C/g# = I/#v	11 + 2 En	2 + 2 En
9) 4 hrs c-c	C/e = I/iii	10	5
10) 5 hrs c	C/c# = I/#i	12 + 1 En	2 + 1 En
11) 5 hrs c-c	C/b = I/vii	11	4
12) 6 hrs c	C/f# = I/#iv	11 + 1 En	3 + 1 En

Now we can make some observations. Looking at the third column, we see that there are basically four groups: Cardinalities of 9, 10, 11, and 12 or 13. Of these, the first group is particularly noteworthy, because in all three nonatonic sets, the major key has 6 notes in common with its minor-key partner. Set seven is, of course, the traditional pairing of a major key with its relative minor, and it is good to see that set one (our original uni-tonal set) shares this characteristic with the traditional one. But what is really thrilling to discover is that **set five, the I/ii combination, is just as good!** This means that, in a way, ii can be considered to be another relative minor of I. (Readers are cautioned at this point not to pay attention to traditional key signatures of minor keys, because they do not accurately reflect the set of tones being used). We can also say that there exist two nonaphonic, bi-tonal, bi-modal systems: I/vi and I/ii. (In I/vi, had we used vi harmonic minor, the set would have been an 8-note set.)

We have three decatonic sets: Nos. 2, 3, and 9. Of these, no. 3, which pairs I with its minor dominant, produces the closest relationship to I/i, because its partners have 6 common tones. Next comes no. 9 because, had we used the harmonic form of e-minor, the set would have been nonatonic, so in that sense, we can add I/iii to our nonatonic sets, although it is a bit weaker, because its partners have only five tones in common. Finally, set two is a decatonic set (even if the harmonic form of iv is used) whose partners have five tones in common. So far, the total number of well-matched bi-modalities is six: One uni-tonal (I/i) and five bi-tonal (I/vi, I/ii, I/v, I/iii, and I/iv), in that order of proximity. This means that semi-modulations to any of the bi-tonal bi-modalities within this group are all closely related to the central, uni-tonal bi-modality I/i.

Our next group contains sets 4 and 11. At first sight, these pairs look about the same, but if we examine them more closely, we can see that there is a significant difference between them. The roots in the former pair are a whole tone apart; in the latter, they are a semitone apart. This makes the former set much more "user friendly" than the latter, as we shall see in the next chapter. For this reason, we can add I/♭vii to our group of closely related bi-tonal bi-modalities, but we cannot add I/vii.

The members of our last group are the least impressive in appearance — all of them. First of all, they all have enharmonics, without which they have only two or three tones in common, so they are not well-matched bi-modalities. Secondly, they are large sets, having a cardinality of 12 or 13 notes. In Chapter Twenty, we will construct more workable 12-note sets than these, when we choose our notes strategically and carefully. For now, let's take a quick look at these four sets, anyway.

Set 6 is a twelve-note set, but not a twelve-tone set, since b= c♭, and d♭ is missing. Also, there are chromatic clashes between the third of I and the root of ♭iii, again between the fifth of I and the third of ♭iii, and again between the leading note of I and the fifth of ♭iii. (Chromatic clashes will be discussed in the next chapter). Set 8 is actually a 13-note set, with e# = f, and f double-sharp = g. (Had we used g# harmonic minor, the e# would not be there). In either case, only two of the common tones are not enharmonics, which is a very low ratio of truly common tones. This last statement also holds true for set 10. It is a 13-note set, with b# = c. Had we used the harmonic form of c#-, the a# would not be there, so it would be an 11-tone set with 12 notes (b# = c). Finally, in set 12, had we used f# harmonic minor, the d# would be missing, so it would have been a decatonic set with 11 notes (e# = f).

It would, of course, be possible to perform extraneous semi-modulations from I/i to any of these sets, but we could hardly expect them to be smooth ones. Such semi-modulations would be comparable to regular modulations directly from C+ to B+, or to C#+, or to F#+. If any of these six turned out to sound smoother than the others, it would be nos. 11 and 4, which have four tones in common, no enharmonics, and, in the case of no. 11, can be written as a decatonic set.

* * *

We now have to perform the other 11 possible semi-modulations in which i (= c-) stays put, and its major-key partner changes. As soon as we write out the results, we can immediately find their equivalents along the radius of the quintcircle to which C+ belongs. This is true for two reasons. First, what is now a rotation of x hours clockwise, was previously the same rotation x hours counter-clockwise. Second, when we performed each of the eleven rotations, we could have located c- along another radius, and found its new partner right then and there. In any event, each resulting bi-modality of the form X/i has exactly the same properties as one of our original 12 sets of the form I/x, because it is a transposition of it, as shown in Example 14-3.

Ex. 14-3 Semi-Modulations of the form X/i where c- = i

ROTATION	RESULT	EQUIVALENT TO:	CLOSELY RELATED?
1) none	C/c = I/i	C/c = no. 1 in Ex. 14-2	yes
2) 1 hr c	F/c = IV/i	C/g = no. 3 "	yes
3) 1 hr c-c	G/c = V/i	C/f = no. 2 "	yes
4) 2 hrs c	B♭/c = ♭VII/i	C/d = no. 5 "	yes
5) 2 hrs c-c	D/c = II/i	C/b♭ = no. 4 "	yes
6) 3 hrs c	E♭/c = ♭III/i	C/a = no. 7 "	yes
7) 3 hrs c-c	A/c = VI/i	C/e♭ = no. 6 "	no
8) 4 hrs c	A♭/c = ♭VI/i	C/e = no. 9 "	yes
9) 4 hrs c-c	E/c = III/i	C/g# = no. 8 "	no
10) 5 hrs c	D♭/c = ♭II/i	C/b = no. 11 "	no
11) 5 hrs c-c	B/c = VII/i	C/c# = no. 10 "	no
12) 6 hrs c	F#/c = #IV/i	C/f# = no. 12 "	no

The six corresponding well-matched bi-tonal bi-modalities are ♭III/i, ♭VII/i, IV/i, ♭VI/i, V/i and II/i, in that order. Now, our family of semi-modulations that are closely related to I/i is as shown in the first two columns of Example 14-4 below. In addition to C/c, four other uni-tonal bi-modalities can be extracted from the above; they are G/g, F/f, D/d, and B♭/b♭, the four closest neighbors of C/c on the nonaphonic bi-modal quintcircle. Also, four other relative major/relative minor pairings are inherent in the above; they are F/d, B♭/g, G/e, and A♭/f. All nine of these are shown in the third column of the example.

Ex. 14-4 Semi-Modulations and modulations closely related to I/i where C/c = I/i

I/vi = C/a	♭III/i = E♭/c	I/i = C/c
I/ii = C/d	♭VII/i = B♭/c	V/v = G/g
I/v = C/g	IV/i = F/c	IV/iv = F/f
I/iii = C/e	♭VI/i = A♭/c	II/ii = D/d
I/iv = C/f	V/i = G/c	♭VII/♭vii = B♭/b♭
I/♭vii = C/b♭	II/i = D/c	IV/ii = F/d
		♭VII/v = B♭/g
		V/iii = G/e
		♭VI/iv = A♭/f

We now have our complete family of related bi-modal pairs of keys, consisting of 21 members.

Example 14-5 on the next page shows where and how these keys appear on our double quintcircle. The keys that lay in their home position are underlined. The others have arrived where they are as a result of various rotations. We can see that everything has worked out almost perfectly from the standpoint of symmetry — almost, but not entirely, because the bi-modalities at 10 o'clock and 8 o'clock are not perfect mirror images of those at 2 o'clock and 4 o'clock, respectively.

As is, our family spans nine of twelve stations. However, if we want to make the qualifications for closely related keys stricter, we can always do so, and subtract the two bi-modalities that are in the 4 o'clock position and the two bi-modalities in the 8 o'clock position. We can even exclude the two found at 9 o'clock and 3 o'clock. This would still leave us an immediate family of 15 or 17 pairings, but they would span only five or seven stations.

Ex. 14-5 Family of Bi-Modalities closely related to I/i (C/c = I/i)

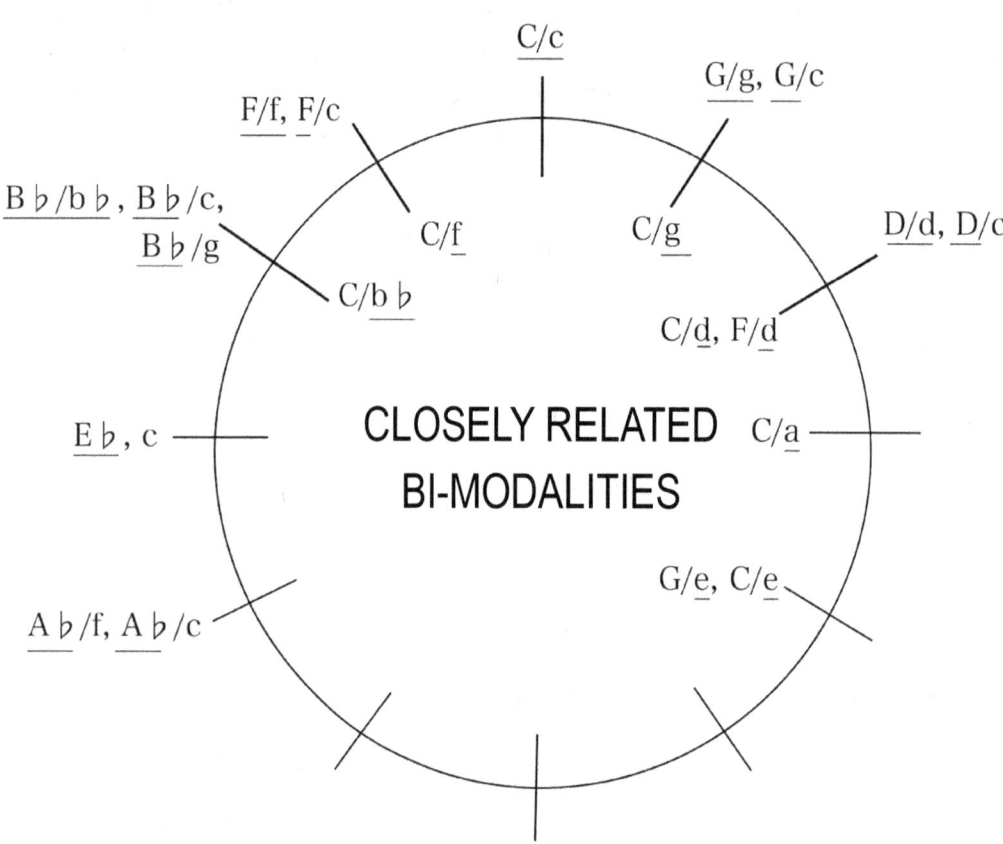

NOTE: Keys which appear in their home position are underlined.

Before we move on to the next topic, we can construct a sample time-line of a composition employing a series of semi-modulations, as shown in Example 14-6 below.

Ex. 14-6 Blueprint of a series of semi-modulations.

C/c → C/f → A♭/f → A♭/c → G/c → G/g → C/g →

C/c/ → F/c → F/d → C/d → C/e → G/e → G/g →

B♭/g → B♭/c → C/c → C/f → F/f → F/d → C/d → C/c

The brackets indicate the half of the bi-modality that stays the same, while the other half changes. Except for the first few and the last few measures, there is always an overlap of keys. Every time C/c (the home key) is reached, the sequence can be stopped, depending on the length of the piece. In this case, 15 of the 21 closely related bi-modalities shown in Example 14-5 are used, and the total number of individual keys appearing is 10.

A composition written as a chain of semi-modulations, such as the one shown above, would have three fantastic features: First, it would never deviate very far from the home key. Second, it would always remain bi-modal, but would not always be bi-tonal, because C/c, G/g and F/f are in the sequence. Third, within a reasonably short time, it would move into and out of a rather large number of keys. All of this can be achieved by slick and smooth sliding around.

Readers can try writing such sequences on their own, and see what happens. Two-voice counterpoint would be a good way to start. The sections can be of equal length, but they don't have to be.

* * *

Our final task in this chapter is to examine the subsets that are hidden within the bi-modalities that result from performing our rotations. The uni-tonal set X/x has no subsets. In all of the examples for the rest of this chapter, tones in common are written in half notes, and the rest are written as quarter notes. We start with our two nona-tonic sets, I/vi and I/ii, written as C/a and C/d in Example 14-7.

Ex. 14-7 Two nonatonic sets

We see that C/a has G+ as a subset, and C/d has F+ as a subset. So the first set is really a tri-tonal set (C/G/a OR G/C/a), and the second one is also a tri-tonal set (C/F/d OR F/C/d). **But both of these are of the form I/V/vi OR I/IV/ii — they are actually the same set! We have just proven, by using Set Theory, that ii is equivalent to vi!** This interchangeability can be verified as shown in Example 14-8 below.

In this process, we have created our first tri-tonal, bi-modal set. More accurately speaking, it created itself for us — we just had to observe that it is there — twice.

Ex. 14-8 Interchangeability of I/V/vi and I/IV/ii

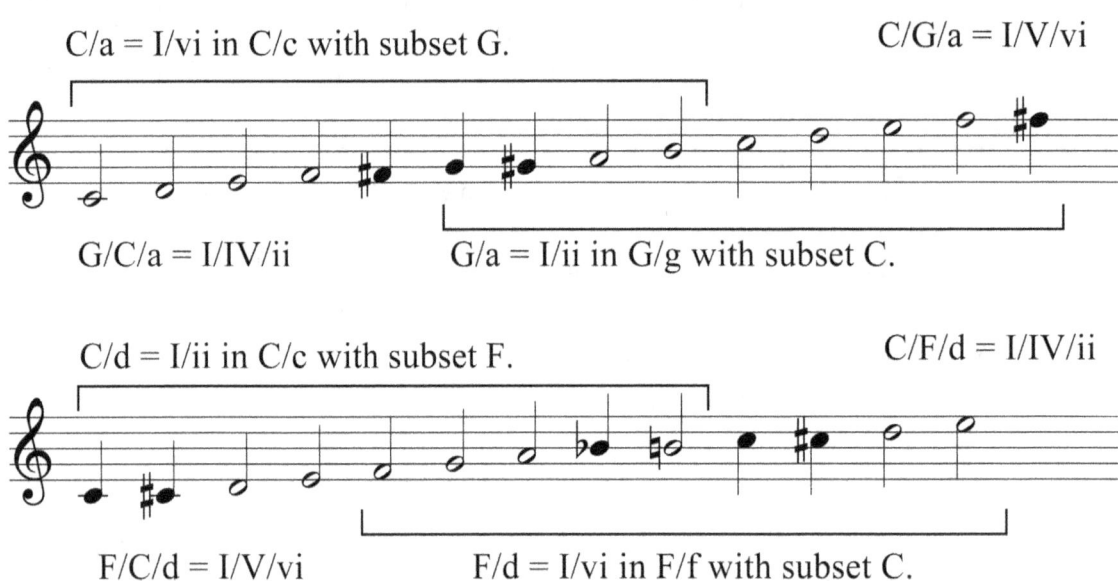

Example 14-8 actually shows a closed system of five keys: C+, a-, F+, d-, and G+. So why is e- not there? The short answer is that d# is not there. The complete answer is that, in our quintcircles, whenever two major keys laying two stations apart are present, then the major key laying in between them is automatically present. (It is impossible to combine F+ and G+ without obtaining C+ in the process). However, there is no minor key on the quintcircle that lays in between a- and d-. Not only that, the "in between" rule does not apply to minor keys. (In a separate case, the presence of d- and e- would not imply the presence of a-).

Next, we examine our three decatonic sets, I/v, I/iii, and I/iv, written in Example 14-9 below as C/g, C/e, and C/f, respectively.

Ex. 14-9 Three decatonic sets

The first set has as subsets G+, F+, B♭+, and, if we add the enharmonic d# (= e♭), e- also. So here, G may be considered the real tonal center, because we have G/g, plus the relative minor of G+, plus the relative major of g-. In general form, this is the set I/i/vi/♭III. These keys form a complete set in themselves, so we do not really need C+ or F+. The compatible keys have highlighted themselves for us to see them, while the incompatible ones have slid into the background. More will be said about this type of situation in later chapters.

The set C/e contains G+ as a subset and, if we include the c#, it also contains D+. For that reason, in order to keep the set more tightly knit, we are actually better off to use e harmonic minor, and leave it at I/iii/V, which is a nonatonic, tri-tonal, bi-modal set.

The third set contains the subsets F+ and d- (if the enharmonic c# = d♭ is included), so it can be re-written as F/f/C/d or, in the general form I/i/V/vi, stating the uni-tonal bi-modality first. Here we have a very interesting tri-tonal, bi-modal combination: F+ takes over centre stage because it is joined by its tonic minor, and the dominant key of both, and its relative minor. We can predict a great future for this set.

* * *

We have now looked at all the bi-modal sets that are well-matched and closely related to C/c. Now, in order to keep track of everything, we need to see what happens when we examine the subsets of our remaining five sets from Example 14-2. These are I/vii, I/♭iii, I/#v, I/#i, and I/#iv.

In Example 14-10 below, we have our first two sets, I/vii and I/♭iii, written out as C/b and C/e♭ respectively.

Ex. 14-10

C/b has the subsets G+, D+, and A+. If we add the enharmonic of f, e#, then f#- also becomes a subset. C/e♭ has the subsets F+, B♭+, E♭+, and c-. If we add the enharmonic of g♭, f#, then g- also becomes a subset. So the total number of keys contained in these sets has now grown to six and seven.

The next set becomes very cumbersome to work with when written out as C/g#, so it is written out in Example 14-11 as I/♭vi (= C/a♭).

Ex. 14-11

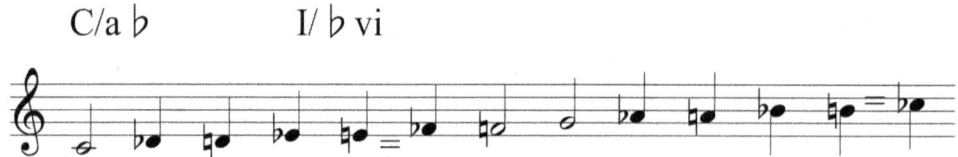

It has the subsets F+, B♭+, E♭+, A♭+, c-, and f-. If we add the enharmonic c# (= d♭), then d- is also a subset. This gives us a total of 8 keys (5 major and 3 minor).

The next set is I/#i, shown as C/c# in Example 14-12.

Ex. 14-12

This set has as subsets G+, D+, A+, E+, B+, a-, e-, and b-. If we add the enharmonic e# (= f), then F#+, C#+, and f#- become subsets. Then, adding fx (= g) gives us G#+ (theoretically) and g#-. So we have, in total, 8 or 9 major keys and 6 minor keys.

Finally, Example 14-13 shows the set I/#iv written out as C/f#.

Ex. 14-13

Here, the subsets are G+, D+, A+, E+, and e-. If we add the enharmonic b# (= c), then c#- also becomes a subset, for a total of 8 keys, 5 major and 3 minor.

We see now that with these five sets, things get out of hand. In each case, enharmonics are involved, and that means that the number of notes is higher than the number of tones; the note in question is not there, but the tone is. And "things get out of hand" means that these sets have two main undesirable characteristics. First, from the practical standpoint, the number of keys present is much too large. Second, because that is the case, we cannot ascertain which is the superset, and which are the subsets! Ours are not mathematical sets; they are musical sets. So the elements of our sets are not numbers (even or uneven, prime or not prime), but notes, tones, and keys and modes. In mathematical set theory, the order of elements is irrelevant, so the seven Church modes would be considered as the same, single set. In music theory, we consider a transposition to be the same set; in mathematics, this is not the case.

The undesirable characteristics just mentioned cause complexities. For example, in the last set shown, someone could claim that E/f# (a transposition of I/ii) is the superset, and C+, G+, D+, A+, e-, and c#- are the subsets, and we could not argue with them. Someone else could claim that E/e is the superset, and C+, G+, D+, A+, f#, and c#- are the subsets, and we could not argue with them, either.

It is not necessary to examine subsets of bi-modalities of the form X/i, because we know that each of these has an equivalent bi-modality in the form I/x, and we have just examined all of those. But just to assure ourselves that sets and their subsets remain consistent, and to have them in front of us, we write out the five closely related bi-modalities of the form X/i in Example 14-14 below.

Ex. 14-14 Five corresponding closely related bi-modalities of the form X/i

E♭/c Subset: B♭ = I/V/vi (c.f. Ex. 14-8)

B♭/c Subset: E♭ = I/IV/ii (c.f. Ex. 14-8)

F/c Subsets: C, B♭, E♭, a (g# = a♭) = I/v (c.f. Ex. 14-9)

A♭/c Subsets: E♭, B♭ = I/iii (c.f. Ex. 14-9)

G/c Subsets: C, a, (g# = a♭), e, (d# = e♭) = I/iv (c.f. Ex. 14-9)

This completes our examination of all sets and subsets formed by all 22 possible semi-modulations as listed in Examples 14-2 and 14-3. There is no question that the results of quintcircle rotations vary a lot, and that we have had several surprises — both pleasant and unpleasant ones. The pertinent fact here is that some combinations of keys yield desirable results, some yield undesirable ones, and still others yield a combination of both. We must sort these things out somehow, and that is the objective of the next chapter.

CHAPTER FIFTEEN

Compatibility of Keys

*The following chapter contains mature subject matter.
Viewer discretion is advised!*

So far, we have examined keys and key combinations from a number of different angles. In Chapter Nine of Part One, we evaluated closeness and remoteness of keys with respect to each other by using a system of proximity points. The approach there was from the standpoint of the number of tones keys had in common with each other. We assigned one proximity point for each note in common, and half a point for each enharmonic, for a total number of tones in common.

In Chapter Thirteen above, we used the acoustical approach in order to come up with a hierarchy of intervals from most consonant to most dissonant. Now, if we were to take this same order of notes, as notated in Example 13-4, and think of each one as the root of its own key, then we would end up with the order of proximities of keys with respect to C+, or c-, or C/c, as shown in Example 15-1.

Ex. 15-1 Order of proximity of keys

C → G, F, E, A, E♭, A♭, D, B♭, B, D♭, F#

C → g, f, e, a, e♭, a♭, d, b♭, b, d♭, f#

C/c → G/g, F/f, E/e, A/a, E♭/e♭, A♭/a♭, D/d, B♭/b♭, B/b, D♭/d♭, F#/f#

While not everyone would agree that the order in these series of keys — especially the first two — would be correct, if we re-write the third series, and indicate the number of tones that the partners of each bi-modality have in common with C/c, then the results are excellent, in that at least the total number of proximity points is in the order: 7, 7, 6, 6.5, 6.5, 6, 6, 6, 5, 5, 4.5, as shown in Example 15-2.

Ex. 15-2 Tones in common between C/c and the other 11 uni-tonal bi-modalities

C/c and:
1) G/g — 7 common tones
2) F/f — 7 common tones
3) E/e — 5 common tones and 2 enharmonics
4) A/a — 6 common tones and 1 enharmonic
5) E♭/e♭ — 6 common tones and 1 enharmonic
6) A♭/a♭ — 5 common tones and 2 enharmonics
7) D/d — 6 common tones
8) B♭/b♭ — 6 common tones
9) B/b — 4 common tones and 2 enharmonics
10) D♭/d♭ — 4 common tones and 2 enharmonics
11) F#/f# — 3 common tones and 3 enharmonics

Now we have to take a look at what happens when we write out our 22 possible semi-modulations, in the order given above. Each pairing of C/c with a bi-modality of the form X/x can be done in two ways: C/x and X/c. For example, C/c and G/g can result in C/g and G/c. For the next two pairs, the original minor key, c, is replaced with the next minor key in the column, f, after which the original major key, C, is replaced with the next major key, F. This results in the bi-modalities C/f and F/c, respectively. We keep following that same pattern for the remaining 10 bi-modalities. The 22 results are shown in Example 15-3 below.

Ex. 15-3 The 22 possible bi-modalities resulting from semi-modulations

C/c and:

G/g	→	1) C/g	D/d	→	13) C/d
		2) G/c			14) D/c
F/f	→	3) C/f	B♭/b♭	→	15) C/b♭
		4) F/c			16) B♭/c
E/e	→	5) C/e	B/b	→	17) C/b
		6) E/c			18) B/c
A/a	→	7) C/a	D♭/d♭	→	19) C/d♭
		8) A/c			20) D♭/c
E♭/e♭	→	9) C/e♭	F#/f#	→	21) C/f#
		10) E♭/c			22) F#/c
A♭/a♭	→	11) C/a♭			
		12) A♭/c			

Of these 22, the 12 that we called well-matched, bi-tonal bi-modalities in the previous chapter (see Ex. 14-4) are: The first five, the seventh, tenth, and twelfth to sixteenth inclusive. It is not surprising that the last six combinations did not make the list, but we must figure out what is "wrong" with the remaining four in the middle, which are: E/c, A/c, C/e♭, and C/a♭.

We need answers that we do not have. In order to find them, we must venture into what this author thinks is an unexplored subject, that of compatibility of keys. The traditional concepts of closely related keys will help us a bit, but only a bit. One dictionary definition of "compatible" is: "capable of existing together in harmony," and that is a good starting point. But, other than by trial and error, how can we tell whether or not two keys are compatible? Here is this author's theory:

Every key has neutral tones and Sensitive/Assertive tones. In both major and minor keys, the second, fourth and sixth scale degrees are neutral. The root, third, leading note, and fifth scale degrees — in that order — are assertive. The root asserts the tonality, the tonal center, and therefore the key. The third asserts the mode (major or minor). The leading note is the most ardent, most vehement, supporter of the tonic, mainly because of its inherent gravitational force, which makes it desperate to resolve itself by semitone upwards to the tonic. And the fifth is the second-strongest supporter of the tonic, being the root of the dominant function, even though it retains its membership in the tonic triad. Because these four tones are assertive, they are also sensitive, but not to the same degree (hence the order given above).

The assertive and sensitive nature of these four tones means that they go to war when they encounter rivals, these being any of their own kind. The battle cry is any such encounter, or chromatic clash, of sensitive/assertive tones (henceforth designated as SATs). When two keys are involved, there are 16 possible versions of chromatic clashes of SATs, as shown in Chart 15-1 below.

We can assign "clash intensity" point values to each of these combinations, as follows: root — 4, third — 3, leading note — 2, fifth — 1. In this chart, the intervals are listed in decreasing order of clash intensity, as per the point value system outlined above. The chart can be divided into three basic groups of clash intensities: six or higher, five, and four or lower.

Chart 15-1 Chromatic clashes of SATs and their intensities

Chromatic Clash of SATs	Clash Intensity
Root against root	4 + 4 = 8
Root against third	4 + 3 = 7
Third against root	3 + 4 = 7
Root against leading note	4 + 2 = 6
Leading note against root	2 + 4 = 6
Root against fifth	4 + 1 = 5
Fifth against root	1 + 4 = 5
Third against third	3 + 3 = 6 (?)
Third against leading note	3 + 2 = 5
Leading note against third	2 + 3 = 5
Third against fifth	3 + 1 = 4
Fifth against third	1 + 3 = 4
Leading note against leading note	2 + 2 = 4
Leading note against fifth	2 + 1 = 3
Fifth against leading note	1 + 2 = 3
Fifth against fifth	1 + 1 = 2

The case of "third against third" seems out of place in this chart, so it deserves special attention. In general, all chromatic clashes should be regarded in context, but when this particular clash occurs, it is particularly important not to look at it in isolation, and here is why. In the case of C+ and c-, e-natural clashes against e♭, but that is the only chromatic clash of SATs, and it is, in fact, the primary feature of the uni-tonal bi-modality. In the case of c#- and c-, the same clash (e vs. e♭) exists, but this pairing of keys is much different, because the roots, leading notes, and fifths also clash chromatically (as does every other corresponding scale degree).

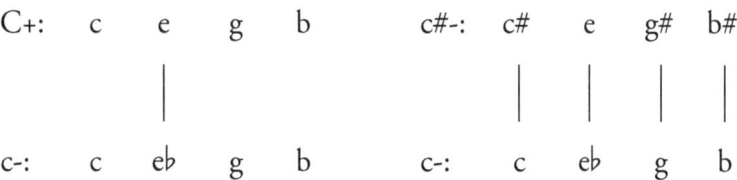

So while the total number of clash intensity points in C/c is only 6 (third against third), the total in the pairing of c#- with c- is 20 (root against root — 8, third against third — 6, l.n. against l.n. — 4, 5th against 5th — 2).

Before we go on, an explanation is in order about what is meant by a "chromatic clash," which could also be considered a "semitone clash." Clearly, any note x against x-sharp (example f against f#), or y against y-flat (example g against g-flat), forms a chromatic clash. But when we consider keys such as F and G against F# or G♭, (or f and g against f# or g♭), then we have to consider the notes f against g♭, and g against f#, to be chromatic clashes also, because, for example, F+ will clash just as much against G♭+ as it will against F#+. In addition, E against F, or B against C, (or e against f, or b against c), must be considered chromatic clashes also, because, for example, the relationship of E+ to F+ is the same as that of any transposition of these (such as A♭+ to A+), in which the chromatic clashes are obvious.

Now we can examine how many chromatic clashes exist in each of the pairings that results from the 22 possible semi-modulations that are outlined in Example 15-3 above. The clash intensities are tallied in Chart 15-2 below. Details of the calculations are shown on the pages that follow.

Chart 15-2 — Page 1 of 3

Chromatic clashes of SATs and their intensities for the 22 possible bi-modalities

Bi-Modality	Chromatic Clashes of SATs	Clash Intensity
1) C/g	l.n. & 3rd	5
2) G/c	none	0
3) C/f	none	0
4) F/c	l.n. & 3rd	5
5) C/e	none	0
6) E/c	root & 3rd, 3rd & 5th	7 + 4 = 11
7) C/a	5th & l.n.	3
8) A/c	3rd & root, 5th & 3rd, l.n. & 5th	7 + 4 + 3 = 14
9) C/eb	3rd & root, 5th & 3rd, l.n. & 5th	7 + 4 + 3 = 14
10) Eb/c	5th & l.n.	3
11) C/ab	root & 3rd, 3rd & 5th	7 + 4 = 11
12) Ab/c	none	0
13) C/d	root & l.n.	6
14) D/c	l.n. & root	6
15) C/bb	l.n. & root	6
16) Bb/c	root & l.n.	6
17) C/b	root & root, 5th & 5th, l.n. & l.n.	8 + 2 + 4 = 14
18) B/c	root & root, 5th & 5th, l.n. & l.n.	8 + 2 + 4 = 14
19) C/db	root & root, 5th & 5th, l.n. & l.n.	8 + 2 + 4 = 14
20) Db/c	root & root, 5th & 5th, l.n. & l.n.	8 + 2 + 4 = 14
21) C/f#	root & 5th, 5th & root	5 + 5 = 10
22) F#/c	5th & root, root & 5th	5 + 5 = 10

Chart 15-2 — page 2 of 3

BI-MODALITY	KEY	SATS	CHROMATIC CLASHES BETWEEN KEYS	POINT VALUE OF CLASHING SATS	CLASH STRENGTH
1) C/g	C+ g-	c e g b g b♭ d f#	b (leading note) b♭ (third)	2 + 3	= 5
2) G/c	G+ c-	g b d f# c e♭ g b	— — — — — — — — — —	0 + 0	= 0
3) C/f	C+ f-	c e g b f a♭ c e	— — — — — — — — — —	0 + 0	= 0
4) F/c	F+ c-	f a c e c e♭ g b	e (leading note) e♭ (third)	2 + 3	= 5
5) C/e	C+ e-	c e g b e g b d#	— — — — — — — — — —	0 + 0	= 0
6) E/c	E+ c-	e g# b d# c e♭ g b	e (root) e♭ (third)	4 + 3	7
	E+ c-	e g# b d# c e♭ g b	g# (third) g (fifth)	3 + 1	+ 4 = 11
7) C/a	C+ a-	c e g b a c e g#	g (fifth) g# (leading note)	1 + 2	= 3
8) A/c	A+ c-	a c# e g# c e♭ g b	c# (third) c (root)	3 + 4	7
	A+ c-	a c# e g# c e♭ g b	e (fifth) e♭ (third)	1 + 3	+ 4
	A+ c-	a c# e g# c e♭ g b	g# (leading note) g (fifth)	2 + 1	+ 3 = 14
9) C/e♭	C+ e♭-	c e g b e♭ g♭ b♭ d	e (third) e♭ (root)	3 + 4	7
	C+ e♭-	c e g b e♭ g♭ b♭ d	g (fifth) g♭ (third)	1 + 3	+ 4
	C+ e♭-	c e g b e♭ g♭ b♭ d	b (leading note) b♭ (fifth)	2 + 1	+ 3 = 14
10) E♭/c	E♭+ c-	e♭ g b♭ d c e♭ g b	b♭ (fifth) b (leading note)	1 + 2	= 3
11) C/a♭	C+ a♭-	c e g b a♭ c♭ e♭ g	c (root) c♭ (third)	4 + 3	7
	C+ a♭-	c e g b a♭ c♭ e♭ g	e (third) e♭ (fifth)	3 + 1	+ 4 = 11

Chart 15-2 — Page 3 of 3

BI-MODALITY	KEY	SATS	CHROMATIC CLASHES BETWEEN KEYS	POINT VALUE OF CLASHING SATS	CLASH STRENGTH
12) A♭/c	A♭+ c-	a♭ c e♭ g c e♭ g b	— — — — — — — — — —	0 + 0	= 0
13) C/d	C+ d-	c e g b d f a c#	c (root) c# (leading note)	4 + 2	= 6
14) D/c	D+ c-	d f# a c# c e♭ g b	c# (leading note) c (root)	2 + 4	= 6
15) C/b♭	C+ b♭-	c e g b b♭ d♭ f a	b (leading note) b♭ (root)	2 + 4	= 6
16) B♭/c	B♭+ c-	b♭ d f a c e♭ g b	b♭ (root) b (leading note)	4 + 2	= 6
17) C/b	C+ b-	c e g b b d f# a#	c (root) b (root)	4 + 4	8
	C+ b-	c e g b b d f# a#	g (fifth) f# (fifth)	1 + 1	+ 2
	C+ b-	c e g b b d f# a#	b (leading note) a# (leading note)	2 + 2	+ 4 = 14
18) B/c	B+ c-	b d# f# a# c e♭ g b	b (root) c (root)	4 + 4	8
	B+ c-	b d# f# a# c e♭ g b	f# (fifth) g (fifth)	1 + 1	+ 2
	B+ c-	b d# f# a# c e♭ g b	a# (leading note) b (leading note)	2 + 2	+ 4 = 14
19) C/d♭	C+ d♭-	c e g b d♭ f♭ a♭ c	c (root) d♭ (root)	4 + 4	8
	C+ d♭-	c e g b d♭ f♭ a♭ c	g (fifth) a♭ (fifth)	1 + 1	+ 2
	C+ d♭-	c e g b d♭ f♭ a♭ c	b (leading note) c (leading note)	2 + 2	+ 4 = 14
20) D♭/c	D♭+ c-	d♭ f a♭ c c e♭ g b	d♭ (root) c (root)	4 + 4	8
	D♭+ c-	d♭ f a♭ c c e♭ g b	a♭ (fifth) g (fifth)	1 + 1	+ 2
	D♭+ c-	d♭ f a♭ c c e♭ g b	c (leading note) b (leading note)	2 + 2	+ 4 = 14
21) C/f#	C+ f#-	c e g b f# a c# e#	c (root) c# (fifth)	4 + 1	5
	C+ f#-	c e g b f# a c# e#	g (fifth) f# (root)	1 + 4	+ 5 = 10
22) F#/c	F#+ c-	f# a# c# e# c e♭ g b	c# (fifth) c (root)	1 + 4	5
	F#+ c-	f# a# c# e# c e♭ g b	f# (root) g (fifth)	4 + 1	+ 5 = 10

Sure enough, our 12 well-matched bi-modalities (which are the first five, the seventh, tenth, and twelfth to sixteenth) have the lowest chromatic clash ratings. This is marvelous, because when we arrive at the same results in two different ways, we have a type of proof of correctness.

Now, in Chart 15-3, we re-write Chart 15-2 in ascending order of clash strength point values.

Chart 15-3

Bi-Modality	No. of Chromatic Clashes of SATs	Clash Strength
2) G/c	0	0
3) C/f	0	0
5) C/e	0	0
12) A♭/c	0	0
7) C/a	1	3
10) E♭/c	1	3
1) C/g	1	5
4) F/c	1	5
13) C/d	1	6
16) B♭/c	1	6
14) D/c	1	6
15) C/b♭	1	6
21) C/f#	2	10
F#/c	2	10
17) C/b	2	10
18) B/c	2	10
19) C/d♭	2	10
20) D♭/c	2	10
6) E/c	2	11
11) C/a♭	2	11
8) A/c	3	14
9) C/e♭	3	14

Plenty has already been said about the first group, that of our 12 well-matched bi-modalities. But it is interesting to note here the position taken by the traditional relative major/relative minor pairings — they came in second out of the eight different rankings that resulted, as shown in the clash strength column in Chart 15-3. Their clash intensity rating is 3, and that is the same as the rating for X/x (C/c for example). We now have to analyze the last ten bi-modalities, in four groups, as illustrated above.

The pairs C/f# and F#/c are unique, because they are the self-reproducing-root invertible pairs, which occur only in the case of the tritone. When looking at these, we should also consider their appearance when F# and f# are substituted by G♭ and g♭ respectively. In any event, if we assigned 4, 3, 2, and 1 intensity of strength points to chromatic clashes of SATs, then how many points should we allot to the three tritone clashes (of the roots and leading notes and fifths) that are found in both these pairs?

Readers can decide this for themselves, but it is clear that only four or five more points would take these two bi-modalities to the bottom of the list.

Our next group is the one in which the roots in each pair are a semitone apart. Here again, we must remember that a semitone can be a minor second or an augmented unison, depending on the specific keys involved. Whatever the case, this is the very reason why these four bi-modalities ended up close to the bottom of our original list: The corresponding notes of keys whose roots are a semitone apart clash with each other in almost every case, so we can hardly expect such keys to be compatible.

In the case of the next group, E/c and C/a♭, it is not the fact that the roots of the keys in each pair are a major third apart that is the problem at hand. Rather, it is the fact that the roots of the major key clash with the thirds of the minor key. If we compare these pairings to C/e and A♭/c respectively, we see that there is a world of difference. Although the roots in those are also a major third apart, these pairs contain no chromatic clashes of the type defined in Chart 15-2! This is a prime example in which close observation of what is there really pays off for us.

Finally, we have the notorious combinations of A/c and C/e♭. This time, the roots of the keys in each pair are a minor third apart, but the problem is the same as before, in that the modes clash. And there is more to it: these combinations are possibly even fiercer than Stravinsky's Petroushka Chord. In it, the two triads being combined are diametrically apart on the traditional quintcircle. Here, the roots of each pair are not just diametrically apart, but of the opposite mode as well. And if we compare these to C/a and E♭/c respectively, we see that those are the traditional relative major — relative minor pairings. Conclusion: When choosing a partner for a key, what a difference it makes to go a major third up instead of down, or a minor third down instead of up!

At this point, some general comments about SATs and chromatic clashes are in order. From the foregoing, readers may get the impression that "intensity of strength points" are "demerit points." In a way, they are, but only when their number is large (9 or higher). When their number is low (6 or less), that is actually a desirable characteristic. After all, if these numbers always came out equal (or almost equal), then all pairings would lay on the same level of intensity, and semi-modulations would not be felt much.

What we have seen so far is a large part of the picture of compatibility of keys, but it is not the whole picture; there is more. Although this whole study is about bi-modality, since subsets are such a frequent and common occurrence, inevitably, the issue of compatibility of two major keys, or of two minor keys, with respect to each other, comes up. So we have to examine the situation of chromatic clashes of SATs within the family of major keys, and then within the harmonic minor key family. To do this, we reproduce Chart 9-2 from Part One (consisting of two columns), and add the "Chromatic Clashes of SATs" and "Clash Strength" columns, to obtain the results shown in Chart 15-4 on the next page.

Notes regarding Chart 15-4

C+ with B+ or C+ with D♭+ should be regarded as the equivalent of X with X-flat or X with X-sharp, in which all SATs clash chromatically. The same applies to c- with b- or c- with d♭-.

Tritone clashes are not taken into account. If they were, since all four SATs clash, the total number of points would probably be somewhere between 15 and 20.

Details of the calculations are shown on the pages after the chart.

Chart 15-4 — Page 1 of 3

Chromatic clashes of SATs in pairings of two major keys or two minor keys

KEY	NUMBER OF TONES IN COMMON WITH C+	CHROMATIC CLASHES OF SATS	CLASH STRENGTH
G+	6	0	0
F+	6	0	0
D+	5	root & l.n.	6
B♭+	5	l.n. & root	6
A+	4	root & 3rd, 5th & l.n.	10
E♭+	4	3rd & root, l.n. & 5th	10
E+	3	5th & 3rd	4
A♭+	3	3rd & 5th	4
B+	2	roots, 3's, 5's, l.n.'s	20
D♭+	2	roots, 3's, 5's, l.n.'s	20
F#+	1 + 1 En	root & 5th, 3rd & l.n.	10
G♭+	1 + 1 En	5th & root, l.n. & 3rd, root & 5th	15
KEY	NUMBER OF TONES IN COMMON WITH c-	CHROMATIC CLASHES OF SATS	CLASH STRENGTH
g-	4	l.n. & 3rd	5
f-	4	3rd & l.n.	5
d-	3	root & l.n.	6
b♭-	3	l.n. & root	6
a-	4 + 1 En	3rd & 5th, 5th & l.n.	7
e♭-	4 + 1 En	5th & 3rd, l.n. & 5th	7
e-	3 + 1 En	3rd & root	7
a♭-	3 + 1 En	root & 3rd	7
b-	3	roots, 3's, 5's, l.n.'s	20
d♭-	3	roots, 3's, 5's, l.n.'s	20
f#-	2 + 2 En	root & 5th	5
g♭-	2 + 2 En	5th & root	5

Chart 15-4 — Page 2 of 3

KEY COMBINATION	KEY	SATS	CHROMATIC CLASHES BETWEEN KEYS	POINT VALUE OF CLASHING SATS	CLASH STRENGTH
1) C/G	C+ G+	c e g b g b d f#	— — — — — — — —	0 + 0	= 0
2) C/F	C+ F+	c e g b f a c e	— — — — — — — —	0 + 0	= 0
3) C/D	C+ D+	c e g b d f# a c#	c (root) c# (leading note)	4 + 2	= 6
4) C/B♭	C+ B♭+	c e g b b♭ d f a	b (leading note) b♭ (root)	2 + 4	= 6
5) C/A	C+ A+	c e g b a c# e g#	c (root) c# (third)	4 + 3	= 7
6) C/E♭	C+ E♭+	c e g b e♭ g b♭ d	e (third) e♭ (root)	3 + 4	= 7
7) C/E	C+ E+	c e g b e g# b d#	g (fifth) g# (third)	1 + 3	= 4
8) C/A♭	C+ A♭+	c e g b a♭ c e♭ g	e (third) e♭ (fifth)	3 + 1	= 4
9) C/B	C+ B+	c e g b b d# f# a#	c (root) b (root)	4 + 4	8
	C+ B+	c e g b b d# f# a#	e (third) d# (third)	3 + 3	+ 6
	C+ B+	c e g b b d# f# a#	g (fifth) f# (fifth)	1 + 1	+ 2
	C+ B+	c e g b b d# f# a#	b (leading note) a# (leading note)	2 + 2	+ 4 = 20
10) C/D♭	C+ D♭+	c e g b d♭ f a♭ c	c (root) d♭ (root)	4 + 4	8
	C+ D♭+	c e g b d♭ f a♭ c	e (third) f (third)	3 + 3	+ 6
	C+ D♭+	c e g b d♭ f a♭ c	g (fifth) a♭ (fifth)	1 + 1	+ 2
	C+ D♭+	c e g b d♭ f a♭ c	b (leading note) c (leading note)	2 + 2	+ 4 = 20
11) C/F#	C+ F#+	c e g b f# a# c# e#	c (root) c# (fifth)	4 + 1	5
	C+ F#+	c e g b f# a# c# e#	e (third) e# (leading note)	3 + 2	+ 5 = 10

Chart 15-4 — Page 3 of 3

KEY COMBINATION	KEY	SATS	CHROMATIC CLASHES BETWEEN KEYS	POINT VALUE OF CLASHING SATS	CLASH STRENGTH
12) c/g	c- g-	c e♭ g b g b♭ d f#	b (leading note) b♭ (third)	2 + 3	= 5
13) c/f	c- f-	c e♭ g b f a♭ c e	e♭ (third) e (leading note)	3 + 2	= 5
14) c/d	c- d-	c e♭ g b d f a c#	c (root) c# (leading note)	4 + 2	= 6
15) c/b♭	c- b♭-	c e♭ g b a c e g#	b (leading note) b♭ (root)	2 + 4	= 6
16) c/a	c- a-	c e♭ g b a c e g#	e♭ (third) e (fifth)	3 + 1	4
	c- a-	c e♭ g b a c e g#	g (fifth) g# (leading note)	1 + 2	+ 3 = 7
17) c/e♭	c- e♭-	c e♭ g b e♭ g♭ b♭ d	g (fifth) g♭ (third)	1 + 3	4
	c- e♭-	c e♭ g b e♭ g♭ b♭ d	b (leading note) b♭ (fifth)	2 + 1	+ 3 = 7
18) c/e	c- e-	c e♭ g b e g b d#	e♭ (third) e (root)	3 + 4	= 7
19) c/a♭	c- a♭-	c e♭ g b a♭ c♭ e♭ g	c (root) c♭ (third)	4 + 3	= 7
20) c/b	c- b-	c e♭ g b b d f# a#	c (root) b (root)	4 + 4	8
	c- b-	c e♭ g b b d f# a#	e♭ (third) d (third)	3 + 3	+ 6
	c- b-	c e♭ g b b d f# a#	g (fifth) f# (fifth)	1 + 1	+ 2
	c- b-	c e♭ g b b d f# a#	b (leading note) a# (leading note)	2 + 2	+ 4 = 20
21) c/d♭	c- d♭-	c e♭ g b d♭ f♭ a♭ c	c (root) d♭ (root)	4 + 4	8
	c- d♭-	c e♭ g b d♭ f♭ a♭ c	e♭ (third) f♭ (third)	3 + 3	+ 6
	c- d♭-	c e♭ g b d♭ f♭ a♭ c	g (fifth) a♭ (fifth)	1 + 1	+ 2
	c- d♭-	c e♭ g b d♭ f♭ a♭ c	b (leading note) c (leading note)	2 + 2	+ 4 = 20
22) c/f#	c- f#-	c e♭ g b f# a c# e#	c (root) c# (fifth)	4 + 1	= 5

What different pictures have resulted! In the major-key set, the compatible pairings turn out to be, in order, (I/V and I/IV), (I/III and I/♭VI), and (I/II and I/♭VII). In the minor-key set, the order follows the quintcircle: First (i/v and i/iv), next (i/ii and i/♭vii), and then (i/vi, i/♭iii, i/iii, and i/♭vi). And, for those who do not mind tritone clashes, (i/#iv and i/♭v) have turned out to be extremely compatible, ranking equal to the top two keys. The reason that the bottom half of the chart differs so much from the top half is, of course, that, in harmonic minor keys, the leading note is "artificially manufactured."

After seeing these results, and getting back to the subject of subsets, we can see that choosing a compatible pair of keys is one thing, but the question of whether or not the subsets that automatically come with our choice will be compatible is quite another. There is a positive and a negative side to this situation. The positive side is that we know now to be even more careful in choosing keys. The negative side is that this whole business of compatibility of keys is by no means consistent or straightforward.

In particular, it is arguable that two keys can be too compatible, for example, those combinations of keys for which both the number of chromatic clashes of SATs and the intensity of strength is zero. This is especially true if, in addition, the number of tones that the two keys have in common is high, for example, in I/V and I/IV. The relationships C/G, or C/F, or F/C or G/C are like those of siblings: They can make a great team in many ways, but they better not get married … On the other hand, the bi-modalities **G/c and C/f have no chromatic clashes either, but because they are of different modes, they complement each other, and for that reason, make an excellent pair. This is why, in key combinations, bi-modalities work better than do combinations of two major, or two minor, keys.**

The bi-modalities C/d, D/c, C/b♭, and B♭/c deserve special attention. In all four of these, there is only one chromatic clash, and it is between the root and leading note (or leading note and root). This particular clash just does not seem to be an obstacle to compatibility. It looks more like a complementary situation, one in which one key has what the other does not. More will be said about clashes versus complements in Chapter Nine, on Dodecaphonic Tonalities. For now, we can take note that analysis of chromatic clashes of SATs helps us a great deal in determining the degree of compatibility of two (or more) keys with each other, but other aspects of key relationships must be taken into account as well.

Here is an example. Of the three tones described earlier as neutral (the second, fourth, and sixth scale degrees), the fourth scale degree is perhaps not 100% neutral. It is the root of the subdominant, and when it is the seventh of the V^7 chord, it wants to resolve downward. So we could have categorized it as a SAT and assigned to it an intensity value of .5. But since we did not do that, we could at least consider whether or not it is diatonic in the partner key.

Given the results obtained throughout this chapter, we can see that very many key combinations can be analyzed from the standpoint of compatibility. So, as a partial summary of our findings in this chapter, we draw up one final chart, Chart 15-5, which presents a comparison of various basic groups of key combinations.

Chart 15-5 Compatibility of Keys comparison chart

PAIRS OF KEYS	RATIO OF TONES IN COMMON	CHROMATIC CLASHES OF SATS	CLASH INTENSITY
a) Keys With Roots a Perfect Fifth or Perfect Fourth Apart			
C/g (I/v, IV/i)	4/10	l.n. & 3rd	5
G/c (I/iv, V/i)	4/9	none	0
C/G (I/V)	6/8	none	0
c/g (i/v)	4/10	l.n. & 3rd	5
b) Keys With Roots a Minor Third or Major Sixth Apart			
C/a (I/vi, ♭III/i)	6/8	5th & l.n.	3
A/c (I/♭iii, #VI/i)	2/11	3rd & 5th, 5th & 3rd, l.n.& 5th	14
C/A (I/VI)	4/10	root & 3rd, 5th & l.n.	10
c/a (i/vi)	5/9	3rd & 5th, 5th & l.n.	7
c) Keys With Roots a Major Third or Minor Sixth Apart			
C/a♭ (I/♭vi, #III/i)	3/11	root & 3rd, 3rd & 5th	11
A♭/c (I/iii, VI/i)	5/9	none	0
C/A♭ (I/♭VI)	3/11	3rd & 5th	4
c/a♭ (i/vi)	4/9	root & 3rd	7
d) Keys With Roots a Major Second or Minor Seventh Apart			
C/d (I/ii, ♭VII/i)	5/9	root & l.n.	6
D/c (I/♭vii, II/i)	3/11	l.n. & root	6
C/D (I/II)	5/9	root & l.n.	6
c/d (i/ii)	3/11	root & l.n.	6
e) Keys With Roots a Minor Second or Major Seventh Apart			
C/d♭ (I/♭ii, VII/i)	3/12	root & root, 5th & 5th	10
D♭/c (I/vii, ♭II/i)	4/10	root & root, 5th & 5th	10
C/D♭ (I/♭II)	2/12	roots, 3's, 5's, l.n.'s	20
c/d♭ (i/♭ii)	3/11	roots, 3's, 5's, l.n.'s	20
f) Keys With Roots a Tritone Apart			
C/f# (I/#iv, I/♭v)	4/10	root & 5th, 5th & root	10
F#/c (I/♭v, I/#iv)	4/10	5th & root, root & 5th	10
C/F# (I/#IV, I/♭V)	2/12	root & 5th, 3rd & l.n.	10
c/f# (i/#iv, i/♭v)	4/10	root & 5th	5

NOTES: In d) above, since the intensities came out equal, we can dig deeper, and consider the fourth scale degrees. If we do, then we see that the f in C+ clashes chromatically with the f# (third) of D+, so the pairs D/c and C/D end up with higher intensity levels.

In f) above, tritone clashes apply, but they are not incorporated into the chart. Even so, we can see that the only possible compatible combination of the four presented is c/f#.

It is clear that the only way that we could have discovered all these properties of key combinations was by doing all this work. But now that it is done, readers should take a good, long look at all the charts in this chapter, and compare, compare, and compare! Compare things more, and compare more things. Compare anything and compare everything. The reason that it is necessary to do so is that, in this chapter, we have considered only pairs of keys, but in subsequent chapters, we will have to consider sets of three keys or more. When we do encounter various combinations of keys, we will refer back to the charts in this chapter, as needed, and as applicable. When we determine how compatible various key combinations are, we will be able to figure out which combinations are user-friendly, and which are not.

It is not of particular importance to rank all key combinations in order of clash intensity, although readers can easily do that if they want to do so. What is important is to memorize that **for two-key combinations, a rating below 8 is low, and above 8 is high.** It is **relative compatibility of keys** that is the significant factor in key relationships.

In the light of what we have seen in this chapter, it would be interesting to examine the key combinations that composers of polytonal music have used, and to see if any of them habitually chose either compatible or incompatible combinations. Maybe someone could visit their graves and ask them, but then the answer would probably be silence…

The last three chapters should be regarded as a grand accumulation of analytical tools that we will use in the next five chapters. Some of these tools are home-made, but then, so is our system … We now have all our raw materials, and a full toolbox, too. In the next four chapters, we will do our construction work.

INTERMISSION

CHAPTER SIXTEEN

Nonaphonic Tri-Tonal, Bi-Modal Systems

If we refer back to Chapter Fourteen, then we can recall that so far, we have encountered four nonatonic sets: I/i, I/vi, I/ii, and I/iii (when the harmonic form of iii is used). The first of these has no subsets, and only one tonal centre; it is our original uni-tonal, bi-modal set. The second one has V as a subset, and the third has IV. Both of these can be written in the form I/V/vi and I/IV/ii (for example, C/G/a and C/F/d or F/C/d and G/C/a). Since there are nine tones, three tonal centres (no other subsets), and two modes, these are our first two nonaphonic, tri-tonal, bi-modal systems.

The fourth set, I/iii, is a bit different. It has V as a subset, so it can be written in the general form I/V/iii, or, by interchangeability, I/IV/vi (for example, C/G/e or C/F/a). Since there are no other subsets, we have here our third nonaphonic, tri-tonal, bi-modal system.

Now, if we write out all our key combinations (without unnecessary duplication), we can see how many tones the members of our tri-tonalities have in common. We can also see how many chromatic clashes of SATs there are. The results are shown in Example 16-1 below.

Ex. 16-1 Common tones and chromatic clashes of SATs in Nonatonic, Tri-tonal sets

											Chromatic clashes of SATs
I/V/vi = C/G/a	C:	c		d	e	f		g		a	b	C and G: 0
	G:	c		d	e		f#	g		a	b	G and a: root, l.n.
	a:	c		d	e	f	(f#)		g#	a	b	C and a: 5th, l.n.
Common:		**c**		**d**	**e**					**a**	**b**	
I/IV/ii = C/F/d	C:	c		d	e	f		g		a		b	C and F: 0
	F:	c		d	e	f		g		a	bb		F and d: 5th, l.n.
	d:		c#	d	e	f		g		a	bb	(b)	C and d: root, l.n.
Common:				**d**	**e**	**f**		**g**		**a**			
I/V/iii = C/G/e	C:	c		d	e	f		g		a	b	C and G: 0
	G:	c		d	e		f#	g		a	b	G and e: 5th, l.n.
	e:	c		d#	e		f#	g		a	b	C and e: 0
Common:		**c**			**e**			**g**		**a**	**b**	

Ex. 16-1 Cont'd.

	Chromatic clashes of SATs								
I/IV/vi = C/F/a	C:	c	d	e	f	g		a		b	C and F: 0
	F:	c	d	e	f	g		a	b♭		F and a: 0
	a:	c	d	e	f		g#	a		b	C and a: 5th, l.n.
Common:		c	d	e	f			a			

There are several desirable results to be observed here. In each case, the three keys involved have five tones in common. There are not many chromatic clashes of SATs, and they are of two types only. (Reminder from Chart 15-1: Root against leading note has an intensity of strength of 6, and fifth against leading note has a rating of 3). We can safely claim that the three keys within each of these sets are compatible with each other. Also, when we consider that three keys are involved, we can be well pleased that, in each case, five of the nine tones are common.

Now, let us go beyond common tones, and see all the possible triads and seventh chords that can be built in each of our two basic sets, I/V/vi and I/V/iii. These are shown in Example 16-2 below.

Ex. 16-2 Triads and seventh chords in I/V/vi and I/V/iii

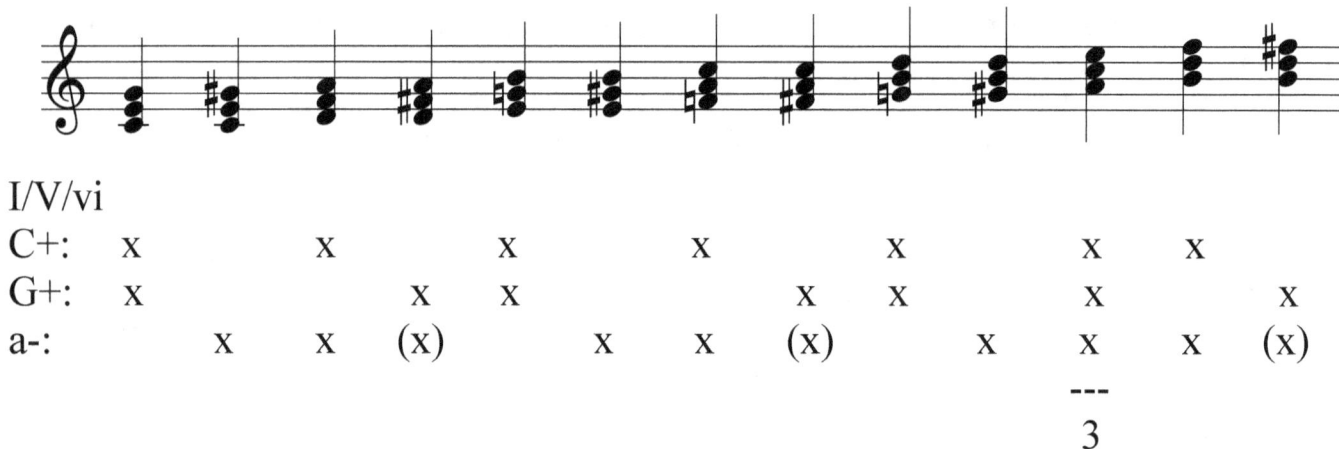

I/V/vi
C+: x   x   x   x   x   x   x
G+: x   x x   x x   x   x
a-: x x (x)   x   x (x)   x   x   x (x)

                                               3

Ex. 16-2 Cont'd.

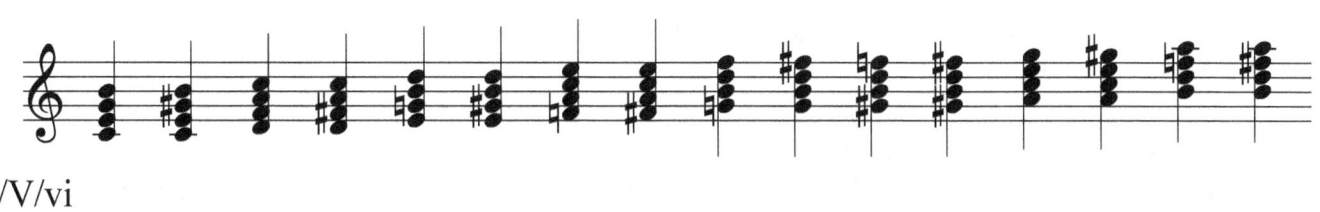

I/V/vi
C+:	x		x		x		x		x				x		x
G+:	x			x	x			x		x			x			x
a-:		x	x	(x)		x	x	(x)		x	(x)		x	x	(x)

I/V/iii
C+:	x	x			x	x		x		x	x		
G+:	x		x		x		x	x		x			x
e-:	x			x	x		x		x	x			x
	---			---	---				---	---		
	3			0	3				3	0		

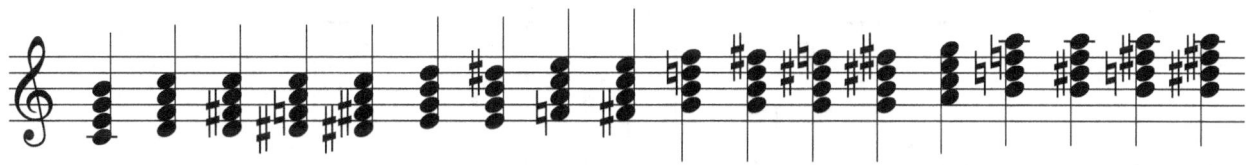

I/V/iii
C+:	x	x		x		x		x		x	x	
G+:	x		x		x		x		x		x		x
e-:	x		x	x		x		x		x	x		x
	---								---	---	---	
	3	(=Gr6)							0	3	0	

Readers can make the obvious observations on their own; the less obvious ones are pointed out in the example. First, had we not used the octatonic form of a-minor, the x's that are in parentheses would not be there. This would mean that a-minor would have only one chord in common with G-major (the a-minor triad); this way, the two keys have seven common chords.

Second, there are not many chords that are common to all three keys involved — only six out of 62. Third, only four of the 62 chords do not belong to any of the three keys involved.

These are all desirable results, but the best feature of the whole picture is that we have ended up with a healthy proportion of chords that belong to only one, or only two, of the three keys involved (30/62 and 22/62 respectively). This is marvelous, because it means that we have at our disposal plenty of chords that we can use to steer a composition towards, or away from, any one key, or any pair of keys (of the three), as we wish. These features make all of these tri-tonal, bi-modal, nonaphonic systems very user-friendly, indeed.

* * *

Our next task in this chapter is to ascertain whether or not there exist any other nonatonic, bi-modal sets. There are at least three ways to approach this problem: mathematically, musically, and by using a combination of these two approaches. If we used the mathematical approach only, we would be examining a very large number of sets unnecessarily. If we used the music theory approach only, we might inadvertently fail to find an existing set. So the third option is by far the best one for us, because by using it, we will save ourselves a lot of unnecessary work (and, of course, time) and we can still be certain that we have found all usable sets.

We begin by fixing the seven white-key notes of C-major, and adding to them every possible two-note combination of the five black-key notes that remain, as shown in Example 16-3 below.

Ex. 16-3 Diagram of black-key tones numbered

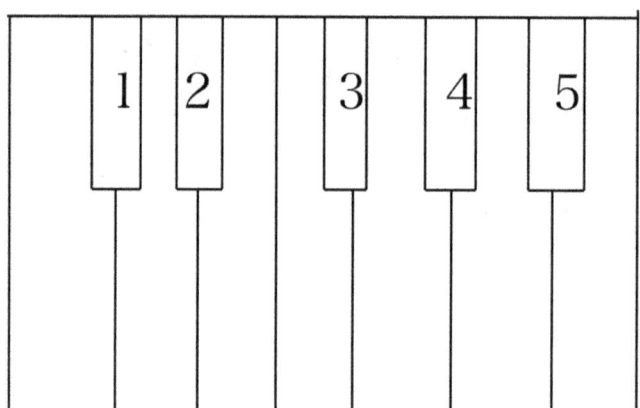

If we consider tones only, then there are only 10 possible pairs to add. They are: (1,2), (1,3), (1,4), (1,5), (2,3), (2,4), (2,5), (3,4), (3,5), and (4,5). However, each of these five tones has two different names (x-sharp and y-flat), so each of these pairs can be written in four different ways. For example, the pair (1,2) can be written as (c#, d#), or (c#, eb), or (db, d#), or (db, eb). So we have 40 cases in all to consider, as shown in Example 16-4 on the next page.

Ex. 16-4 Forty cases of pairs of black-key notes added to C+

C+ (= c, d, e, f, g, a, b) plus:

1) c#, d#
2) c#, e♭
3) d♭, d#
4) d♭, e♭
5) c#, f# = C+ plus D+ = I/II
6) c#, g♭
7) d♭, f#
8) d♭, g♭
9) c#, g#
10) c#, a♭
11) d♭, g#
12) d♭, a♭

13) c#, a#
14) c#, b♭ = C+ plus F+ plus d- = I/IV/ii
15) d♭, a#
16) d♭, b

17) d#, f# = C+ plus G+ plus e- (harm.) = I/V/iii
18) d#, g♭
19) e♭, f#
20) e♭, g♭

21) d#, g#
22) d#, a♭
23) e♭, g#
24) e♭, a♭ = C+ plus c- (octatonic) = I/i

25) d#, a#
26) d#, b♭
27) e♭, a#
28) e♭, b♭ = C+ plus B♭+ = I/♭VII
29) f#, g# = C+ plus G+ plus a- = I/V/vi
30) f#, a♭
31) g♭, g#
32) g♭, a♭

33) f#, a#
34) f#, b♭ = C+ plus F+ plus G+ = I/IV/V
35) g♭, a#
36) g♭, b♭

37) g#, a#
38) g#, b♭ = C+ plus F+ plus a- (harm.) = I/IV/vi
39) a♭, a#
40) a♭, b♭

128 • Dodecaphonic Tonality

This example also illustrates that we obtain concrete results (meaning results definable in terms of major and minor keys) in only eight cases. We can summarize these in one paragraph.

Case 5) yields C+ plus D+, which is bi-tonal, but not bi-modal. Case 14) is the set I/IV/ii, which we have already defined. Case 17) is the set I/V/iii, which has also been previously derived. Case 24) is our original uni-tonal, bi-modal set, I/i. Case 28) is actually the same set as case 5). Case 29) is our already familiar set I/V/vi. Case 34), I/IV/V, is tri-tonal, but not bi-modal. Finally, case 38) is the last of our previously derived sets, I/IV/vi.

The remaining 32 cases do not yield any nonatonic, bi-modal sets, so we have our answer: There do not exist any other such sets that we did not define before doing this check. This means that we are now finished with this part of our study.

Our final task in this chapter is to designate key signatures for each of our five nonaphonic, bi-modal systems. This is done in Example 16-5 below.

Ex. 16-5 Key signatures for five nonaphonic, bi-modal systems

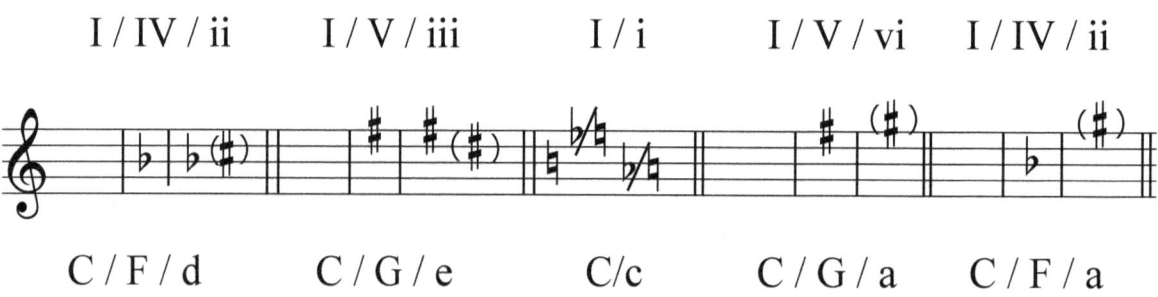

The key signature for C/c is copied from Example 3-8 (of Part One). For the tri-tonal systems, we simply separate the three key signatures with bar lines. This makes it clear that three tonal centres are involved. An invisible key signature is, of course, that of C+. For minor keys, we use the traditional key signature, plus the leading note in brackets.

CHAPTER SEVENTEEN:

Two Fundamental Decaphonic Bi-Modalities

The subject of Decaphonic (10-tone) tonal systems is rather complex, so it is necessary to devote two chapters to 10-tone sets. We begin by dealing only with the first two systems, which are truly out-standing in their field (just like farmers) … This chapter, more than any other one, makes use of all four overall approaches to our subject: back to basics, History of Music Theory, one thing leads to another, and musical acoustics.

The "back to basics" approach compels us to choose more than seven tones, or notes, to form our basic set. Having done 8- and 9-tone sets, we now move on to 10. The "History of Music Theory" approach tells us that the oldest, most frequently used bi-modality is I/vi, and second in importance is I/i. This approach, together with our "one thing leads to another" approach, leads us naturally to combine a given major key with both its relative minor and tonic minor keys. After that, we will combine a given minor key with both its relative major and tonic major keys. In the latter instance, our fourth approach, that of musical acoustics, will serve us very well, indeed.

Our first task, that of creating the I/i/vi set, is extremely simple. All we have to do is to take our basic, nonatonic, uni-tonal set, and add to it the leading note of the relative minor key of I, as shown in Example 17-1 below.

Ex. 17-1

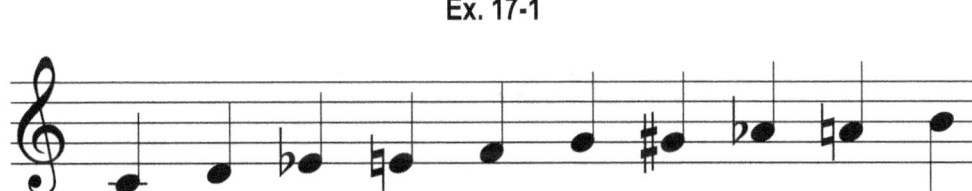

This set is unique, because it consists of nine tones, so it is nonatonic, but it has ten notes, or sounds, so it is decaphonic. Those who claim that g# sounds the same as a♭ should listen to pairs of chords such as the one shown in Example 17-2 below. Do these two triads have their third in common?

Ex. 17-2

No, they do not. Nor can we do a harmonic analysis of them using symbols from any single key. Also, if we think of these chords as I in E+, and i in f-, respectively, then we realize that these two tonalities have no chords in common with each other; they represent two different worlds. The only way in which we can expect the set I/i/vi to be usable is if we make I the centre of attention, and regard i and vi as two close relatives of I, but from opposite sides of the family. This means that these two rarely speak to each other, they should never be left alone in the same "room" for long without I being far away, and, even when being in the same "room," they should maintain a linear (not triangular) relationship, as illustrated in Example 6-3 below.

Ex. 17-3

vi ← I → i

The set of triads and seventh chords in the bi-modality I/i/vi consists of all the chords listed in Chapter Four of Part One, plus all the ones shown in Example 17-4 on the next page.

Ex. 17-4

If we recall what was said about "secret tunnels" in Chapter Eight of Part One, we can see that in the present case there are two chords that can take us through the "secret tunnel" that connects 12 o'clock to 9 o'clock, and, therefore, a-minor to c-minor. These are the first triad and the first seventh chord, re-written as shown in Example 17-5 below.

Ex. 17-5

To complete our study of the set I/i/vi, we designate a standard key signature for this bi-tonal bi-modality. This is also simple; we just use the key signature for I/i, as previously, followed by a bar line, followed by the key signature for vi, plus its leading note indicated in brackets, as shown in Example 17-6 below for C/c/a and A/a/f#.

Ex. 17-6 Key signatures for C/c/a and A/a/f#

C/c/a   A/a/f#

The task of combining a given minor key with its relative major and tonic major keys becomes considerably more complicated than the one which we have just completed, because with it come several surprises. We already have our basic, nonatonic set I/i. However, had we used the natural minor, or the melodic minor, form of i, that basic set would have been decatonic, as shown in Example 17-7 on the next page.

Ex. 17-7 C/c Deca scale

Had we done that, we would have done exactly the same thing which we presently need to do in order to combine i with I and ♭III. So, at this point, we do exactly that, and henceforth call this set I/i Deca. The big difference, though, is that while our original, nonatonic, set I/i was uni-tonal, I/i Deca is not. It contains not just ♭III (the relative major key of i), but two other subsets as well: IV and ♭VII (in the key of C/c, F+ and B♭+). We got much more than we bargained for; our tonic minor key ended up alone in the company of four major keys, and, therefore, four tonal centres.

How did this happen, considering that we added only one tone? It happened because in our original set C/c, the notes e♭ and a♭ were without their leader, "The Commander-in-Chief of the Flat-Key Army, Major General b-flat!" But as soon as he showed up, he brought with him not just the key of E♭+, but F+, and B♭+ as well. (We can recall here the "in between rule" for major keys, which states that it is impossible to add two major keys without adding the one(s) that lay(s) between them on the quintcircle).

Some readers might be skeptical or suspicious that this is an exception, and that it happened in this particular bi-modality only because the first three flats are involved. Be assured that no transposition will change this situation one bit.

For example, let us take a look at A/a Nonaphonic as compared to A/a Deca. A/a Nonaphonic consists of the notes a, b, c, c#, d, e, f, f#, g#, and A/a Deca has all these notes plus g-natural. A/a Nona has no subsets, but A/a Deca has three: C+, D+, and G+. It's always that way.

What can we do about it? If "it" means "the existence of the subsets," then the answer is: "Not a thing." However, if we want to write a composition in C+, c-, and E♭+ only, then we can do exactly that, and refrain from using F+ or B♭+. In this instance, the same things apply that were said above with regard to vi/I/i, and illustrated in Example 17-3. Of course, here, i takes centre stage.

The basic set I/i Deca is a most fascinating set, indeed. There are at least three ways to derive it. The first of these is melodic. As Example 17-7 above shows, it can be regarded as the union of the C+ and c natural minor scales, or the union of the C+ and c melodic minor scales, or the union of the C+ and E♭+ scales. In addition, the I/i Deca scale can be seen as consisting of two overlapping hexachords, with the dominant being in common. (We call them hexachords, because there are six tones in each one, even though there are only five and four letter names, respectively). This is seen in Example 17-8 below, in which the first half of the scale consists of the first five notes of the major and minor scales, while the second half moves by semitones only.

Ex. 17-8

We can also observe here the seeds of three bi-modalities: I/i, IV/iv, and V/v. And here again, one thing has led to another. We began our expansions by using both the major and minor sixths in our octatonic minor scale. Next, we used both major and minor thirds to form our basic nonatonic I/i set. Now, we are using both major and minor sevenths to form the fundamental I/i Deca system.

It is interesting to see what happens when we extract every second note of the C/c Deca scale shown in Example 17-7. Tones 1, 3, 5, 7, and 9 equate to the black-key pentatonic scale beginning with a#, as shown in Example 17-9 below.

Ex. 17-9

Tones 2, 4, 6, 8, and 10 equate to the black-key pentatonic scale beginning with c#, as shown in Example 17-10 below.

Ex. 17-10

So actually, the I/i Deca scale consists of two (black-key) pentatonic scales, with different starting points, interwoven with each other.

Whether we regard the I/i Deca scale as consisting of two overlapping hexachords or two interwoven pentatonic scales, we have a pleasantly sing-able scale, and melodic fragments thereof, at our disposal.

In Chapter Two of Part One, we examined many scales in considerable detail. At this point, we can compare our new Deca scale to those. We know that the greatest feature of the Major scale is that, to a child, or to the untrained ear, the steps up or down the "ladder" seem equal. Well, the same can be said for the I/i Deca scale. It helps to present it in 2/4, 3/4, 4/4, and 5/4 meters, as shown in Example 17-11 on the next page. When we do this, we discover 3-, 4-, and 5-note melodic cells, which have great potential for expansion and development.

Ex. 17-11

The second possible derivation of the I/i Deca set is harmonic. It is fascinating to observe that if we take the union of the six triads I, IV, V, i, iv, and v, then subtract the intersection (the duplicates, shown in quarter notes), we end up with the very same ten tones, as shown in Example 17-12 below (c.f. Ex. 3-9 of Part One).

Ex. 17-12 Harmonic derivation of the I/i Deca set

These two approaches together provide a convincing argument that the Deca scale, as we have constructed and defined it — that is, **by addition** — is based on two solid foundations: melodic and harmonic. These are practical approaches, and it is good to see that they worked. But in order to appreciate fully how extraordinary the I/i Deca set is, we must refer back to Chapter Thirteen.

Chapter Thirteen was written primarily to serve as a preface to this one. Example 13-4 was drawn up to illustrate that the two tones which are the most distantly related to the tonic are the augmented fourth (or tritone) and the minor second (or augmented unison). And these are precisely the same two tones that are not included in our fundamental Deca set, I/i. *So, from the acoustical standpoint, there is no better scale than this one.*

It should also be noted that the first eight notes, or the first nine notes, of Example 13-4 (counting c only once) do not comprise ideal octatonic or nonatonic sets, because the leading note is not among them. We must use at least 10 tones before we can have our leading note included and the least closely related tones excluded.

It is important to realize that this acoustical derivation of our I/i Deca scale is our first instance of **derivation by subtraction**. When the cardinality of a set is 10 or higher, it becomes increasingly important which tone(s) or note(s) are excluded. And this leads us directly into the topic of key signatures for Deca keys.

If we regard I/i Deca as I/i/♭III, and ignore the subsets IV and ♭VII, then we can use the key signature of I/i, followed by a bar line, followed by the key signature for ♭III, as shown in Example 17-13 below, in which I/i is C/c.

Ex. 17-13 Key signature for C/c/E♭ Deca

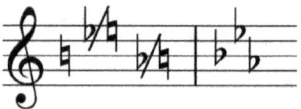

Because this is the special case of a tonic minor key joined by its tonic major and relative major, and because we may deliberately wish to avoid using the subsets IV and ♭VII, we can get away with doing this. However, if we wished to use this format to indicate every key that is included in the set, then our key signature would have to look as shown in Example 17-14 below.

Ex. 17-14 Hypothetical key signature for C/c/F/B♭/E♭

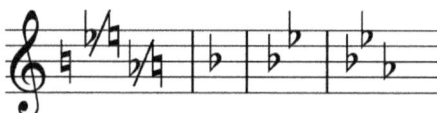

Now this is starting to look downright ridiculous, and, what is worse, terribly confusing. Not only that, what would we do in cases of subsequent sets, which will contain even more subsets? Our key signatures would end up being several "measures," and at least half a line, in length.

There must be a better way — and there is. We indicate the Deca form of I/i by showing the two sevenths (major and minor) as well as the two thirds and sixths. Then we indicate the two excluded tones, which, in the case of C/c Deca, are f# and c#, and their enharmonics, as shown in Example 17-15 below.

Ex. 17-15 Key signature for C/c Deca, showing excluded tones

The slashed circle is the universal symbol for "No," referring to whatever is in the circle. There is no need to duplicate and write another symbol designating "no d-flat and no g-flat," because "Deca" means that two tones of the twelve are to be excluded, which automatically means that these tones cannot appear as enharmonics, either.

The key signatures for all 12 Deca keys of the form I/i are shown in Example 17-16 below. On the pages following, in Example 17-17, all 12 corresponding Deca scales are written out, together with two enharmonics, G♭/g♭ Deca and D♭/d♭ Deca. (Note: The reason that these two scales end up with such unwieldy spelling is that the Deca scale includes the tonic minor scale).

Ex. 17-16 Key signatures for all 12 Deca bi-modalities, showing excluded tones

NOTE: Because extensive use of accidentals within the score is inevitable, it would be appropriate to start a new trend, and state the key signature only once, at the beginning of a composition.

Ex. 17-17 Scales of 14 Deca Bi-modalities — p. 1 of 2

138 • *Dodecaphonic Tonality*

Before we continue on, we can make an observation regarding comparison of Deca key signatures to traditional ones. Deca key signatures designate two excluded tones. But traditional key signatures also indicate excluded tones — in a way. The two key signatures that can best be used for comparison are two sharps and two flats. "F-sharp and c-sharp" also means "no f-natural and no c-natural." And this is the key signature for B/b Deca, just as it is for b-minor. "B-flat and e-flat" also means "no b-natural and no e-natural." And this is the key signature for B♭/b♭ Deca, just as it is for B-flat major.

* * *

Our next task is to examine the triads and seventh chords of I/i Deca, and to analyze them. This section should be read in conjunction with Chapter Four (of Part One). We begin, as we did there, by building diatonic triads on each scale degree, as shown in Example 17-18 below.

Ex. 17-18 Triads contained in C/c Deca

i   I   ii°   ii   ♭III   ♭III⁺   iii°   iii   iv

IV   v   V   ♭VI   ♭VI⁺   vi°   vi   ♭VII   vii°

There are four new triads that are not included in Example 4-1 (of Part One). They are the ones which contain the note b-flat.

Next, we build seventh chords on each scale degree, as shown in Example 17-19 on the next page.

Ex. 17-19 Seventh chords contained in C/c Deca

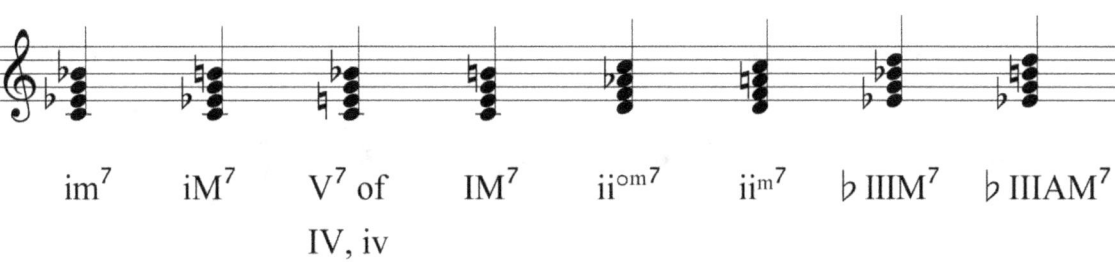

im⁷   iM⁷   V⁷ of   IM⁷   ii°ᵐ⁷   iiᵐ⁷   ♭IIIM⁷   ♭IIIAM⁷
                  IV, iv

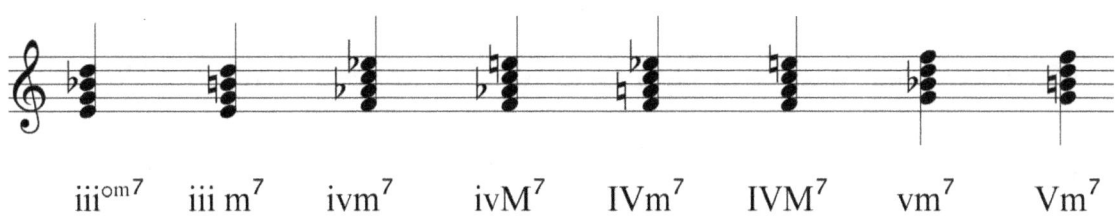

iii°ᵐ⁷   iii m⁷   ivm⁷   ivM⁷   IVm⁷   IVM⁷   vm⁷   Vm⁷

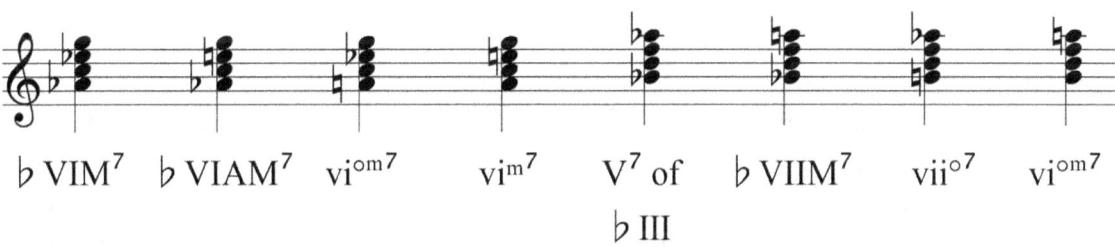

♭VIM⁷   ♭VIAM⁷   vi°ᵐ⁷   viᵐ⁷   V⁷ of   ♭VIIM⁷   vii°⁷   vi°ᵐ⁷
                                      ♭III

There are seven new chords that are not included in Example 4-2 (of Part One). Again, they are the ones which contain the note b-flat. So in the I/i Deca system, the composer has 42 different triads and seventh chords (excluding duplicates) from which to choose. The eleven new chords are shown in Example 17-20 on the next page.

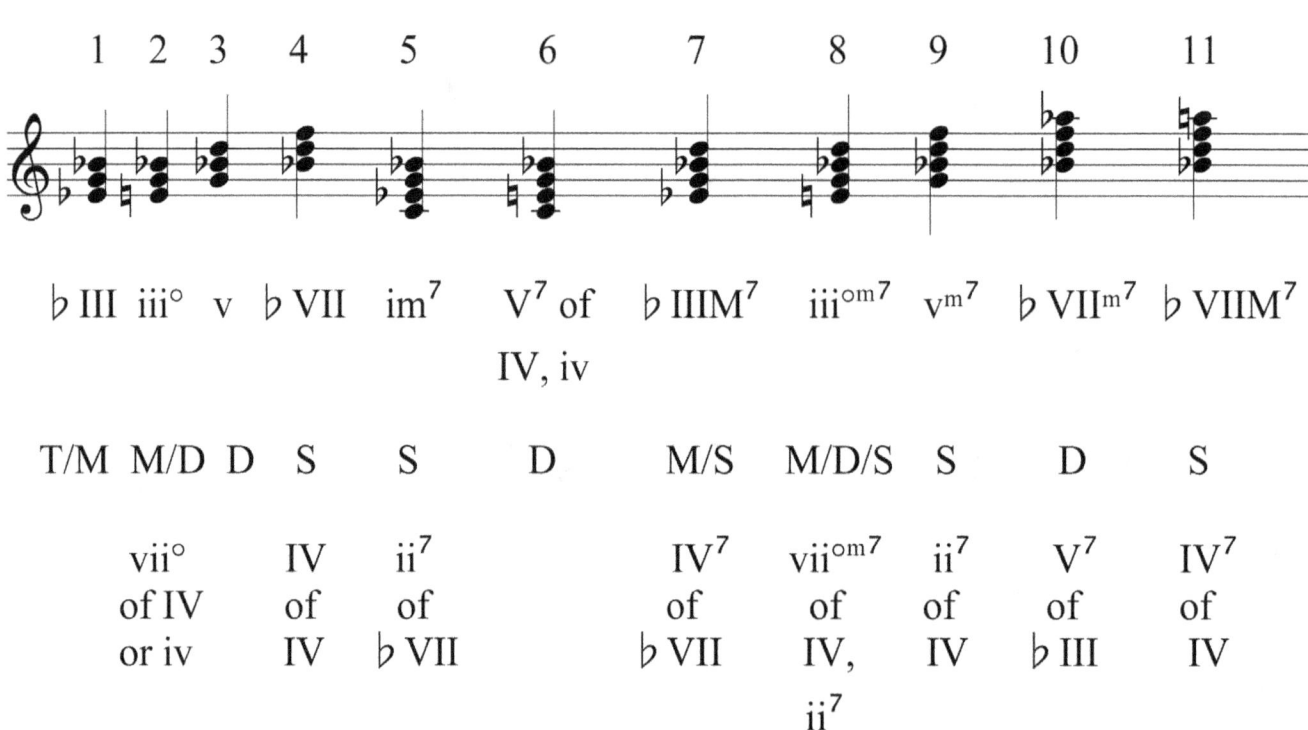

Ex. 17-20 Eleven chords of C/c Deca containing the note b-flat

When we sort these by functions, we find the following: The first chord has a **Tonic** function as the relative major of i. Five chords have **Dominant** functions: The second chord is vii° of IV or iv; the third chord is a minor dominant of i; the sixth chord is V^7 of IV or iv; the eighth chord is vii$^{\text{o}m7}$ of IV, and the tenth chord is V^7 of ♭III (the relative major of i). The remaining five chords (4, 5, 7, 9, 11), and the eighth chord, have **Subdominant** functions: The fourth chord is IV of IV; the fifth chord is ii^7 of ♭VII; the seventh chord is IV^7 of ♭VII; the eighth chord is ii^7 of ii; the ninth chord is ii^7 of IV, and the last chord is IV^7 of IV.

In addition, four of these eleven chords have a **Mediant** function: The first chord is ♭III; the second chord is iii°; the seventh chord is ♭IIIM^7, and the eighth chord is iii$^{\text{o}m7}$. There are no new chords in the Submediant group, because adding the note b-flat did not affect any **Submediant** chords. But now, the chords in the Mediant and Submediant groups match one for one.

We can now draw up our model of Decaphonic Bi-Modality by adding these eleven chords to the House of Nonaphonic Bi-Modality, presented in Example 6-2 (of Part One). This model appears in Example 17-21 on the next page. The total number of chords, including duplicates, is 59, distributed as follows: Tonic: 5, Dominant: 18, Subdominant: 22, Mediant: 7, Submediant: 7. Twenty-two chords have one function only, eleven have two possible functions, and five have three possible functions (ref. Example 17-22). As was the case in Part One, it is not a goal here to list every chord possible under the sun. The goal is to compare triads and seventh chords found in traditional functional tonality to those found in Nonaphonic Bi-Modality, and presently to those found in Decaphonic Bi-Modality.

Ex. 17-21

DECAPHONIC BI-MODALITY

SUBDOMINANT GROUP	SUBMEDIANT GROUP	TONIC GROUP	MEDIANT GROUP	DOMINANT GROUP
ii°, ii,	♭VI, ♭VI⁺,	i,	♭III⁺,	vii° of ♭III,
iv, IV,	vi°, vi,	I,	iii,	♭III = $V^{13}_{13\ 7}$
♭VI,	♭VIM⁷,	♭VI,	iii^{m7}	iii = $V^{6}_{6\ 8}$
			4 new in Ex. 17-21:	
ii° of v,	vi°^{m7},	vi		V, vii°, V⁷,
IV⁷ of V,	vi^{m7}		♭III,	$V^{13}_{13\ 7}$ of iv,
ii°^{m7}, ii^{m7},		**1 new in Ex. 17-21:**	iii°,	
ii⁷ of II,			♭IIIM⁷	vii° of ♭VII,
iv^{m7},		♭III	iii°^{m7}	V⁷ of ♭VII,
ii^{m7} of ♭III,				vii°^{m7} of ♭VII,
IV⁷,				vii⁷ of ♭VII,
IV⁷ of ♭III,				vii°⁷,
ii°^{m7} of v,				vii°^{m7}
ii⁷ of V				
6 new in Ex. 17-21:				**5 new in Ex. 17-21:**
IV of IV,				vii° of IV,
ii⁷ of ♭VII,				v,
IV⁷ of ♭VII,				V⁷ of IV,
ii⁷ of ii,				vii⁷ of IV,
ii⁷ of IV,				V⁷ of ♭III
IV⁷ of IV				
22	7	5	7	18

Here, now, is a brief summary of this comparison. If we look back at the House of Functional Tonality shown in Example 5-9 (of Part One), we see that the total number of chords was 35: 4 Tonic, 15 Dominant, and 16 Subdominant. This was for the system which we now call I/vi. There were only three pillars, but the house had two floors (one for each tonal centre).

The House of Nonaphonic Bi-Modality was illustrated in Example 6-2 (of Part One). We began with 31 triads and seventh chords, as shown in Example 6-1 (of Part One). Four of these chords were declared to be non-functional, leaving us with 27 chords. Of these, 15 were found to have one function only, eight were found to have two possible functions, and four had three possible functions. So we ended up with a final total of 43 chords: (15 x 1) + (8 x 2) + (4 x 3) = 15 + 16 + 12 = 43. These were distributed as follows: Tonic: 4, Dominant: 13, Subdominant: 16, Mediant: 3, Submediant: 7.

Presently, in the House of Decaphonic Bi-Modality, shown in Example 17-21, we have 59 chords. The first 43 are exactly the same ones that were listed in Example 6-2 (of Part One). In this chapter, we added eleven chords, but three of them have two possible functions, and one chord has three, so the number of chords added to the house was: (7 x 1) + (3 x 2) + (1 x 3) = 7 + 6 + 3 = 16. The 59 chords in the House of Decaphonic Bi-Modality are distributed as follows: Tonic: 5, Dominant: 18, Subdominant: 22, Mediant: 7, Submediant: 7.

To help us keep track of chords having more than one function, Example 17-22 below shows all the chords that have been identified so far as having two or three functions. Readers can perhaps find more.

> **Ex. 17-22 Bi-functional and tri-functional chords**
>
> **Bi-functional chords from Ex. 6-1 (from Part One):**
> ii°, ♭III+, iii, ♭VI+, vi, iii^{m7}, iv^{m7}, ♭VIM^7
>
> **Tri-functional chords from Ex. 6-1 (of Part One):**
> ♭VI, vi°, vi$^{°m7}$, vi^{m7}
>
> **Bi-functional chords from Ex. 17-20 above:**
> ♭III, iii°, ♭IIIM^7
>
> **Tri-functional chord from Ex. 17-20 above:**
> iii$^{°m7}$

* * *

Our last task in this chapter is to construct the Decaphonic Quintcircle and to make some observations about it. This quintcircle is shown in Example 17-23 on the next page.

Once again, we use 12 o'clock, which is now C/c Deca, as the starting point, and take a look around. It can readily be seen that adjacent Deca keys have one of their two excluded tones in common. So C/c Deca and G/g Deca both have c# excluded, and f# is excluded from both C/c Deca and F/f Deca. This means that the keys of three adjacent stations form the family of most closely related keys — just as they do in the traditional quintcircle. It also means that semi-modulations from C/c to C/g, and to C/f, and to G/c, and to F/c will be simple semi-modulations.

If we compare C/c Deca to any other Deca key, then we see that, in each case, both excluded tones are different. So now, the question arises whether or not the two excluded tones are somehow more remote the farther away we get from 12 o'clock. In the cases of 5 o'clock, 6 o'clock, and 7 o'clock, they are. B/b Deca and F#/f# Deca both exclude c-natural, which is the tonic of C/c Deca. C/c Deca excludes f# and c#, which are the tonic notes of F#/f# Deca and C#/c# Deca respectively.

Ex. 17-23 Decaphonic Quintcircle with 6 "secret tunnels"

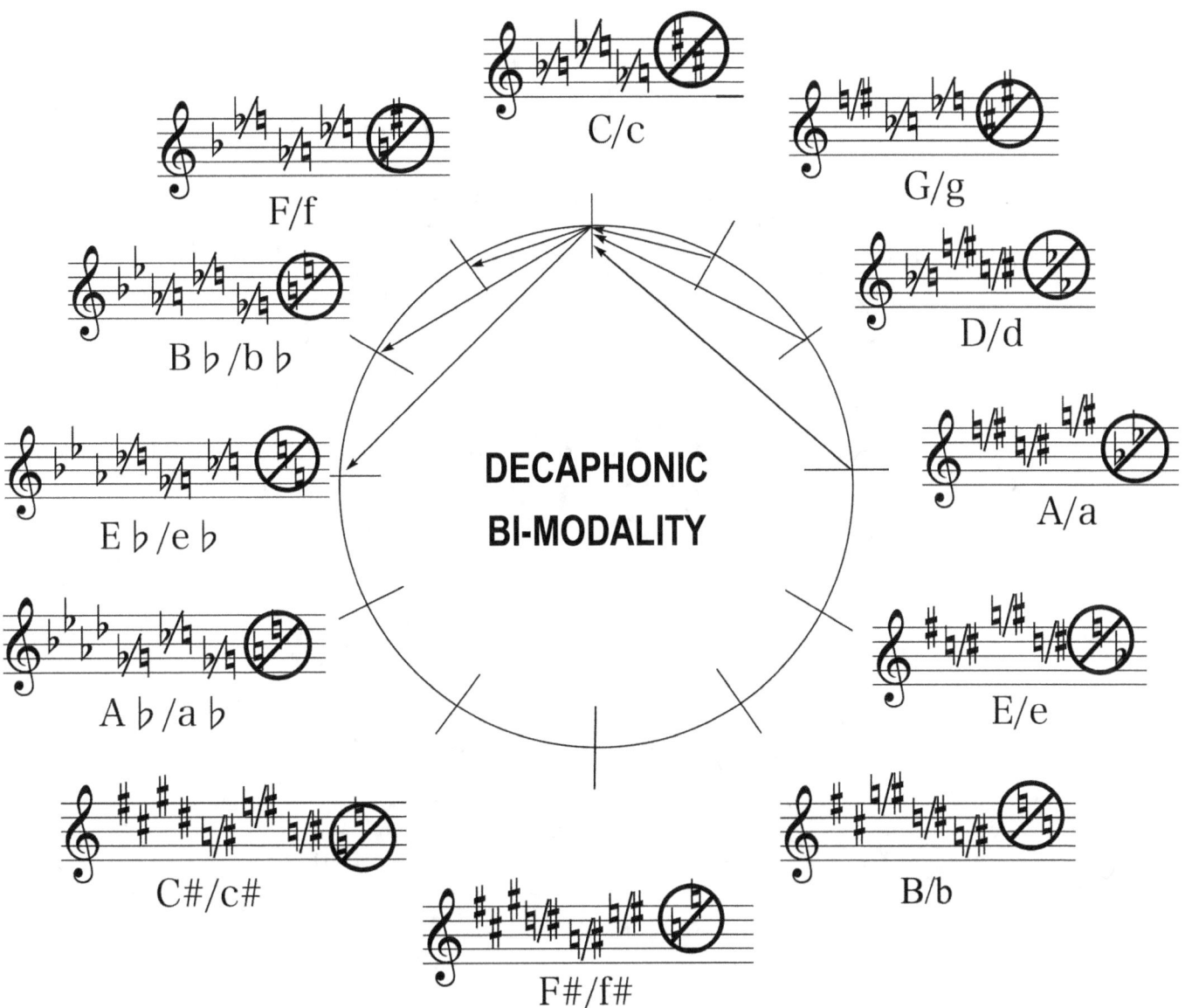

When it comes to relating C/c Deca to the other Deca bi-modalities, however, things are not so simple. For within the Decaphonic Quintcircle, the network of "secret tunnels" is peculiar, indeed. First of all, the tunnels are not so secret, because we already know that C/c Deca contains F+ and B♭+ and E♭+ as subsets. So the tunnels naturally lead to the nearest three stations in the counter-clockwise direction. Secondly, the tunnels do not truly connect C/c Deca to f- or b♭- or e♭-. And thirdly, these tunnels are one-way routes. If we begin at 9 o'clock, we cannot claim that any key at 10 o'clock, or 11 o'clock, or 12 o'clock is a subset of E♭/e♭ Deca, because this bi-modality excludes the leading notes of those six keys. (B-natural is not in E♭/e♭ Deca either; c-flat is).

To make up for this lopsidedness, we can claim that C/c Deca is *inversely related* to A/a Deca, D/d Deca and G/g Deca, because harmonic traffic flows **towards** it through the tunnels leading **from** these three bi-modalities. In order to see how this is so, it is necessary to illustrate the full network of 36 "secret tunnels." This is done in Example 17-24 below.

Ex. 17-24

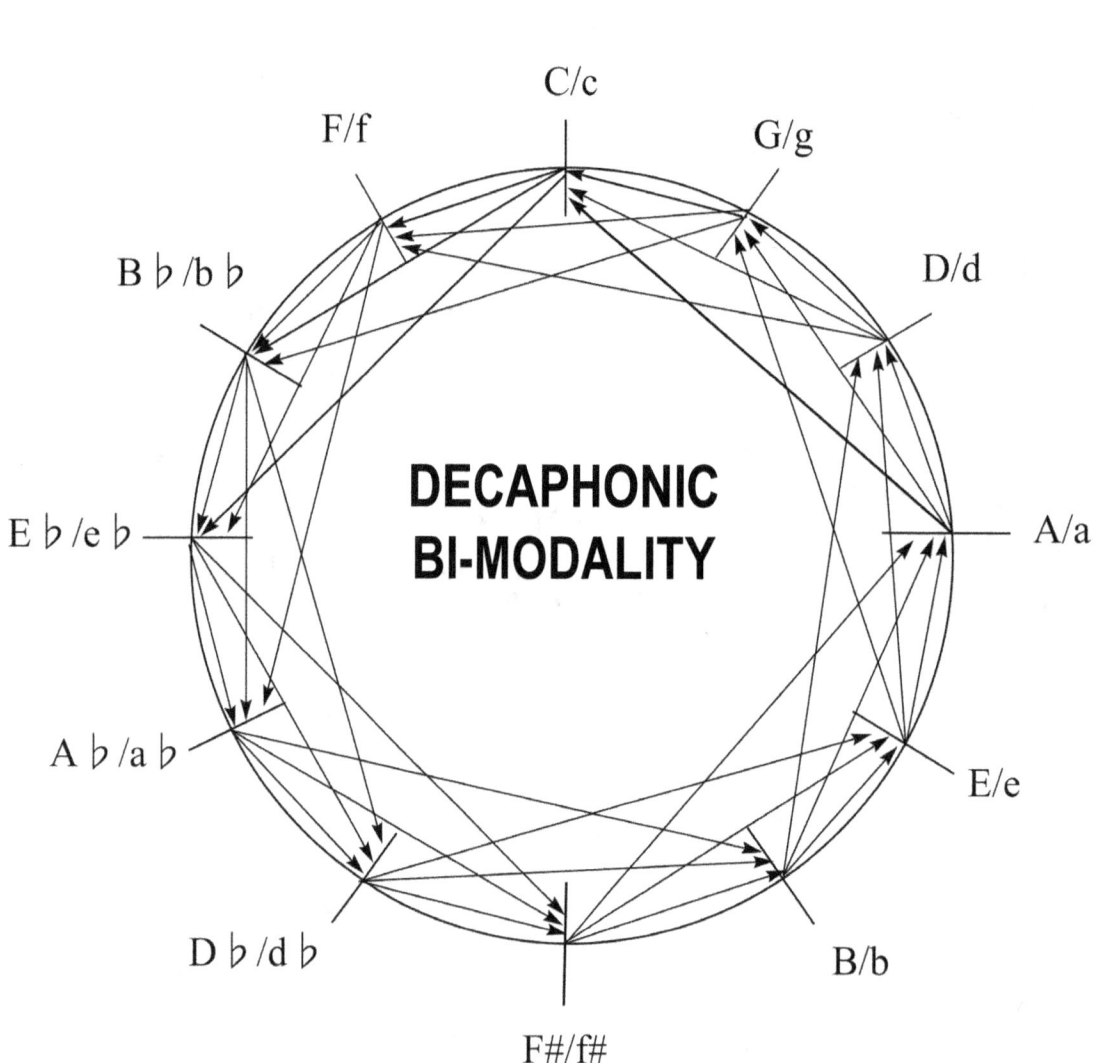

The "Revenge" of the Subdominant

In light of what we have just seen, let us end this chapter by taking a look at the role of the subdominant key in the history of music theory, specifically, in the classical period. We know that in Sonata Allegro form, it was not the subdominant, but the dominant key that played a prominent role. In sonatas written in minor keys, the second theme was usually in the relative major key, so again the subdominant was ignored. The second (slow) movement was often in the subdominant key, but that, of course, was a completely different method of employing the subdominant.

In cadences, even though the plagal cadence existed at least since the Baroque period (and probably earlier, even if it was not called that), it was V - I who was the Prince of Cadences. In fact, when one considers the age-old

IV - V - I progression, one could argue that the subdominant actually steers the harmony *away* from the tonic, because it moves to the dominant. So when IV moves to V, the musical journey is still in progress, not quite ready to come home just yet.

We also know that the Prince of Cadences was often accompanied by his Princess, V of V, and when that happened, she replaced IV, so again the subdominant was absent from the picture. In the case if ii - V - I, the subdominant appeared, but it did so disguised as either the supertonic triad or as ii^7. On the other hand, in the case of the plagal cadence, one thing that did not happen, (although it could have), was extensive, or even frequent, use of the final progression IV of IV - IV - I.

Interestingly enough, if we analyze many melodies written over the centuries, we find that the climax often occurs on (or in) the subdominant. But here again, this is yet another different method of employing IV.

In summary, we must admit that over the centuries, the subdominant has been short-changed. It has always had to fight its way into the musical landscape, and in order to do so, it even went to the extreme measure of disguising itself as the Neapolitan Sixth. What a struggle! Miss Subdominant was always there, but she always had to push her way in.*

As we have seen, our system has had a different evolution. By adding tones successively (to the basic seven) in the order that we did, and for the reasons that we did, what came out in the wash was the ever-increasing appearance of IV, IV of IV, and ♭III (= IV of IV of IV). This happened because we paid attention to acoustics, specifically, to the relative proximity of the remaining eleven tones to the fundamental. And with c as the fundamental, e-flat, a-flat, b-flat, and d-flat appeared (in that order) before f#, and c# never did appear in the hierarchy.

That is why our system can be dubbed The "Revenge" of the Subdominant.

We next move on to Decaphonic Bi-modalities of the form X/y and their counterparts of the form Z/x.

---

* Something similar to the other woman in some marriages...

CHAPTER EIGHTEEN

Other Decaphonic Bi-Modalities

In our study of Nonaphonic Bi-Modalities (Part One), after we drew up the Quintcircle and examined related keys, we moved on to the topic of Rotating Quintcircles and Semi-Modulation, which was the title of Chapter Fourteen. This time around, we will do some of that also, but it is more important to address first another issue which comes up at this point.

Suppose that we were to perform semi-modulations and end up in keys such as I/ii, I/iii, I/iv, I/v, etc. …, and their counterparts of the form X/i, such as ♭VII/i, ♭VI/i, V/i, IV/i, etc. … What would be the cardinalities of the resulting sets? We know that they would not be all the same, because we already saw that in Example 3-2 of Part One. In that instance, we used the octatonic minor, and we focused on nonatonic sets. Presently, we will do something similar, but use the harmonic minor instead. The goal here is to determine the minimum number of tones required to form each of the 22 possible resulting bi-modalities. The results are given in Example 18-1 below.

Ex. 18-1 Cardinalities of I/x and X/i Sets

C+ (= c, d, e, f, g, a, b) plus:	Total no. of tones
1) d- = ii: + b♭ + c# =	9
2) e- = iii: + f# + d# =	9
3) f- = iv: + b♭ + a♭ + d♭ =	10
4) g- = v: + b♭ + e♭ + f# =	10
5) a- = vi: + g# =	8
6) b- = vii: + f# + c# + a# =	10
7) c#- = #i: + f# + c# + g# + d# + b# =	11 + 1 En
8) e♭- = ♭iii: + b♭ + e♭ + a♭ + g♭ + c♭ =	11 + 1 En
9) f#- = #iv: + f# + c# + g# + e# =	10 + 1 En
10) a♭- = ♭vi: + b♭ + e♭ + a♭ + d♭ + c♭ + f♭ =	11 + 2 En
11) b♭- = ♭vii: b♭ + e♭ + d♭ + g♭ =	11

Ex. 18-1 Cardinalities of I/x and X/i Sets CONT'D.

Counterparts: c- (= c, d, e♭, f, g, a♭, b) plus:	Total no. of tones
12) B♭+ = ♭VII: + b♭ + e♭ =	9
13) A♭+ = ♭VI: + b♭ + d♭ =	9
14) G+ = V: + a + e + f♯ =	10
15) F+ = IV: + a + e + b♭ =	10
16) E♭+ = ♭III: + b♭ =	8
17) D♭+ = ♭II: + b♭ + d♭ + g♭ =	10
18) B+ = VII: + f♯ + c♯ + g♯ + d♯ + a♯ =	10 + 2 En
19) A+ = VI: + a + e + f♯ + c♯ + g♯ =	11 + 1 En
20) G♭+ = ♭V: + b♭ + d♭ + g♭ + c♭ =	10 + 1 En
21) E+ = III: + e + a + f♯ + c♯ + g♯ + d♯ =	11 + 2 En
22) D+ = II: + e + a + f♯ + c♯ =	11

This example provides us with an accurate overall picture of where we have already been, where we are now, and where we should go later. We have already studied sets 1, 2, 5, and their counterparts, sets 12, 13, and 16. It is clear that in this chapter, the next Deca bi-modalities that we should examine are I/iv, I/v, and I/vii, and their counterparts V/i, IV/i, and ♭II/i (= sets 3, 4, 6, 14, 15, 17). We can also consider I/♯iv and its counterpart, ♭V/i (= sets 9, 20). After this chapter, we can look at the eight remaining sets: 7, 8, 10, 11, and their counterparts 18, 19, 21, and 22.

Sets 3, 4, 6, and 9, followed by their counterparts, sets 14, 15, 17, and 20, are written out in Example 18-2 on the next page. The two excluded tones are indicated for each bi-modality, using the symbol for "No."

148 • *Dodecaphonic Tonality*

Ex. 18-2 Other Decaphonic Bi-Modalities: Comparison

𝅗𝅥 = common tones,   𝅘𝅥 = non-common tones,   ♫ = enharmonics

Set
3 C/f Deca
4 C/g Deca
6 C/b Deca
9 C/f# Deca

14 G/c Deca
15 F/c Deca
17 D♭/c Deca
20 G♭/c Deca

At first sight, all of this looks like quite a mess, and almost impossible to decipher, because … it is! Looking at the pairs of excluded tones helps a bit, because we can see that in sets 3 and 14, they are a minor third apart, and in all the remaining sets they are a perfect fifth apart (as they are in C/c Deca). Also, if we refer back to Example 14-9, we know that we have encountered sets 3 and 4 before. At that point, we noted that if we add the note c# to C/f Deca, the result is the combination F/f/C/d (or I/i/V/vi, if we let F= I). Furthermore, we said that if we add d# to C/g Deca, the result is G/g/e/B♭ (or I/i/vi/♭III, if we let G = I), with C+ and F+ (IV and ♭VII) as leftover subsets. These are both beautiful bi-modalities, but they are 11-note sets! In fact, set 4 is the same as sets 9 and 20, which are: A/a/f#/C (with D+ and G+ left over), and E♭/e♭/c/G♭ (with A♭+ and D♭+ left over), respectively. Do any readers recognize what this "mega-set" is? It is the union of the two sets presented in Chapter Seventeen: I/i/vi plus I/i/♭III. We will deal with all of these in the next chapter on 11-note systems.

For now, we should take a closer look at our three bi-tonal 10-note sets, I/iv, I/v, and I/vii. The first of these is the best one, from the practical standpoint, because it contains only one subset, IV. So it is a tightly knit, closed set of the form I/IV/iv. We can certainly combine the tonic key with its major and minor subdominant keys. However, if we let IV/iv take over as I/i, then I becomes V, and instead of I/IV/iv (C/F/f) we have I/i/V (F/f/C), which is much better, because we end up with our fundamental Deca set plus its Dominant key. (The bi-modality takes priority).

Incidentally, did any reader notice that C/g Deca is an exact transposition of C/c Deca moved up a perfect fifth, and that F/c Deca contains the exact same notes as C/c Deca, but beginning on f? Each of these two sets is like a reversible coat: If you wear it inside out, you have the same coat, but with an added feature.

The next set, I/v, has subsets IV, V, and ♭VII. The set of keys is C+, g-, F+, G+, and B♭+. This makes for a very lopsided bi-modality, but we already know that we will fix this by letting G/g = I/i, and then creating our "mega-set."

Finally, the set I/vii has subsets II and V, so the set of keys consists of C+, b-, D+, and G+. In this case again, we can add the note b-flat, and thus the keys F+ and d-. Then we let D/d = I/i, and end up with the "mega-set."

There are many other possible decaphonic sets. The only way that we can be certain that we find all the ones definable in terms of major and minor keys is if we examine all the possible cases. So, once again, we use the same method that we used in Chapter Sixteen: We fix the seven white-key notes of C-major and add to them every possible three-note combination of the five black-key notes that remain, as per Example 16-3.

If we consider tones only, then there are only 10 possible triples to add. They are: (1,2,3), (1,2,4), (1,2,5), (1,3,4), (1,3,5), (1,4,5), (2,3,4), (2,3,5), (2,4,5), and (3,4,5). However, since each tone has two names, each of these triples can be written in 2x2x2 = 8 different ways. So this time we have 80 cases in all to consider, as shown in Example 18-3 on the next page.

It should be noted that this list contains every possible 10-note set, but only if each triple is comprised of three different numbers. We know that there is a special case in which we add e♭, g#, and a♭ to the C+ scale to get the set I/i/vi. This, however, is an exception, in which we add the triple (2,4,4), so this case is not on the list.

Ex. 18-3 Eighty cases of triples of black-key notes added to C+

C+ (= c, d, e, f, g, a, b) plus:

		Category				Category
1)	c#, d#, f#	(2)		25)	c#, f#, g#	(1)
2)	c#, eb, f#	(2)		26)	c#, gb, g#	(5)
3)	c#, eb, gb	(4)		27)	c#, gb, ab	(4)
4)	c#, d#, gb	(4)		28)	c#, f#, ab	(3)
5)	db, d#, f#	(5)		29)	db, f#, g#	(3)
6)	db, eb, f#	(3)		30)	db, gb, g#	(5)
7)	db, eb, gb	(4)		31)	db, gb, ab	(4)
8)	db, d#, gb	(5)		32)	db, f#, ab	(3)
9)	c#, d#, g#	(3)		33)	c#, f#, a#	(1)
10)	c#, eb, g#	(3)		34)	c#, gb, a#	(4)
11)	c#, eb, ab	(3)		35)	c#, gb, bb	(3)
12)	c#, d#, ab	(3)		36)	c#, f#, bb	(1)
13)	db, d#, g#	(5)		37)	db, f#, a#	(4)
14)	db, eb, g#	(3)		38)	db, gb, a#	(4)
15)	db, eb, ab	(3)		39)	db, gb, bb	(4)
16)	db, d#, ab	(5)		40)	db, f#, bb	(3)
17)	c#, d#, a#	(4)		41)	c#, g#, a#	(3)
18)	c#, eb, a#	(4)		42)	c#, ab, a#	(5)
19)	c#, eb, bb	(2)		43)	c#, ab, bb	(3)
20)	c#, d#, bb	(2)		44)	c#, g#, bb	(1)
21)	db, d#, a#	(5)		45)	db, g#, a#	(3)
22)	db, eb, a#	(4)		46)	db, ab, a#	(5)
23)	db, eb, bb	(2)		47)	db, ab, bb	(1)
24)	db, d#, bb	(5)		48)	db, g#, bb	(3)

Ex. 18-3 Cont'd

C+ (= c, d, e, f, g, a, b) plus:

		Category				Category
49)	d#, f#, g#	(1)		65)	d#, g#, a#	(3)
50)	d#, g♭, g#	(5)		66)	d#, a♭, a#	(5)
51)	d#, g♭, a♭	(4)		67)	d#, a♭, b♭	(3)
52)	d#, f#, ♭	(3)		68)	d#, g#, b♭	(3)
53)	e♭, f#, g#	(3)		69)	e♭, g#, a#	(4)
54)	e♭, g♭, g#	(5)		70)	e♭, a♭, a#	(5)
55)	e♭, g♭, a♭	(3)		71)	e♭, a♭, b♭	(1)
56)	e♭, f#, a♭	(1)		72)	e♭, g#, b♭	(2)
57)	d#, f#, a#	(3)		73)	f#, g#, a#	(3)
58)	d#, g♭, a#	(4)		74)	f#, a♭, a#	(5)
59)	d#, g♭, b♭	(4)		75)	f#, a♭, b♭	(2)
60)	d#, f#, b♭	(2)		76)	f#, g#, b♭	(3)
61)	e♭, f#, a#	(4)		77)	g♭, g#, a#	(5)
62)	e♭, g♭, a#	(4)		78)	g♭, a♭, a#	(5)
63)	e♭, g♭, b♭	(4)		79)	g♭, a♭, b♭	(4)
64)	e♭, f#, b♭	(1)		80)	g♭, g#, b♭	(5)

In order to save his readers a lot of time, the author examined these for several days, and divided them into five categories, as marked in the example. Let us go through them together now, beginning with the worst first, and ending with the best.

Category (5) consists of 18 sets, each of which contains the combination x-flat and x-sharp (for example d-flat and d-sharp). These 18 sets are numbers 5, 8, 13, 16, 21, 24, 26, 30, 42, 46, 50, 54, 66, 70, 74, 77, 78, and 80. Except for one special case, which we will encounter in Chapter Twenty, none of these sets are usable.

Category (4) consists of 20 sets. Ten of these contain the note a-sharp; they are numbers 17, 18, 22, 34, 37, 38, 58, 61, 62, and 69. Fourteen contain the note g-flat; they are numbers 3, 4, 7, 27, 31, 34, 38, 39, 51, 58, 59, 62, 63, and 79. (Four of these sets, 34, 38, 58, and 62 contain both a-sharp and g-flat, so the total is 10 + 14 — 4 = 20). None of these sets provide us with useable systems. In a way, this is not surprising, either, because a-sharp is the last of the black-key sharps, and g-flat is the last of the black-key flats, and we are adding all these sets to C+.

The world's worst sets surely must be numbers 77) and 78), because they have the characteristics of Category (5) and contain both a-sharp and g-flat besides. Also, there is no point using set 31) because set 25), the enharmonic equivalent, is available instead.

Category (3) consists of 25 sets, numbered as follows: 6, 9, 10, 11, 12, 14, 15, 28, 29, 32, 35, 40, 41, 43, 45, 48, 52, 53, 55, 57, 65, 67, 68, 73, and 76. None of these sets appear to show any potential for providing us with new, useable systems. They are not as hopeless as the sets of Categories (4) and (5), but they are still not good enough to be of much use to us, and here is why: Every one of these sets, except set 12), produces exactly one subset, and with that, has at least one note left over (unused). The subsets produced are: a- (eleven times), G+ (four times), c- (three times), F+ and e- (twice each), and D+ and d- (once each). As for set 12), it is rather peculiar, because it looks user-friendly, but actually has yet to prove itself.

Category (2) contains eight sets, which are the following numbers: 1, 2, 19, 20, 23, 60, 72, and 75. Some of these are already usable as they are, others are potentially usable if we tamper with them. This can be seen most clearly if we examine them both individually and in combination.

Set 1) is I/iii, using e octatonic minor, or I/iii harmonic minor without the note c#. Set 75) is I/IV/V, without the note a-flat. These two sets together form set 60), which is I/iii/IV/V, without the notes c-sharp or a-flat. Meanwhile, set 2) forms I/II/V, without the note e-flat. So the union of sets 2) and 75) = I/II/IV/V. These have subsets I, ii, v, VII, and bIII. But our goal is to achieve bi-modality and, ideally, balanced bi-modality, so we take the union of all these sets together in order to form the set I/i/II/ii/V/v, with subsets IV, bIII, bVII, and iii, which we can avoid using. More will be said about all of this in Chapter Twenty. For now, we just summarize it all in Example 18-4 below.

Ex. 18-4 Summary of Category (2) Sets

Set	Notes												Keys
1)	c	(c#)	d	d#		e	f	f#	g		a		b	I/iii
75)	c		d			e	f	f#	g	(ab)	a	bb	b	I/IV/V
60) = 1), 75)	c		d	d#		e	f	f#	g		a	bb	b	I/iii/IV/V
2)	c	c#	d		(eb)	e	f	f#	g		a		b	I/II/V
2), 75)	c	c#	d		(eb)	e	f	f#	g	(ab)	a	bb	b	I/II/IV/V
Union of 1), 75), 60), 2)	c	c#	d	d#	eb	e	f	f#	g	ab	a	bb	b	I/i/II/ii/V/v Subsets: IV, bVII, bIII, iii

Set 19) without the note eb = set 20) without the note d# = I/ii/IV, a nonatonic set. Probably the best thing that we can do with this set is to balance the bi-modality by adding the note g#, to get set 44), which equals I/vi/IV/ii, and belongs in Category (1). Another good possibility is to add the note f#, to get set 36), which also belongs in Category (1).

Set 23) without the note d-flat gives us I/IV/bVII. This is actually a subset of our original Deca set, I/i. If we substitute g# for d-flat, we get set 72), which yields I/vi/IV/bVII. Now, in order to balance this bi-modality, we need a rabbit out of a hat…

We come now to the nine sets of Category (1). These are numbers 25, 33, 36, 44, 47, 49, 56, 64, and 71, and they are the stars of this Decaphonic show. We have already seen some of these: Number 71 is our original I/i Deca set; number 47) is I/iv with subset IV; number 33) is I/vii with subsets II and V. Number 64) is I/v with subsets IV, V, and bVII. If in this set we let V/v (which is G/g) = I/i, then the subsets are bIII, IV, and bVII. This is also our original Deca set.

The remaining five sets are shown in Example 18-5 below, in the following order: Numbers 25, 36, 56, 44, and 49.

Ex. 18-5 Category (1) Sets

Set	Notes											Keys
25)	c	c#	d		e	f	f#	g	g#		a		b	I/vi/VI/V/II
36)	c	c#	d		e	f	f#	g			a	bb	b	I/II/ii/IV/V
56)	c		d	eb	e	f	f#	g		ab	a		b	I/i/V
44)	c	c#	d		e	f		g	g#		a	bb	b	I/vi/IV/ii
49)	c		d	d#	e	f	f#	g	g#		a		b	I/vi/V/iii

Set 25) consists of the keys C+, a-, A+, G+, and D+. As soon as we see X+ and x- in the group, we must make X/x = I/i and transpose the rest of the keys accordingly (because if X/x is present, then it takes priority). This gives us A/a/C with D and G as subsets, or I/i/bIII, with IV and bVII as subsets. Set 36) is comprised of the following keys: C+, D+, d-, F+, and G+. Here again, we must let D/d = I/i; then, C+ becomes bVII, F+ becomes bIII, and G+ becomes IV. The result is I/i/bIII with subsets IV and bVII. So both of these equate to our original Deca set, I/i! This may not be immediately obvious, but it can be easily verified by transposition, as follows: Set 25), beginning on a, is: a b c c# d e f f# g g#; this, transposed up a minor third, equals C/c Deca. Set 36), beginning on d, is: d e f f# g a bb b c c#, and this, transposed down a major second, also equals C/c Deca.

Set 56) consists of the keys C+, c-, and G+, and no others. It is a clear case of I/i/V with no subsets. This set is a 24-carat gem, and we have seen it before, also. No? Yes, we have, but it first appeared as I/iv with subset IV. In this set, if we let G+ = I, then C/c becomes IV/iv. This is our "reversible coat" set.

Set 44) is comprised of the keys C+, a-, F+, and d-, and no others. If we list the keys in this order, then we can see the key relationships clearly as I/vi/IV/ii. This is a beautiful, well-balanced bi-modality, having four tonal centres, and no subsets. Set 49) is similar; it contains the keys C+, a-, G+, and e-, which together create the set I/vi/V/iii. While our original Deca set I/i/bIII is polytonal if we use the subsets IV and bVII, **sets 44) and 49) are our best polytonal bi-modalities of all, because they are balanced, and have no subsets.**

We now have to calculate clash intensities of SATs for all nine of our Category (1) sets. Sets 25), 36), 64), and 71) are all I/i Deca; the only clash there is "third against third," which has a rating of 3 + 3 = 6. The other five calculations are done in Example 18-6.

Ex. 18-6 Clash Intensities of SATs in Category (1) Sets

33)	I/vii/II/V	=	I/vii	+	I/II	+	I/V	+	vii/II	+	vii/V	+	II/V	=
			10	+	6	+	0	+	3	+	0	+	0	= 19
44)	I/vi/IV/ii	=	I/vi	+	I/IV	+	I/ii	+	vi/IV	+	vi/ii	+	IV/ii	=
			3	+	0	+	6	+	0	+	5	+	3	= 17
47)	I/IV/iv	=	I/IV	+	I/iv	+	IV/iv	=	0 + 0 + 6 = 6					
	or I/i/V	=	I/i	+	I/V	+	i/V	=	6 + 0 + 0 = 6					
49)	I/vi/V/iii	=	I/vi	+	I/V	+	I/iii	+	vi/V	+	vi/iii	+	V/iii	=
			3	+	0	+	0	+	6	+	5	+	3	= 17
56)	I/i/V	=	I/i	+	I/V	+	i/V	=	6 + 0 + 0 = 6					
	or I/IV/iv	=	I/IV	+	I/iv	+	IV/iv	=	0 + 0 + 6 = 6					

These results are not difficult to interpret. The three-key combinations (47, 56) all ended up with a clash intensity of 6. These combinations all involve closely related keys only. Not only that, they involve only three two-key combinations. However, when four keys are involved, the number of two-key combinations doubles to six. So we ended up with clash intensity ratings in the teens. Here again, it is the relative compatibility of the keys that is the most important factor to consider. And the well-balanced bi-modalities (44, 49) ended up having lower ratings than that of the unbalanced one (33).

Summary and Analysis

Our Decaphonic treasure-hunting expedition unfortunately forced us to look through a very large amount of junk. But now that we have done it, we should put our findings into perspective. It is not a goal to produce as long a final list of sets as possible, just for the sake of doing so. Rather, the goal is to extract only the "good stuff." After all, we already have nonatonic sets, and in the next two chapters we will produce 11- and 12-tone sets as well.

We started out in Example 18-2 with three sets whose two excluded tones are a perfect fifth apart, and one set having the two excluded tones a minor third apart. That one set, I/iv, turned out to be our "reversible coat" set. I/v and I/#iv led to the formation of the "mega-set" I/i/vi/♭III. The set I/vii remains unbalanced — at least for now.

We next found that the eight sets belonging to Category (2) are clearly identifiable, but terribly imbalanced when taken one at a time, because, with the exception of sets 1 and 60, they contain major keys only. In combination, however, they have a fair amount of potential for creating larger, well-balanced sets, so for this purpose, they will serve us well.

The nine sets of Category (1) are the finalists in this competition. Since sets 71, 47, 64, and 33 are previous winners, we already know about them, so we focus on the five sets listed in Example 18-5. Sets 25) and 36) turn out to be I/i Deca in disguise. Set 56) turns out to be our "reversible coat" set, also in disguise, but identifiable by its two excluded tones being a minor third apart (in this case, b-flat and d-flat).

But now, if we take a closer look at sets 44) and 49), we observe that their excluded tones also lay a minor third apart (d# and f# in the former, a# and c# in the latter). In fact, set 44) transposed a perfect fifth up is equivalent to set 56), and set 49) is equivalent to set 56) without transposition.

So why is it that set 56) is designated as I/i/V or I/IV/iv, and is bi-tonal, while sets 44) and 49) each have four tonal centres and relative major/relative minor key relationships? The answer is: Enharmonics. We can see clearly now that sets 49) and 56) produce considerably different offspring, even though the only differences between the two are d# vs. e♭ and g# vs. a♭.

Conclusion: We declare the winners of this beauty contest to be Contestants No. 44 and No. 49. Congratulations to both!

CHAPTER NINETEEN

Hendecaphonic (Eleven-Note) Bi-Modalities

Prelude

Before we get into the topic of 11-note sets, I would like to make a type of editorial comment on this entire project in general, and this chapter in particular. At the end of Part One, it became clear that it would be possible to create and define other nonaphonic sets besides the basic set I/i, and furthermore, that it would be possible to do the same with 10-note sets. I also could visualize the possibility of constructing and defining at least one bi-modal, tonal dodecaphonic set. These were the only original objectives of Part Two.

The idea of working with 11-tone sets, however, made me very uncomfortable. It seemed like such a "crack-brained notion" (crazy idea). I imagined people asking: "Why not just use all 12 tones, and forget about 11-tone sets entirely?" So this chapter was not even going to be written.

However, after working with 10-tone sets, I had to change my attitude towards 11-note sets. It became clear that there exist specific sets consisting of 10 notes plus one enharmonic, and other specific sets consisting of 11 tones. It also became clear that there exist some scenarios in which 10 notes are not enough, and 12 notes are too many (because undesirable subsets result).

I had to accept that the number 11 is just as legitimate as a total as are the numbers 9, 10, and 12, so now I must ask readers to accept this, also. Not only that, 11-note sets really do fall in between decaphonic and dodecaphonic sets. So to omit this chapter would be to leave a gap in the whole picture. But even at this point, my approach is not: "Let's create some 11-note sets." Rather, it is my continuous "one thing leads to another" approach.

It will be easier to see this chapter in perspective after we get through with studying dodecaphonic sets. At that point, it will become clear that 11-note sets form a stepping stone between 10- and 12-note sets. For now, we get a preview of that idea if we treat sets consisting of 10 notes plus one enharmonic as a stepping stone between 10- and 11-note sets.

In the preceding chapter, it was confirmed that there exist two cases of decatonic sets in which it is worth our while to add one enharmonic, because by doing so we can create attractive, well-balanced tri-tonal bi-modalities. The first of these is the set I/iv, which contains the subset IV, so if C+ = I, then the set is C/F/f. However, if we let F+ = I, then the set is I/i/V, or F/f/C. Now, if we add the enharmonic c# (=db), we add the key of d-, and our final result is F/f/C/d, or I/i/V/vi, as shown in Example 19-1.

Ex. 19-1 Set I/i/V/vi (enharmonics are indicated in eighth notes)

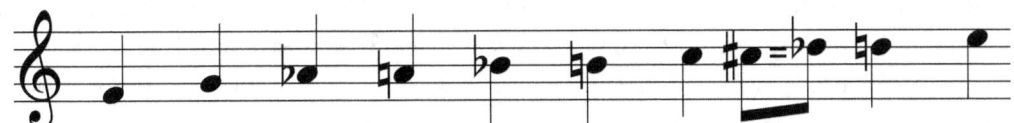

This is a tri-tonal, 10-tone, 11-note set, and it is characterized by three desirable features. First, it is a closed set (having no subsets). Second, the modes are balanced (two of each). Third, and most important, the key relationships are very healthy and compatible.

The second case is the set I/v, which contains the subsets IV, V, and ♭VII, so if C+ = I, then the set is C/G/g/F/B♭. As is, the modes in this combination are terribly imbalanced. However, we can see instantly that of the five keys present, if g- is to be included, then the three keys that are best related to each other are G+, g-, and B♭+. So we let G/g = I/i, and that gives us I/i/♭III (with subsets IV and ♭VII, as always). This, of course, is our basic I/i Deca set. Now we add the note d# in order to add e-(= vi), the relative minor of G+. The final result is I/i/vi/♭III, as shown in Example 19-2 below.

Ex. 19-2 Set I/i/vi/♭III

This is our "Mega-set," consisting of tonic major/minor, the relative minor of I, and the relative major of i. It is the same as the set I/#iv, as shown in Ex. 19-3 below, where I = B♭+ and #iv = e-.

Ex. 19-3 Set I/#iv (common tones are indicated in half notes)

The subsets here are II, V, VI, and vi (= C+, F+, G+, and g-). Clearly, I/II/V/#iv/VI/vi is hardly a set that we would ever aim to produce. When regarded as I/i/vi/♭III, though, it does make a usable set if the linear relationship, as shown in Example 19-4 below, is maintained.

Ex. 19-4 Linear relationship of vi, I, i, and ♭III

vi ← I ←→ i → ♭III

Next, we look back at Example 18-5, and recall that the only differences between sets 49) and 56) are d# vs. e♭ and g# vs. a♭. Now that we are looking at 11-tone sets, it is worth our while to check what possibilities would exist if we added the eight tones common to sets 49) and 56), (c, d, e, f, f#, g a, and b), to the six possible two-note combinations of the four tones (d#, e♭, g#, a♭) that are not common: (d#, e♭), (d#, g#), (d#, a♭), (e♭, g#), (e♭, a♭), (g#, a♭).

Case One gives us the notes c, d, d#, e♭, e, f, f#, g, a b. If we add b-flat to these, we get the Mega-set I/i/vi/♭III, as shown in Example 19-2 above.

Case Two yields c, d, d#, e, f, f#, g, g#, a, b, which is C/a/G/e (= I/vi/V/iii). This is set 49) in Example 18-5, a winner of our Decaphonic set competition of the previous chapter. So we leave it as it is.

Case Three gives us c, d, d#, e, f, f#, g, a♭, a, b. If we add e♭ to this set, we get C+, c-, G+, and e-, which is I/i/V/iii. BINGO! How did this happen? It happened because without the b-flat (which we do not need), we ended up with C/c Nonaphonic, plus f# and d#. This is a lovely, well-balanced closed set. It is closed because b-flat is absent; if b-flat was present, we would also have F+, B♭+, and g-.

Case Four adds up to c, d, e♭, e, f, f#, g, g#, a, b. As is, we have C+, a-, and G+ without making any use of the e♭. (There is no c- because a♭ is absent.) If we add b♭, we gain F+, B♭+, and g-. Now, we must let G/g = I/i, and when we do, we get I/i/♭III (with subsets IV and ♭VII, as usual), which is our basic Deca Set. But we also end up with ii (= a-) as a subset, and it makes a good partner for IV. So we end up with I/i/IV/ii, with ♭VII and ♭III as leftover subsets. This is both an 11-note (hendecaphonic) and an 11-tone (hendecatonic) set, because no enharmonics are involved.

Case Five with d# added is the same as Case Three with e♭ added, as described above (the Bingo set).

Finally, Case Six gives us c, d, e, f, f#, g, g#, a♭, a, b. The keys present are C+, a-, and G+. If we add e♭, we get C/c Nonaphonic (with a- and G+), and the result is I/i/V/vi with no subsets. This set was already anticipated way back in Chapter Fourteen, when we looked at Example 14-9. It is the set shown in Example 19-1 (transposed).

This is about as far as we should go in examining sets consisting of ten tones and one enharmonic. More such sets certainly do exist, but most of them are apt to be of the type described in Case Four. We have most likely already seen the best of the lot. Now we must move on to considering hendecaphonic sets consisting of eleven different tones.

We already know about one set of this type. It appears in Example 18-1, and it is the set I/♭vii, and its counterpart, II/i, as shown in Example 19-5 below. Here, C+ can be regarded as I, or b♭- can be regarded as i.

Ex. 19-5 Sets I/♭vii and II/i (common tones indicated in half notes)

The missing tone is a♭, because it disappears when the leading note of b♭- is created. There are two subsets (F+ and B♭+), so the set is I/IV/♭VII/♭vii. If we let B♭+ = I, the set becomes I/i/II/V. If we let F+ = I, it becomes I/IV/iv/V. In the next chapter, we will see how these equivalent sets can be regarded as stepping stones towards a twelve-tone tonal set.

This leaves us with four more cases to consider. Each one consists of the notes of C+ plus four of the five keyboard black-key notes. We saw in Chapter Thirteen that, from the acoustical standpoint, f# (= g♭) should be the first note to omit. But there was also a case to be made for including the f# and omitting the d♭ (= c#), so we will start with these two cases. After that, we will look at what possibilities exist if we omit b♭ (= a#), and finally, if we omit e♭ (= d#).

Example 19-6 shows the eleven tones that remain when f# (= g♭) is excluded. In the first case we include c#, and in the next case, d♭.

Ex. 19-6 Eleven-tone sets with f# excluded

The first case gives us the basic C/c Deca set (with its default subsets, and c# left over) plus … nothing! However, in the next chapter, it will be very easy to work with this set and to create … something. Can any readers anticipate the two things that we will do in order to create this "something?"

In the second case, we end up with C/c Deca, with subsets F+, B♭+, and E♭+, plus F/f Deca, with subsets B♭+, E♭+, and A♭+. So A♭+ is a new subset. If C/c = I/i, then the set is I/i/IV/iv. If F/f = I/i, then the set is I/i/V/v. This has to be compared to the situation illustrated in the next example, Example 19-7.

Example 19-7 includes C+ plus the black-note keys except for c# (= d♭).

Ex. 19-7 Eleven-tone set with c# excluded

Now we have C/c Deca, with its subsets IV (F+), ♭VII (B♭+), and ♭III (E♭+), plus G/g Deca, with its subsets IV (= C+), ♭VII (= F+), and ♭III (= B♭+). So if C+ = I, the set is I/i/V/v, and if G+ = I, it is I/i/IV/iv.

This set, and the previous one, is like a British bus — a Double-Deca … The subsets are like the stairs that connect the two levels. However, in this set, the subsets all overlap each other. In the previous set, the subset A♭+ does not belong to the group. In the next chapter, we will take these two "buses" farther.

Example 19-8 below shows first what happens when we exclude b♭, but add e♭, a♭, d♭, and f# to C+. Second, it shows the result of C+ plus e♭, a♭, f#, and c#. Third, we have C+ plus e♭, a♭, f#, c#, and g#.

Ex. 19-8 Eleven-tone sets with b♭ excluded

In the first instance, we have C/c Nona plus G+. The note d♭ does us no good. In the next case, there is C/c Nona, G+, and D+, which again is nothing to get excited about. Finally, in the third case, we try using one enharmonic. The result is C/c Nona, A/a Deca, plus G+ and D+. So if C+ = I, the set is I/i/VI/vi/II/V, and if A+ = I, it is I/i/♭III/♭iii/IV/♭VII. This is just I/i Deca with ♭iii thrown in to cause pain. We do not need the e♭ or the a♭.

So why is it so difficult to create good sets with these notes? It is because b♭ is missing, and it has not been replaced by a#, and c# or d♭ have been added instead. With both b♭ and a# absent, the other accidentals become orphaned, and do not contribute to the cause.

Finally, in Example 19-9 below, we omit e♭ (=d#), and include C+ plus f#, c#, and g#. To these, we try adding a# first, and then b♭ instead.

Ex. 19-9 Eleven-tone sets with e♭ excluded

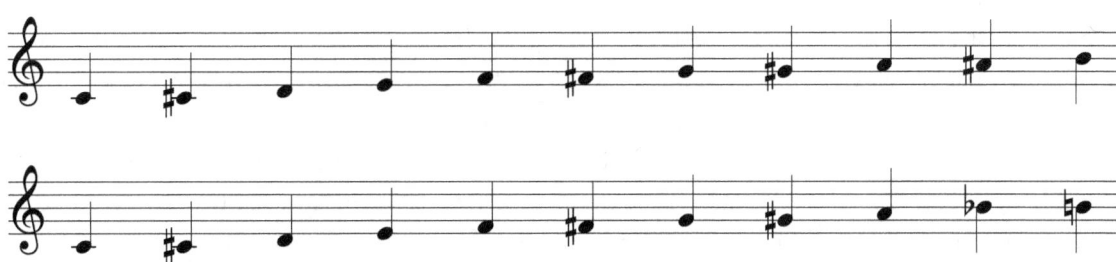

In the first case, we have A/a Deca, plus C+, D+, b-, and G+. This is just A/a Deca with its regular subsets (IV, ♭VII, and ♭III), plus ii. It is the same set as Case Four, seen earlier, which is I/i/IV/ii with subsets ♭VII and ♭III.

In the second case, we have A/a Deca with its regular subsets (D+, G+, and C+), plus ♭VI/iv (= F/d). But if we let D/d = I/i, then the set becomes I/i (with its subsets G+, C+, and F+), plus V/v (= A/a). This is the Double-Deca set, which will assume its rightful place, in context, in the next chapter.

We can now summarize the six different 11-note sets examined in this chapter. These are listed in Example 19-10.

Ex. 19-10 Six different eleven-tone sets, all starting on C

1)	I/i/V/vi ex. C/F/f → F/f/C → F/f/C/d	(c.f. Ex. 19-1)
	10 tones (f#, e♭ missing) + 1 En (c# = d♭)	
2)	I/i/vi/♭III ex. C/c/a plus C/c/E♭	(Mega-set)
	10 tones (c#, f# missing) plus 1 En (g# = a♭)	
3)	I/i/V/iii ex. C/c Nonaphonic plus G+ plus e-	(Bingo set)
	10 tones (c#, b♭ missing) + 1 En (d# = e♭)	
4)	I/i/IV/ii ex. C/c/F/d	(c.f. Ex. 19-9)
	11 tones (f# missing)	
5)	I/♭vii ex. C/b♭	(c.f. Ex. 19-5)
	11 tones (a♭ missing)	
6)	I/i/V/v OR I/i/IV/iv ex. C/c/G/g OR C/c/F/f	(Double-Deca)
	11 tones (d♭ missing OR f# missing)	

Set 1) evolved from the "reversible coat" set. We started with I/iv, which had IV as a subset. So we let the subdominant equal I/i, and the tonic equal V. Then we added one enharmonic in order to add vi to balance the bi-modality.

Set 2) consists of the sum of I with its tonic minor and relative minor plus i with its tonic major and relative major. It contains one enharmonic. This is our "Mega-set."

Set 3) was a surprise which happened because we began with C/c Nona, so we could still add two notes. Adding f# gave us G+, plus one of the two notes needed to add e-. Then, to get e-, it was necessary to add only one enharmonic. (This is easier to follow in Case Five above than in Case Three.)

Set 4) is the set derived in Case Four earlier, and seen again as the first set in Example 19-9. It consists of the fundamental Deca set plus ii. Here, because ii is a perfect mate for IV, we can balance the bi-modality by using I/i/IV/ii, and avoiding ♭VII and ♭III.

Set 5) was first seen back in Example 18-1, where it turned out to be the only 11-tone and 11-note set (without enharmonics) resulting from a semi-modulation.

Finally, Set 6) is the Double-Deca set, which is a real gem. It can also be seen as a "reversible coat" set if we regard it as I/i/V/v = I/i/IV/iv, where C/c/G/g = G/g/C/c, with the note c# missing in both cases. Either way, this is a perfectly balanced bi-modality and a closed set, having no subsets.

We now have to list the chromatic clashes of SATs found in these six sets, and calculate the total for each. In the case of set 6), we already know from Chart 15-2 that the answer is 6. But in the other five cases, things are not so simple, because when more than three keys are involved, duplications are involved, so we must be very careful.

Set 1) consists of the combinations I/i + I/V + I/vi + i/V + i/vi + V/vi. I/i has the clash of e/eb for a point value of 6; I/vi has g/g# for a point value of 3. But i/vi also has eb/e, this time for 4 points, and g/g#, again for 3 points.

Now, on the one hand, it is "not fair" to count the same pair of notes more than once, and accumulate points the same way as if there were chromatic clashes of two different pairs of notes present. On the other hand, since the same clash occurs more than once, we should use the highest point value that appears for it. So we choose 6 points for each of eb/e and g/g# for a total of 12.

Set 2) consists of the combinations I/i + I/vi + I/bIII + i/vi + i/bIII + vi/bIII. I/i has the clash e/eb for 6 points; I/vi has g/g# for 3 points; I/bIII has e/eb for 7 points, and b/bb for 3 points. So far, we have 3 + 7 + 3 = 13 points, but then, these same pairs appear again, so we must check them again, in case the corresponding values are higher. In i/vi, g/g# also counts for 3 points, and in i/bIII, b/bb also counts for 3 points, so there are no changes to make. In vi/bIII, eb/e appears for 5 points, which we do not count, because we already counted 7 points for this pair. But g#/g appears for 5 points, so we must add 2 points for a final total of 15.

Set 3) is a bit easier. It consists of the combinations I/i + I/V + I/iii + i/V + i/iii + V/iii. The clash e/eb appears in I/i for 6 points, but in i/iii, eb/e counts for 7 points. In V/iii, d/d# counts for 3 points, so the total here is 10.

Set 4) consists of the combination I/i + I/IV + I/ii + i/IV + i/ii + IV/ii. I/i, as always, has e/eb for 6 points. I/ii has c/c# for 6 points, as does i/ii.* i/IV has eb/e for only 5 points, so we do not count it. IV/ii has c/c# for only 3 points, so we do not count it, either. So in this case, our total of 12 remains unchanged.

Set 5) is the simplest. The only clash is b/bb for 6 points.

In set 6), I/i/V/v and I/i/IV/iv come out the same. I/i/V/v consists of the combination I/i + I/V + I/v + i/V = i/v + V/v. I/i has e/eb for 6 points, and V/v has b/bb for 6 points. I/v has b/bb for 5 points, as does i/v, so we do not count either of these. The total remains at 12.

Our totals came out to be 12, 15, 10, 12, 6, and 12, respectively. In looking at these, we must keep in mind not just the number of keys involved, but also the number of tones and enharmonics (if any) involved. Sometimes, we must put up with a comparison of apples to oranges; just let us not compare lemons ... Example 19-11 on the next page compares the sets of Example 18-6 to those of Example 19-10.

Our "mega set," I/i/vi/bIII, clearly has an "attitude," in that bIII just does not get along with I or vi. Not only that, the total number of clash intensity points is even higher than the 15 shown, because vi/bIII involves three tritone clashes (between roots, fifths, and leading notes). This is what happens when we go to combine I/vi with i/bIII, which is what our "mega-set" does. On the positive side, the rest of our sets have turned out to be very user-friendly.

---

*NOTE: I/II, I/ii, i/II, i/ii, and I/bVII, I/bvii, i/bVII, and i/bvii all have the same one and only clash of root against leading note, for a total of 6 points. It is very easy to memorize this; **it applies to any two keys that have roots one tone apart.**

Ex. 19-11 Comparison or Ex. 18-6 to Ex. 19-10

SET	KEYS	TONAL CENTRES	CARDINALITY	CLASH INTENSITY
I/vii/II/V	4	4	10	19
I/vi/IV/ii	4	4	10	17
I/i/v and I/IV/iv	3	2	10	6
I/vi/V/iii	4	4	10	17
I/i/V/vi	4	3	10 + 1 En	12
I/i/vi/♭III	4	3	10 + 1 En	15
I/i/V/iii	4	3	10 + 1 En	10
I/i/IV/ii	4	3	11	12
I/♭vii	2	2	11	6
I/i/V/v and I/i/IV/iv	4	2	11	12

* * *

We move on now to defining and explaining the fundamental Hendecaphonic, Bi-Modal system in very much the same way that we did for 9- and 10-note sets.

The basic set is the Double-Deca set, or I/i/V/v. (We could choose I/i/IV/iv, but then if C/c = I/i, then IV/iv includes an extra subset, A♭+.) To begin, let us look back at Example 17-16, in which the key signatures for all 12 Deca keys are listed. What we have to do now is to combine every consecutive pair of those key signatures. There is a fair amount of overlap between each of these pairs. For example, for the first pair, we copy C/c, and then add only "f-natural/f-sharp" from G/g. The two pairs have only one excluded tone in common, and it is indicated next (and last).

The key signatures for all 12 Double-Deca keys are shown in Example 19-12 on the next page. In key combinations which have a large number of accidentals, these start to get difficult to decipher. So it is a good idea to write "X/x/Y/y" in each case. The fact that only one tone (and its enharmonic) is excluded in each case indicates that these are 11-tone sets.

Ex. 19-12 Key Signatures for all 12 Double-Deca Sets

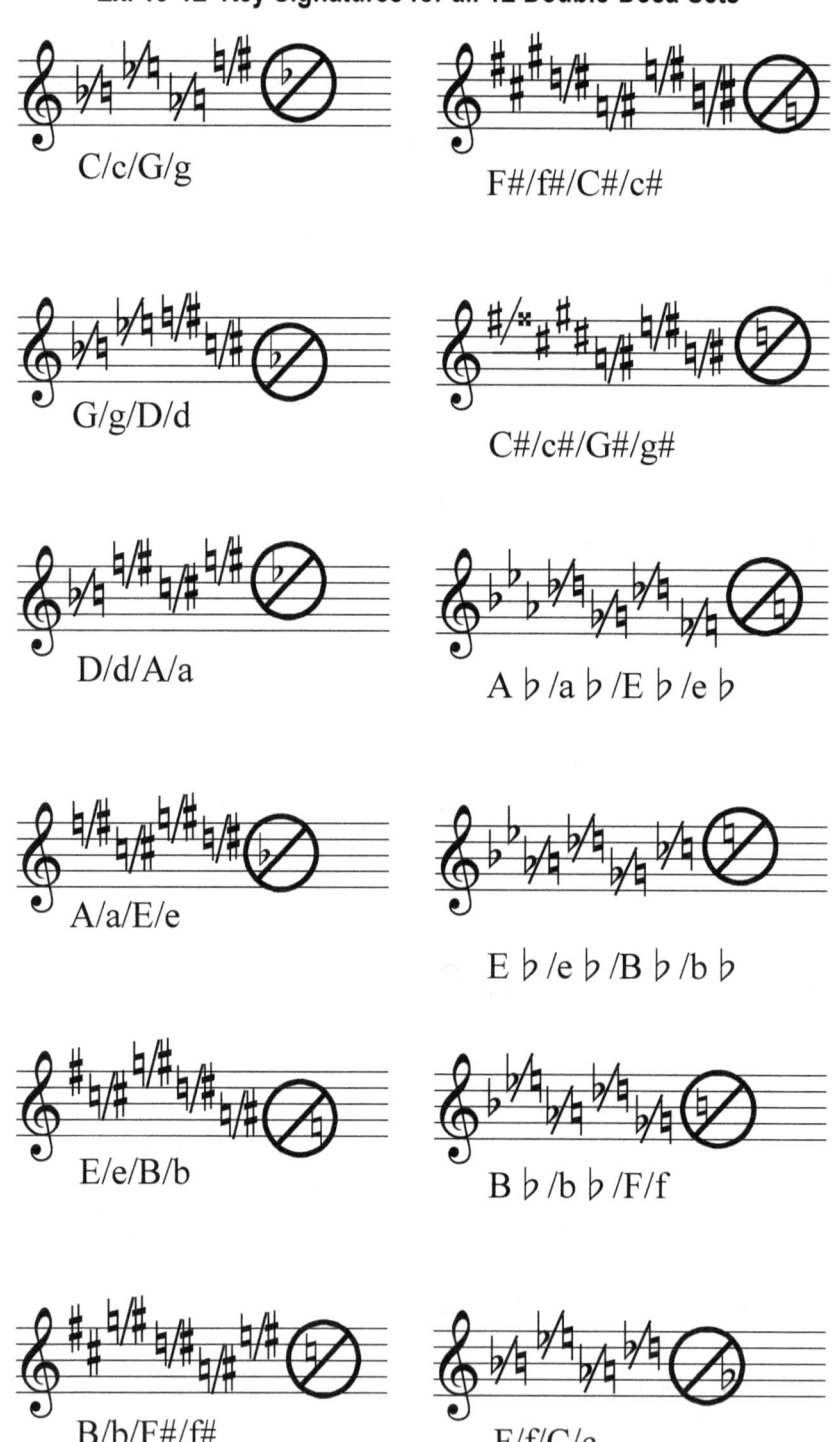

NOTE: Here again, the key signatures indicate precisely the specific sets of tones which comprise the given keys. But since accidentals must be used constantly throughout the score anyway, it is sufficient to state the key signature only once, at the beginning.

We next look back at Example 17-17 to compare what Double-Deca scales will look like. It is very easy to write these. We just take the Deca scale, and add to it the augmented fourth. For example, C/c Deca becomes C/c plus the note f#, which makes it C/c Double-Deca. (C#/c# Double-Deca contains the note fx).

Our next task is to identify and analyze all new chords that are gained as a result of the addition of our eleventh tone, the augmented fourth (f# in C/c). This tone can be the root, third, or fifth of triads, or the root, third, fifth, or seventh of seventh chords. How many new chords will there be? More than seven, as shown in Example 19-13.

Ex. 19-13 New chords in C/c Double-Deca including the note f#

Triads having f# as root:	(f#, ab, c),	(f#, a, c)
Triads having f# as third:	(d, f#, ab),	(d, f#, a)
Triads having f# as fifth:	(bb, d, f#),	(b, d, f#)
Sevenths having f# as root:	(f#, ab, c, eb),	(f#, ab, c, e)
	(f#, a, c, eb),	(f#, a, c, e)
Sevenths having f# as third:	(d, f#, ab, c),	(d, f#, a, c)
Sevenths having f# as fifth:	(bb, d, f#, ab),	(bb, d, f#, a)
	(b, d, f#, ab),	(b, d, f#, a)
Sevenths having f# as seventh:	(g, bb, d, f#),	(g, b, d, f#)

We have six new triads and twelve new seventh chords. The six new triads are written out and analyzed in Example 19-14 below.

Ex. 19-14 Six new triads in Double-Deca

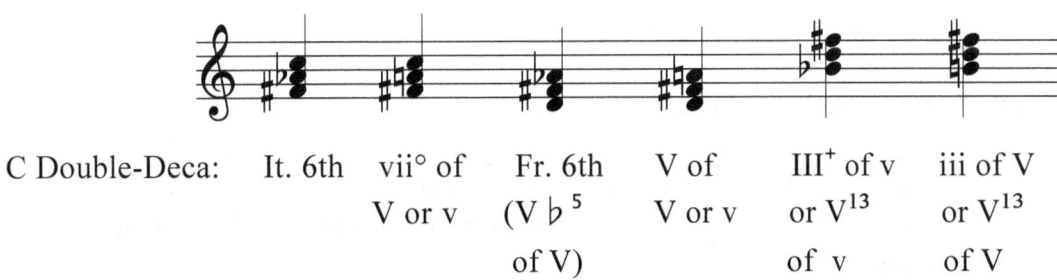

C Double-Deca: It. 6th   vii° of   Fr. 6th   V of   III⁺ of v   iii of V
                 V or v   (V♭5   V or v   or V¹³   or V¹³
                            of V)   of v   of V

All these triads have dominant functions; the last two have mediant functions in addition. Now we examine the twelve new seventh chords in Example 19-15.

Ex. 19-15 Twelve new seventh chords in Double-Deca

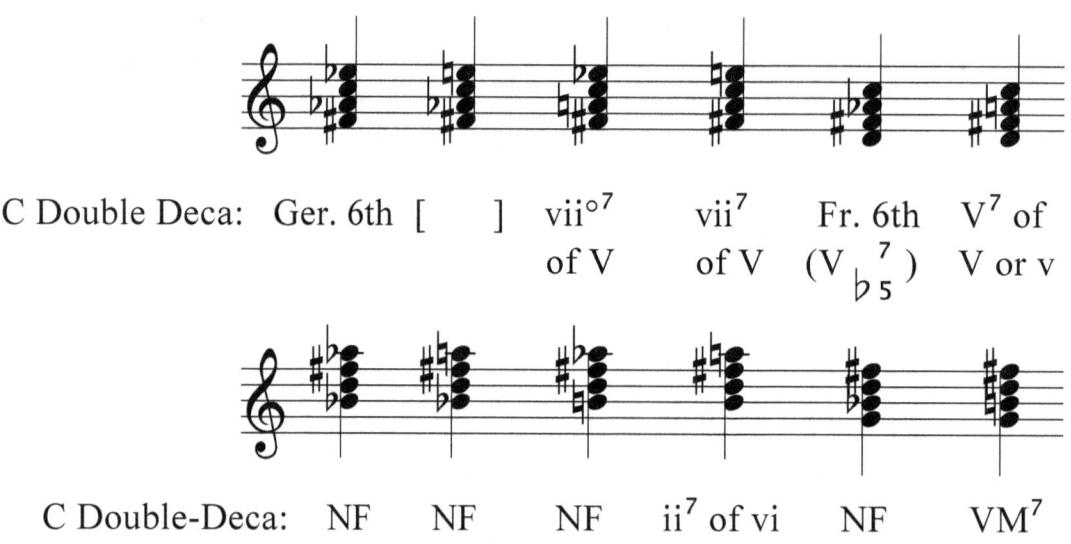

The third-last chord has a subdominant function; four chords are non-functional, and the remaining seven have a dominant function.

Of these, the second chord requires an explanation. In Chapter Five of Part One, the German Sixth chord was explained as follows: In C/c, the double-dominant minor ninth chord consists of the notes d, f#, a, c, eb. When the root is omitted and the fifth is flattened, the result is ab, c, eb, f#. In the second chord of Example 19-15, the note "e" is natural, not flat. But that just means that we can trace its derivation back to the double-dominant major ninth chord, instead. It still has a dominant function. This chord does not have a name. But

Whereas: the characteristic note of the French sixth is d, and d is next to e-flat, and e-flat is next to e-natural, and

Whereas: France is next to Germany, and Germany is next to Poland,

Therefore: Let us call this the Polish Sixth!...*

In any event, we have no new tonic chords, and no new submediant chords. There is one new subdominant chord, and 13 new dominant chords, of which two are bi-functional, they are also new mediant chords. So the total number of new chords is 1 + 13 + 2 = 16.

We can now draw up our model of Double-Decaphonic Bi-Modality. Example 17-21, our House of Decaphonic Bi-Modality, consisted of 59 chords, distributed as follows: Tonic: 5, Dominant: 18, Subdominant: 22, Mediant: 7, Submediant: 7. Now, we add our 16 new chords, for a grand total of 75. Three sub-totals change: Subdominant increases by 1 to 23, Dominant increases by 13 to 31, and Mediant increases by 2 to 9. Tonic and Submediant remain at 5 and 7, respectively. Example 19-16 is a copy of Example 17-21, with the 16 new chords added.

---

*Of course, the author's ethnic background has nothing to do with this (sic)!

Ex. 19-16

HENDECAPHONIC BI-MODALITY

SUBDOMINANT GROUP	SUBMEDIANT GROUP	TONIC GROUP	MEDIANT GROUP	DOMINANT GROUP
ii°, ii, iv, IV, ♭VI,	♭VI, ♭VI⁺, vi°, vi, ♭VIM⁷,	i, I, ♭VI, vi	♭III⁺, iii, iii^{m7}	vii° of ♭III, ♭III = $V^{13}_{13\ 7}$, iii = $V^6_{6\ 8}$
ii° of v, IV⁷ of V, ii°^{m7}, ii^{m7}, ii⁷ of II, iv^{m7}, ii^{m7} of ♭III, IV⁷, IV⁷ of ♭III, ii°^{m7} of v, ii⁷ of V	vi°^{m7}, vi^{m7}	<u>1 new in Ex. 17-21:</u> ♭III	<u>4 new in Ex. 17-21:</u> ♭III, iii° ♭IIIM⁷, iii°^{m7}	V, vii°, V⁷, $V^{13}_{13\ 7}$ of iv, vii° of ♭VII, V⁷ of ♭VII, vii°^{m7} of ♭VII, vii⁷ of ♭VII, vii°⁷, vii°^{m7}
<u>6 new in Ex. 17-21:</u> IV of IV, ii⁷ of ♭VII, IV⁷ of ♭VII, ii⁷ of ii, ii⁷ of IV, IV⁷ of IV				<u>5 new in Ex. 17-21:</u> vii° of IV, v, V⁷ of IV, vii⁷ of IV, V⁷ of ♭III
22	7	5	7	18

—————————— 16 New in Ex. 19-16: ——————————

ii⁷ of vi			III⁺ of v, iii of V	It. 6th, vii° of V or v, Fr. 6th (= V♭5 of V), Fr. 6th (= V⁷♭5 of V), V¹³ of v, V¹³ of V, Ger. 6th,	"Polish 6th," vii°⁷ of v, vii⁷ of V, V of V or v, V⁷ of V or v, V M⁷
23	7	5	9	31

Some readers might argue that many of our "new" chords are not really new, since double-dominants (such as V of V) and Augmented Sixth chords exist in traditional tonality, not just in bi-modality. Of course, this is true. But f# is not diatonic in C+ or c-. "New" here means that these chords now get to move into the house, because all their component notes now belong to the scale and key signature, so they are diatonic. And that happened only when we added G/g to C/c.

Our final task in this chapter is to construct the Double-Decaphonic Quintcircle. This is done in Example 19-17. Once again, we use 12 o'clock as the starting point; it is now C/c/G/g Double-Decaphonic.

This system could be called double-nonaphonic, because the tenth tone of each bi-modality is always present in its partner bi-modality, anyway. For example, at 12 o'clock, b-flat belongs to g-, and f-natural belongs to C+ and c-.

If we look back at Example 17-23, we can see that what has happened here is that each bi-modal key has taken the shortest "secret tunnel" and joined its neighbor located one station counter-clockwise along the perimeter of the quintcircle. This is why C/c/G/g ended up at 12 o'clock, and not at 1 o'clock. All three subsets of G/g belong to C/c, but only two subsets of C/c belong to G/g.

Ex. 19-17

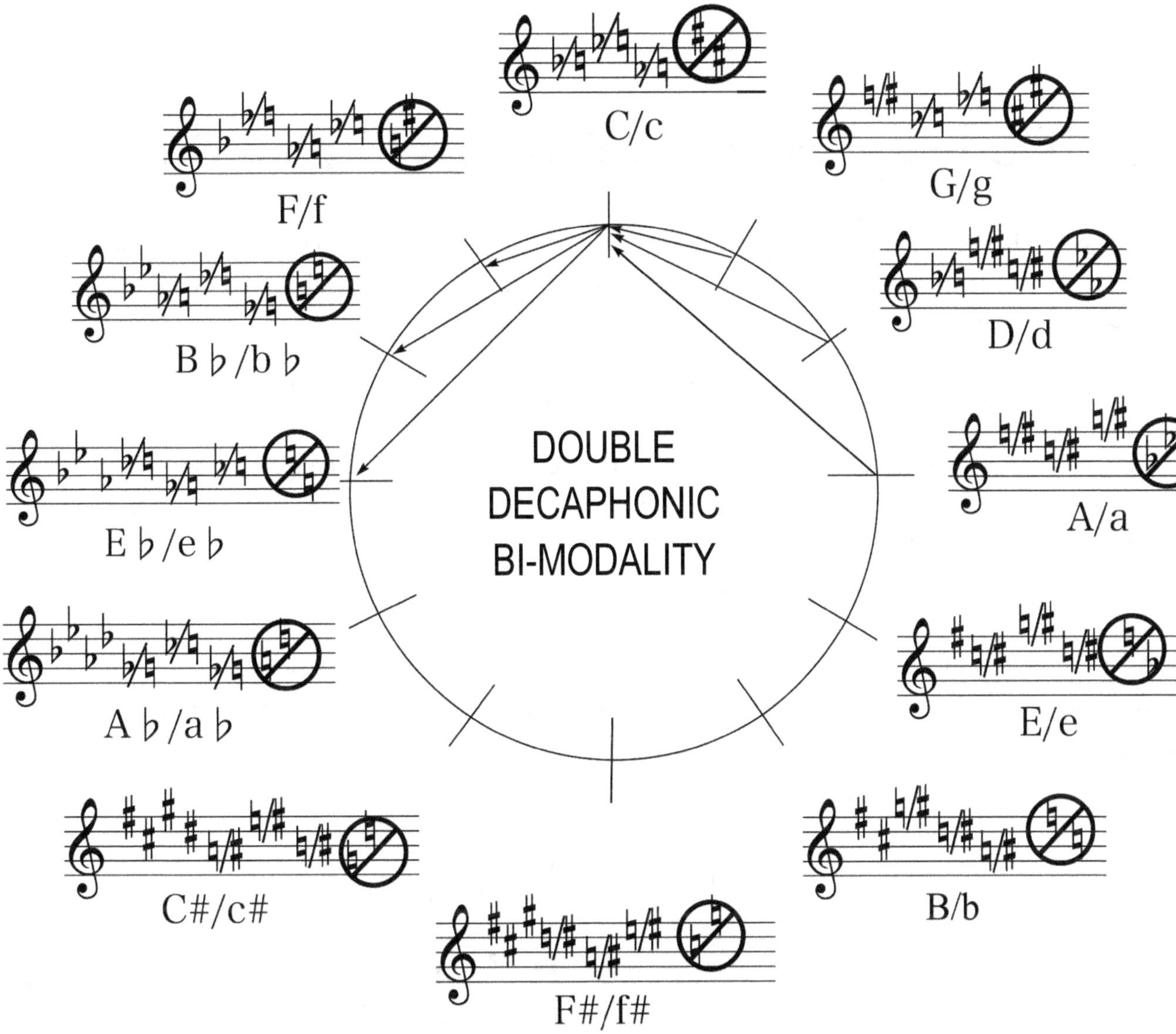

Those readers who like to guess how a movie will end before seeing the ending should now make their guesses how this "movie" will end in the next chapter. Hint: There are two possible endings.

INTERMISSION

CHAPTER TWENTY

Dodecaphonic (Twelve-Tone) Tonalities

The term "dodecaphonic," meaning "twelve-tone," has always been associated with atonal, or serial, music, because that is what its inventor, Arnold Schoenberg, defined and wrote. As a result, many people make the following general assumption:

"When we use all 12 tones, we are in all 12 keys, so we are not in any key, so the music is atonal."

I once read that people remember only 10% of what they read. (This must be true, since I don't remember anything else that was written on the same page) … So if you remember only one sentence of the ten that you are reading right now, let it be this one:

The above statement about 12 tones, 12 keys, and zero keys is false, False, and FALSE, and it is easy to prove this!!!

It is, of course, possible to use all 12 tones in such a way that atonality results (as we well know), but atonality does not come automatically when 12 tones are being used. The raw materials for any twelve-tone system consist of the following 21 notes:

a	b	c	d	e	f	g
a#	b#	c#	d#	e#	f#	g#
a♭	b♭	c♭	d♭	e♭	f♭	g♭

If we added double-sharps and double-flats, the total would be over 21; adding only f-double-sharp, c-double-sharp, and b-double-flat would make 24, so 2 x 12, notes.

The point is that in atonal music, enharmonics are *not* distinct objects, but in tonal music, they *are*. So an atonal composition can make use of all 12 notes, but if 12 notes are being used in a tonal composition, it is not "all" 12 notes, but 12 notes out of 21 (or more) that are in use. And when we use only about 57% of all available notes, we are *not* writing in all available keys! In fact, as we will see, in carefully chosen sets, and without enharmonics involved, the number of keys present is typically 9 out of 24.

This is the point of departure for study of dodecaphonic tonal systems. Some of the questions that arise are: If we use a specific set of 12 notes, exactly how many keys are present, and which ones are they? How many tonal centres are there? Which are the primary sets and which are the subsets? What is the minimum number of keys, and of tonal centres, necessary in order to use all 12 tones *diatonically*? How many 12-tone tonal systems are there, and what are they? How compatible are the keys that comprise these systems?

Before we dive head-first into this vast topic, we have some unfinished business to take care of from Chapters Eighteen and Nineteen, because several references to 12-tone tonal sets were made in those chapters. Completing this will help us considerably, because doing so will make it quite clear where we are headed.

In Example 18-1, we can see that any bi-modality can be achieved without using all 12 tones. Three bi-modalities (and their counterparts) required the use of 11 tones plus one or two enharmonics. These were the sets I/#i, I/♭iii, and I/♭vi. In the first case, if we use the octatonic form of #i, then we end up adding the twelfth tone, a#. This set will be dealt with below in the form of I/♭ii. In the second case, adding the twelfth tone, d♭, would do us more harm than good, because it would just produce more subsets. The same holds true if we added g♭ to I/♭vi. And if we added f#, then G/g would appear on the scene, and that is not a bi-modality that we would want to combine with a-flat-minor. So this is not the way to go. We are looking for better twelve-tone sets than these.

In Example 18-4, we examined Category (2) Deca sets, and mentioned "tampering" with them. The union of sets 1), 75), 60), and 2) produced a 12-tone set with one enharmonic (d# = e♭). But if we now combine sets 2) and 75) only, and eliminate sets 1) and 60), we end up with the notes c, c#, d, e♭, e, f, f#, g, a♭, a, b♭, b, and no others. This gives us I/i/II/ii/V/v, with subsets IV, ♭VII, and ♭III. But these are the automatic, "default" subsets of I/i. NOW we have something to get excited about, because there are no enharmonics, and no new subsets!

Let us continue on to Example 18-5, and try some more set combinations. We see that set 56) contains e♭, and set 49 contains d#. So the thing to do here is to use one or the other of these sets, but not both.

Set 56) needs c# and b♭, which sets 36) and 44) have. The g# contained in set 44) is not needed, so we should add set 36) to set 56). When we do so, the resulting set is {c, c#, d, e♭, e, f, f#, g, a♭, a, b♭, b}, which is identical to the set derived above.

Set 49) is also missing c# and b♭, which sets 36) and 44) have. No matter which one of these we add to set 49), the resulting set is {c, c#, d, d#, e, f, f#, g, g#, a, b♭, b}. The keys that are present in this case are: C, F, G, D, A, and E major and a, d, and e minor. So which are the primary keys and which are the subsets? There are two possible answers to this question, both correct. The first is that there are the three sets A/a/C plus D/d/F plus E/e/G, and no subsets. The second is that C/a and F/d and G/e are the primary sets, and D+, A+, and E+ are the subsets. This equates to I/vi/IV/ii/V/iii with subsets II, VI, and III. This is, of course, a most notable set, and one which we need to study.

We move on now to Chapter Nineteen to see what we can "get out of it," literally. Example 19-5 shows I/♭vii, where either C+ = I or b♭- = i, and the note a-flat is missing. So let's add that a-flat, and form the resulting set {c, d♭, d, e♭, e, f, g♭, g, a♭, a, b♭, b}.

There are three ways to interpret this set. If C+ = I, then we have I/i/IV/iv/♭VII/♭vii, with subsets ♭II, ♭III, and ♭VI, that is, C/c/F/f/B♭/b♭, with subsets D♭, E♭, and A♭. If B♭+ = I, then we get I/i/II/ii/V/v, with subsets ♭III, IV, and ♭VII, which is: B♭/b♭/C/c/F/f, with subsets D♭, E♭, and A♭. Finally, if we let F+ = I, then the set becomes I/i/IV/iv/V/v, with subsets ♭VI, ♭VII, and ♭III, which equals F/f/B♭/b♭/C/c, with subsets D♭, E♭, and A♭.

We have seen the second of these three cases before, but the first and third cases are new. Or are they? Studying these in detail will keep us busy for awhile.

Example 19-6 consists of two cases. In the first case, in order to create a usable 12-tone tonal set, all we have to do is to add f# and change the b♭ to a#. Now the resulting set is: {c, c#, d, e♭, e, f, f#, g, a♭, a, a#, b}, and the keys present are C/c/D/b/G, or I/i/II/vii/V. This is set 74) of Example 18-3, plus c# and e♭; it also requires further attention. In the second case, if we add g♭, then we obtain the same set that we examined just above, where we added a♭ to Example 19-5.

The second case of Example 19-6, and the set of Example 19-7, and the second set of Example 19-9 all illustrate the Double-Deca set. These are transpositions of each other, and all three were illustrated as being of the form I/i/V/v or I/i/IV/iv Double-Deca. This is where we left off in Chapter Nineteen. Our main tasks in this chapter will be to add f# to the second case of Example 19-6, to add c# to Example 19-7, and to add e♭ to the second set of Example 19-9, and to see what happens when we do these three things.

* * *

The tonal 12-tone set derived from the first case of Example 19-6 is truly extraordinary, because there is no other set like it. Not only that, it is the only 12-tone tonal set that does not resemble any of the others.

There is another way to derive this set, and it is in three steps: First, begin with C/c Nona. Second, observe that the three missing tones are c# or d♭, f# or g♭, and a# or b♭. Third, find a key that contains those three black-key tones, and no others. There is only one such key, and it is b-, which has f#, c#, and a#, so it is the key to add.

At this point, we have a "problem," because b- has a high clash intensity rating with both C+ and c-. However, this set contains two subsets; they are D+ and G+. So in the end, we have three possible options. One is C/c/D/b/G, in which C/c and G are partners, as are D and b. The second is to avoid using G, and use only C/c/D/b. The final option is to avoid C, and use G/c/D/b.

Given the traditional structure of keys and key signatures that has existed for centuries, one certainly must think "outside of the box" in order to accept a system that contains all three versions of one letter-name, in this case, a-natural, a-flat, and a-sharp. Yet it is clear that such a system exists, and it is comprised of four tonal centres and five keys.

We can call this set the "Jigsaw puzzle set," because it has the characteristics of pieces (notes/keys) filling in each other's gaps, as shown in Example 20-1 below. The blank pieces belong to C+; the pieces marked with diagonal lines come from b-, and the pieces marked with vertical lines come from c-.

Ex. 20-1 Pictorial illustration of "Jigsaw puzzle set"

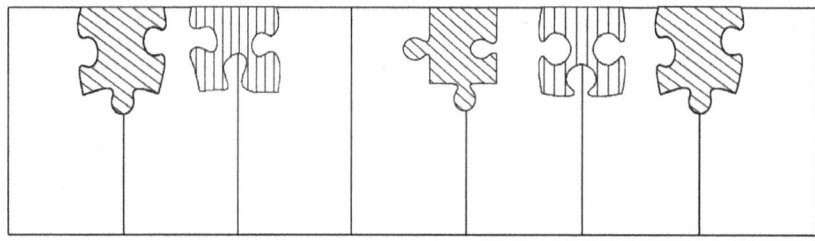

Even though b- has a high clash intensity rating against C/c, there is still a way to achieve "smooth sailing." The chain of semi-modulations shown in Example 20-2 will work very well, because in it, the chromatic clashes of SATs are reduced to a minimum. And note the symmetry!

Ex. 20-2 Workable chain of semi-modulations

C/c → G/c → G/b → D/b → D/c → C/c

* * *

Let us suppose that we found a group of interested musicians who have not seen a single word of this study (neither Part One nor Part Two). And suppose that we asked them to think of any and all possible key combinations which would use all 12 tones. Of those who could come up with any answer, what might they say? In all probability, they would say either "C+ plus B+" (with its five sharps), or "C+ plus D♭+" (with its five flats). Of course, both answers are correct, and they are the same answers, because both mean "I/♭II." They would not say "c- plus b-," because that would exclude a-natural, and they have never heard of our octatonic minor keys or scales. Somebody might say "c-natural-minor plus b-natural-minor," and that would be an excellent answer, as would "c-natural-minor plus c-sharp-natural-minor," which is the same set.

We would then have to get into the topic of subsets, and explain everything shown in Example 20-3 below.

Ex. 20-3 Subsets of certain key combinations

a) Since C+ plus B+ consist of the set {c, c#, d, d#, e, f, f#, g, g#, a, a#, b}, these two keys also include G+, D+, A+, E+, a-, e-, and b-.

b) Since C+ plus D♭+ consist of the set {c, d♭, d, e♭, e, f, g♭, g, a♭, a, b♭, b}, these two keys also include F+, B♭+, E♭+, A♭+, c-, f-and b♭-.

c) Since c-natural-minor plus b-natural-minor consist of the set {c, c#, d, e♭, e, f, f#, g, a♭, a, b♭, b}, these two keys also include the natural-minor keys of g, d, a, and e, plus E♭+, B♭+, F+, C+, G+, and D+.

d) Since c-natural-minor plus c-sharp-natural-minor consist of the set {c, c#, d, d#=e♭, e, f, f#, g, g#=a♭, a, b♭, b}, these two keys also include the natural-minor keys of g, d, a, e, b, and f#, plus C+, G+, D+, A+, E+, F+, B♭+, and E♭+.

After seeing these (especially the last one), what might our group of musicians say? The general consensus would probably be something like: "Let's just forget the whole thing, and use all 12 tones only for atonal music."

In fact, it is this type of experience that leads to the mistaken belief that "When we use all 12 tones, we are in all 12 keys, so we are not in any key, so the music is atonal." However, people who believe this probably have not considered bi-modality. (At this point, some lawyer could yell: "Objection! Speculation!", but never mind that).

The issue of dealing with combinations of keys whose roots lay a semitone apart is an extremely important one in our study of dodecaphonic tonality. After seeing the big mess above, we simply must continue on, and explore all the possible applicable bi-modal combinations. There are five of these; they are: B/b/C/c, B/b/C, C/c/B, B/b/c, and C/c/b.

Since we have already considered C+ plus B+, we can safely eliminate the first three of these, because to add c- or b- (or both) to these would be to add more keys (and more subsets), and that is the opposite of what we want.

The set B/b/c consists of the notes {c, c#, d, d#=e♭, e, f, f#, g, g#=a♭, ( ) a#, b}. The note a-natural is missing, but we could easily fix that by using the octatonic form of c-. But we know by now that the more enharmonics are involved, the more keys (subsets) are involved. In this case, if we used c octatonic minor, the keys present would be: C+, G+, D+, A+, E+, and B+, and a-, e-, b-, and c-.

So we are left with C/c/b, which consists of the notes {c, c#, d, e♭, e, f, f#, g, a♭, a a#, b}, which is our "jigsaw puzzle set." We can also think of it as b- plus c octatonic minor; either way, C+ is present, as are G+ and D+. If we wish to have no subsets, we must omit a-natural, and stay with the 11-tone set c/b, which is not bi-modal.

Conclusion: The set Octatonic i/vii with subsets I, II, and V, or I/i/II/vii/V, our "Jigsaw puzzle set," is the best possible set that combines keys whose roots lay a semitone apart, because it consists of no more than four tonal centres, five keys, and contains no enharmonics.

* * *

At this point, we have completed our study of the extraordinary set I/i/II/vii/V. Also, we know that everything else that we have seen in the last three chapters (including this one) points to the sets I/i/II/ii/V/v, I/i/IV/iv/V/v, I/i/IV/iv/♭VII/♭vii (and their respective subsets), plus the set I/vi/IV/ii/V/iii. But we still need to know for certain whether or not there exist any other workable 12-tone tonal sets. To this end, we use our tried (or "triad")! and true method of combining C+ with all other possible pertinent black-key note combinations. Since there are five black-key tones, and each one can be notated in two different ways, the total number of possible combinations is 2 x 2 x 2 x 2 x 2 = 32; these are written out in Example 20-4 below. They are listed in an orderly fashion, so that sets 17-32 correspond to sets 1-16, but with d♭, instead of c#, present.

Ex. 20-4 32 cases of quadruples of black-key notes added to C+

C+ (= c, d, e, f, g, a, b) plus:

1) c#, d#, f#, g#, a#   *   = C/B
2) c#, e♭, f#, g#, a#
3) c#, d#, g♭, g#, a#
4) c#, d#, g#, a♭, a#
5) c#, d#, f#, g#, b♭   *   = E/F
6) c#, e♭, g♭, g#, a#
7) c#, e♭, f#, a♭, a#   = C/c/D/b/G
8) c#, e♭, f#, g#, b♭   *   = A/B♭
9) c#, d#, g♭, a♭, a#
10) c#, d#, g♭, g#, b♭
11) c#, d#, f#, a♭, b♭
12) c#, e♭, g♭, a♭, a#
13) c#, e♭, g♭, g#, b♭
14) c#, e♭, f#, a♭, b♭   *   = D/E♭
15) c#, d#, g♭, a♭, b♭
16) c#, e♭, g♭, a♭, b♭
17) d♭, d#, f#, g#, a#
18) d♭, e♭, f#, g#, a#
19) d♭, d#, g♭, g#, a#
20) d♭, d#, f#, a♭, a#
21) d♭, d#, f#, g#, b♭
22) d♭, e♭, g♭, g#, a#
23) d♭, e♭, f#, a♭, a#
24) d♭, e♭, f#, g#, b♭
25) d♭, d#, g♭, a♭, a#
26) d♭, d#, g♭, g#, b♭
27) d♭, d#, f#, a♭, b♭   = F/f/G/e/C
28) d♭, e♭, g♭, a♭, a#
29) d♭, e♭, g♭, g#, b♭   = B♭/b♭/C/a/F
30) d♭, e♭, f#, a♭, b♭   *   = G/A♭
31) d♭, d#, g♭, a♭, b♭
32) d♭, e♭, g♭, a♭, b♭   *   = C/D♭

There are only six sets in this list that contain their sharps and flats in their proper order; these are indicated with * in Example 20-4 on the previous page, and described in Example 20-5 below.

Ex. 20-5 Tonal Dodecaphonic sets that can be expressed in terms of Major/minor keys

Set
1) 5 sharps, 0 flats {c, c#, d, d#, e, f, f#, g, g#, a, a#, b}
I/i/IV/iv/V/v, where E+ = I

5) 4 sharps, 1 flat {c, c#, d, d#, e, f, f#, g, g#, a, b♭, b}
I/vi/IV/ii/V/iii, where C+ = I

8) 3 sharps, 2 flats {c, c#, d, e♭, e, f, f#, g, g#, a, b♭, b}
I/i/II/ii/V/v, where G+ = I

14) 2 sharps, 3 flats {c, c#, d, e♭, e, f, f#, g, a♭, a, b♭, b}
I/i/II/ii/V/v, where C+ = I

30) 1 sharp, 4 flats {c, d♭, d, e♭, e, f, f#, g, a♭, a, b♭, b}
I/i/IV/iv/V/v, where C+ = I

32) 0 sharps, 5 flats {c, d♭, d, e♭, e, f, g♭, g, a♭, a, b♭, b}
I/i/IV/iv/♭VII/♭vii, where C+ = I

These are the most important sets with which we will be working in this chapter.

Set 7) is our "Jigsaw puzzle set." Two other sets in the list are transpositions of this set. One is set 27), which is set 7) transposed a perfect fourth up, and it consists of the keys F/f/G/e/C. The other is set 29), which is a transposition of set 7) down a major second. Here, I/i/II/vii/V becomes B♭/b♭/C/a/F. These three sets are marked appropriately in Example 20-4 above.

We now have to look at the remaining 23 sets in groups. The first group consists of three sets which have a specific characteristic in common: if one of their notes is replaced by its enharmonic, then the result is one of our standard dodecaphonic sets listed in Example 20-5. Set 4) needs g# instead of a♭ to create E/e/A/a/B/b, which is set 1). Set 13) needs f# instead of g♭ to become C/c/D/d/G/g, which is set 14). And set 21) needs c# instead of d♭ to create C/a/F/d/G/e, which is set 5). These three sets are transpositions of each other, as shown in Example 20-6.

Ex. 20-6 Three sets that are transpositions of each other

4) {c, c#, d, d#, e, f, f#, g, g#, a, a#, b}, down a M2 =

13) {b♭, b, c, c#, d, e♭, e, f, f#, g, g#, a}, up a P5 =

21) {f, f#, g, g#, a, b♭, b, c, c#, d, d#, e}, up a P5 = set 4).

The next group of four sets has a different characteristic in common. In each case, if we subtract one of the notes, we end up with the same 11-note set, I/i/IV/ii. This is illustrated in Example 20-7 below, in which the excluded note is indicated in parentheses. Here, again, the sets are transpositions of each other.

Ex. 20-7 Four sets that are transpositions of each other

> 2) {a, a#, b, c, c#, d, (eb) e, f, f#, g, g#} = A/a/D/b, up a P4 =
> 11) {d, d#, e, f, f#, g, (ab) a, bb, b, c, c#} = D/d/G/e, down a M2 =
> 16) {c, c#, d, eb, e, f, (gb) g, ab, a, bb, b} = C/c/F/d, up a P5 =
> 24) {g, g#, a, bb, b, c, (db) d, eb, e, f, f#} = G/g/C/a, up a M2 = 2).

Our next four sets are not identical. However, in each case, we cannot make use of two of the notes. If we subtract these two notes, we are left with familiar decatonic sets, as shown in Example 20-8 below. Again, the excluded notes are indicated in parentheses.

Ex. 20-8 Four specific sets

> 10) {c, c#, d, (d#) e, f, (gb) g, g#, a, bb, b} = C/a/F/d
> 17) {c, (db) d, d#, e, f, f#, g, g#, a, (a#) b} = C/a/G/e
> 23) {c, (db) d, eb, e, f, f#, g, ab, a (a#) b} = C/c/G
> 31) {f, (gb) g, ab, a, bb, b, c, db, d, (d#) e} = F/f/C, up a P5 = 23).

Our next four sets can be described as two pairs of familiar nonatonic sets. In all these cases, there are three notes (in parentheses) which we subtract, because they are spares, which do not contribute to any set of any cardinality. These four sets appear in Example 20-9 below.

Ex. 20-9 Two specific pairs of sets

> 15) {c, c#, d, (d#) e, f, (gb) g, (ab) a, bb, b} = C/F/d
> 18) {c, (db) d, (eb) e, f, f#, g, g#, a, (a#) b} = C/a/G
> 20) {c, (db) d, d#, e, f, f#, g, (ab) a, (a#) b} = C/G/e
> 26) {c, (db) d, (d#) e, f, (gb) g, g#, a, bb, b} = C/a/F

The remaining eight sets are rejects. In sets 3), 6), and 22), the only keys present are C+ and a-. In sets 9), 12), 19), 25), and 28), the only key present is C+.

Conclusion: The only tonal dodecaphonic sets that can be expressed in terms of major and minor keys are those listed in Example 20-5, plus our extraordinary set I/i/II/vii/V.

The exercise that we have just completed can be regarded as a reflection of a lot of the work that we have been doing all along, but *in reverse*. In Part One, we dealt with nonatonic sets, and in Part Two we moved progressively to 10-tone, then 11-tone, and then 12-tone tonal sets. In this section, we began by listing the 32 possible 12-tone tonal sets (using the notes of C+ as a "given"), and found that 23 of these cannot be defined as combinations of specific major, plus specific minor, keys.

Next, we went into details, explaining *why* this is so. In three cases, one note had to be replaced by its enharmonic in order to create a workable 12-tone tonal set. But in the next 12 cases, it was not possible to do this. Instead, we had to *subtract* either one, or two, or three tones in order to end up with 11-tone, 10-tone, and 9-tone sets (respectively) that we had previously derived *by addition*. Finally, in the last eight cases, it was not possible to create any specific tonal sets having a cardinality higher than seven or eight.

It would, of course, be possible to list all our previously familiar nonatonic and decatonic tonal sets, as derived by subtraction, by continuing to eliminate a specific tone, or tones, from the 11-tone and 12-tone sets found in Example 20-4. But there is no sensible reason for doing that. The only objective of the present exercise was to show that no additional tonal 12-tone sets exist, and why.

We next take a quick look at set 5), which consists of all the notes contained in C/a/F/d/G/e. These, of course, are the six keys found at 11 o'clock, 12 o'clock, and 1 o'clock on the traditional quintcircle. The subsets here are A+, D+, and E+, or VI, II, and III. So another way to write this set is in the form I/vi/VI plus IV/ii/II plus V/iii/III with no subsets. It is easy to see why no composer has ever written a multi-tonal Sonata in C/a/F/d/G/e, let alone in C/a/A/F/d/D/G/e/E; the number of keys and tonal centres is much too high. Perhaps if Mozart was still living, he could think in six or nine keys at once, but the rest of us do well if we can manage two or three. That is why, if we use this set, we are better off to use it as A/a/D/d/E/e with subsets C, F, and G. Better still, we can suppress C, F, and G entirely.

* * *

We come now to the culminating point in our study of dodecaphonic tonal systems. Here, we will work exclusively with the sets I/i/IV/iv/V/v, I/i/II/ii/V/v, and I/i/IV/iv/♭VII/♭vii. We know from the previous chapter that we will add the twelfth tone to the 11-tone set I/i/V/v. So when C = I, we can add either c# or d♭. Both options must be examined, and the two must be thoroughly compared.

Case One results in the scale shown in Example 20-10 below.

Ex. 20-10 The set I/i/V/v plus the note c# (C = I)

The keys present in this set are C+, G+, D+, F+, B♭+, and E♭+, and c-, g-, and d-. So we have C/c/D/d/G/g, with subsets F, B♭, and E♭, the regular subsets of C/c. This situation is illustrated in Example 20-11 below in the form of a Venn Diagram, the type of diagram used most commonly in Set Theory to illustrate relationships of sets.

Ex. 20-11 Venn Diagram illustrating Ex. 20-10

(Venn diagram: I/i circle contains E♭, c; V/v circle contains g; II/ii circle contains D/d. Intersections: I/i ∩ V/v = B♭; I/i ∩ II/ii = (empty shown); V/v ∩ II/ii = G; center (all three) = C, F.)

Because the subsets of D/d and G/g are G, C, F, and C, F, B♭, respectively, they are all "home-grown;" the only "spare" subset in this system is E♭. This is the fantastic feature here — the system is very tightly knit. It is almost a closed system, but not quite, because of the presence of E♭+, which clashes with D/d.

Obviously, I/i/II/ii/V/v here is C/c/D/d/G/g. To get I/i/IV/iv/ V/v, we must let G = I, and when D = I, the set is I/i/IV/iv/ ♭VII/♭vii.

Case Two results in the scale shown in Example 20-12 below.

Ex. 20-12 The set I/i/V/v plus the note d♭ (C = I)

The keys belonging to this set are C+, G+, F+, B♭+, E♭+, and A♭+, and c-, g-, and f-. So the bi-modalities are C/c/F/f/G/g, and the subsets are B♭, E♭, and A♭. This situation is illustrated in Example 20-13 on the following page.

Ex. 20-13 Venn Diagram illustrating Ex. 20-12

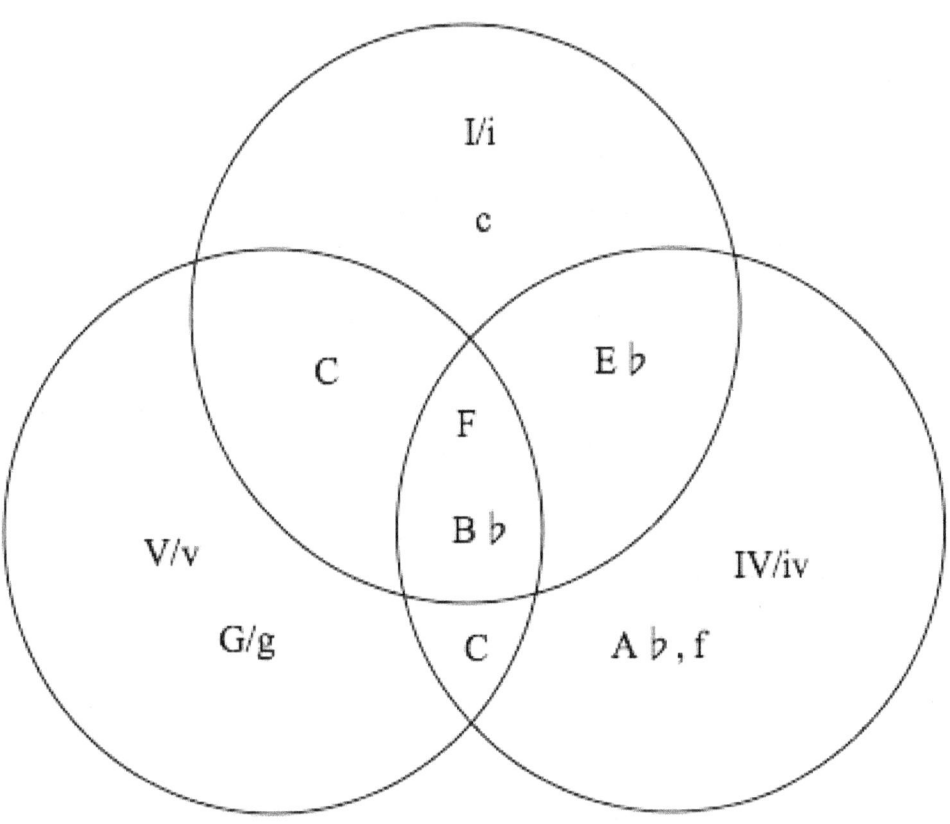

This time, we have C/c with its regular subsets, F, B♭, and E♭, and G/g with its subsets C, F, and B♭. But instead of D/d, the keys added are f- and A♭+. These two keys now become the "spare" subsets. This system is not as tightly knit as that of Case One, but the clash that exists is between G/g and A♭, neither of which is inside the C/c circle.

In this case, I/i/IV/iv/V/v is C/c/F/f/G/g. I/i/II/ii/V/v results if we let F + I, and when G = I, the set is I/i/IV/iv/♭VII/♭vii. So which of these two should we choose as our fundamental Dodecaphonic, Bi-modal system?

There is a story about Igor Stravinsky and a group of his students. It was unclear whether a specific note in a specific chord of one of his scores was supposed to be b-natural or b-flat. The students were about equally divided in their opinions of which it should be, and they had an opportunity to ask him, so they did. Stravinsky sat down at a piano, played the passage one way (with b-natural), then the other way (with b-flat). Then again the first way, and again the second way. First way ... second way ... first way ... second way ... first way ... second way. Finally, after a long pause, he looked up at them and said: "Eet coot be eeter."

Well, here also, it could be either. The reason for this is that in both cases, we have a combination of three consecutive bi-modalities on the Decaphonic quintcircle — these are actually identical sets! However, we are choosing which three bi-modalities we will place in the C/c (12 o'clock) position on the dodecaphonic quintcircle, and that is why there is a decision to be made.

We still have one more test to carry out, and that is the "chemistry experiment," in which we first add c#, and then d♭ instead, to our mixture of chords, and then compare the results, and see which resulting concoction is preferable.

When we add c#, it can be the root, third, or fifth of triads, or the root, third, fifth, or seventh of seventh chords. Example 20-14 below is a list of the chords that are formed.

Ex. 20-14 Resulting chords including c#

Triads having c# as root: (c#, eb, g), (c#, e, g)
Triads having c# as third: (ab, c#, eb), (ab, c#, e), (a, c#, eb), (a, c#, e)
Triads having c# as fifth: (f, ab, c#), (f#, ab, c#), (f, a, c#), (f#, a, c#)

Sevenths having c# as root: (c#, eb, g, b), (c#, eb, g, bb), (c#, e, g, b), (c#, e, g, bb)
Sevenths having c# as third: (ab, c#, eb, g), (ab, c#, e, g), (a, c#, eb, g), (a, c#, e, g)
Sevenths having c# as fifth: (f, ab, c#, eb), (f#, ab, c#, eb), (f, ab, c#, e), (f#, ab, c#, e), (f, a, c#, eb),
 (f#, a, c#, eb), (f, a c#, e), (f#, a, c#, e)
Sevenths having c# as seventh: (d, f, ab, c#), (d, f#, ab, c#), (d, f, a, c#), (d, f#, a, c#)

We can see here that the chords that are functional all relate to D/d. Some relate to G/g, but if we want to analyze them in C/c, the best that we can do is to regard them as V of V of V, or V of ii.

So now, in Example 20-15 below, we write out the triads and seventh chords that result when we use db instead of c#.

Ex. 20-15 Resulting chords including db

Triads having db as root: (db, f, ab), (db, f# ab), (db, f, a), (db, f#, a)
Triads having db as third: (bb, db, f), (bb, db, f#), (b, db, f), (b, db, f#)
Triads having db as fifth: (g, bb, db), (g, b, db)

Sevenths having db as root: (db, f, ab, c), (db, f#, ab, c), (db, f, a, c), (db, f#, a, c)
Sevenths having db as third: (bb, db, f, ab), (bb, db, f, a), (bb, db, f#, ab), (bb, db, f#, a),
 (b, db, f, ab), (b, db, f, a), (b, db, f#, ab), (b, db, f#, a)
Sevenths having db as fifth: (g, bb, db, f), (g, bb, db, f#), (g, b, db, f), (g, b, db, f#)
Sevenths having db as seventh: (eb, g, bb, db), (eb, g, b, db), (e, g, bb, db), (e, g, b, db)

In this case, the resulting chords are more useful, because we have gained augmented sixth chords, and the Neapolitan Sixth. Obviously, we needed that db to be able to achieve this. We have 10 new triads and 20 new seventh chords. The 10 new triads are analyzed in Example 20-16 on the following page.

Dodecaphonic (Twelve-Tone) Tonalities • 179

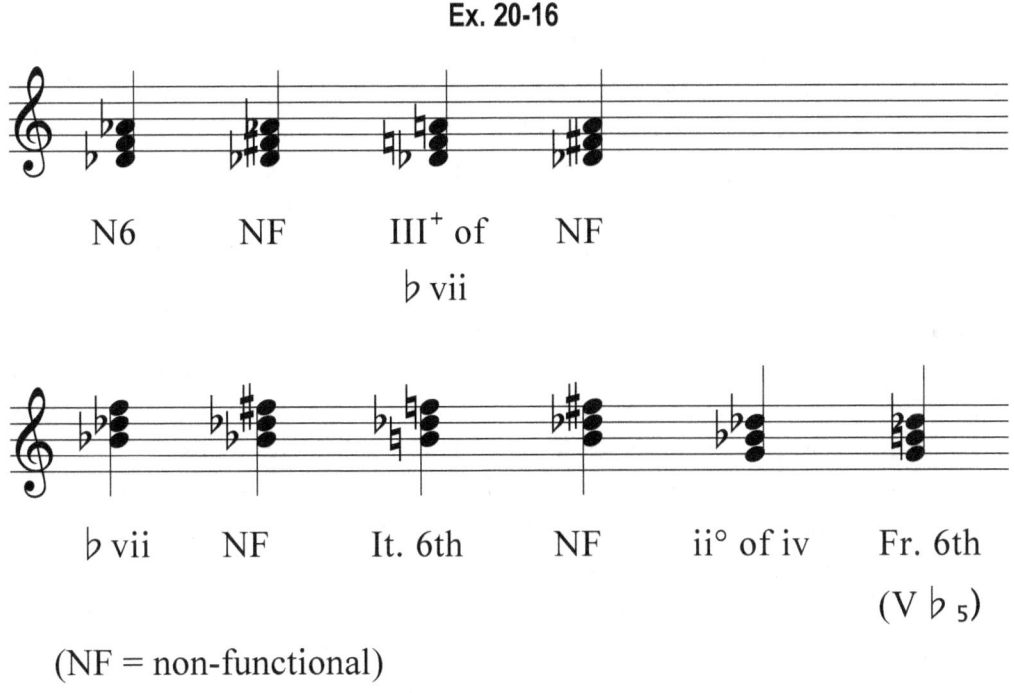

(NF = non-functional)

The 20 new seventh chords are analyzed in Example 20-17 below.

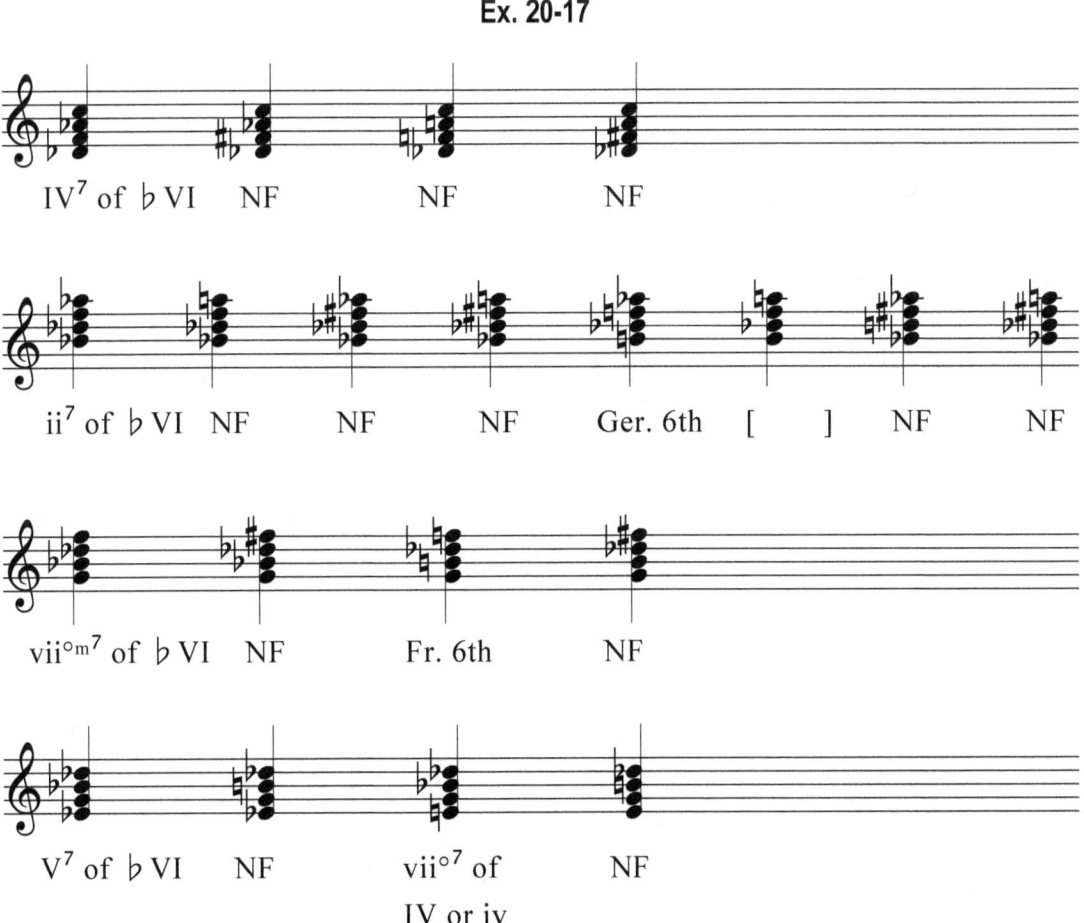

Fourteen of these 30 chords are functional, and sixteen are not. There are five new subdominant chords: the Neapolitan Sixth, ♭vii (= ♭iv of iv), ii° of iv, IV^7 of ♭VI, and ii^7 of ♭VI. The other nine functional chords have a dominant function. One of these is III$^+$ of ♭vii, which also has a mediant function, so we will be adding 15 chords to the house. Two of the triads are the Italian Sixth and the French Sixth (with the note f-natural omitted). Three of the seventh chords are vii°^{m7} of ♭VI, V^7 of ♭VI, and vii°^{7} of IV or iv. We also have the German Sixth and French Sixth (with the note f-natural included). The tenth seventh chord (b, d♭, f, a) is another version of what we called the "Polish Sixth" in Example 19-16 (which consisted of the notes f#, a♭, c, e). More will be said about functionality and non-functionality in the context of dodecaphonic tonality in the next chapter. For now, we add our 15 new chords (5 subdominant, 9 dominant, and 1 mediant), and construct our model of Dodecaphonic Bi-Modality. The final grand total of all chords is 90. The subtotals are as follows: Subdominant increases from 23 to 28, Dominant increases from 31 to 40, and Mediant increases from 9 to 10. Tonic remains at 5, and Submediant remains at 7. Example 20-18 on the next page consists of Example 19-16 plus our 15 new chords.

As was the case in previous chapters, some of the so-called "new" chords are not really new. But it is noteworthy that we had to go so far as to get to chords that relate to ♭VI before we finally encountered the Neapolitan Sixth chord, and the second set of augmented sixth chords, and were able to invite them into our house. With regard to augmented sixth chords in general, technically, these can be constructed on any scale degree, but they almost never are. So we include here only the two most commonly used sets, namely the ones that are derived from V^7 and V^7 of V. With that, at this point, there are no standard, commonly used chords left that are not diatonic, and left homeless.

Ex. 20-18

DODECAPHONIC BI-MODALITY

SUBDOMINANT GROUP	SUBMEDIANT GROUP	TONIC GROUP	MEDIANT GROUP	DOMINANT GROUP	
ii°, ii, iv, IV, ♭VI,	♭VI, ♭VI+, vi°, vi, ♭VIM⁷,	i, I, ♭VI,	♭III+, iii, iiim⁷	vii° of ♭III, ♭III = $V^{13}_{13\ 7}$ iii = $V^6_{\ 6}$	
ii° of v, IV⁷ of V, ii°m⁷, iim⁷, ii⁷ of II, ivm⁷, iim⁷ of ♭III, IV⁷, IV⁷ of ♭III, ii°m⁷ of v, ii⁷ of V	vi°m⁷, vim⁷	vi **1 new in Ex. 17-21:** ♭III	**4 new in Ex. 17-21:** ♭III, iii°, ♭IIIM⁷, iii°m⁷	V, vii°, V⁷, $V^{13}_{13\ 7}$ of iv, vii° of ♭VII, V⁷ of ♭VII, vii°m⁷ of ♭VII, vii⁷ of ♭VII, vii°⁷, vii°m⁷	**9 New in Ex. 20-18** III+ of ♭vii, It. 6th, Fr. 6th (=V♭5), vii⁷ of ♭VI, V⁷ of ♭VI, vii°⁷ of IV or iv, Ger. 6th, Fr. 6th (=V⁷♭5), "Polish 6th"
6 new in Ex. 17-21: IV of IV, ii⁷ of ♭VII, IV⁷ of ♭VII, ii⁷ of ii, ii⁷ of IV, IV⁷ of IV				**5 new in Ex. 17-21:** vii° of IV, v, V⁷ of IV, vii⁷ of IV, V⁷ of ♭III	31+9=40
22	7	5	7	18	
			16 New in Example 19-16:		
ii⁷ of vi,			III+ of v, iii of V	It. 6th, vii° of V or v,	"Polish 6th," vii°⁷ of v,
23			9	Fr. 6th (= V♭5 of V), Fr. 6th (= V⁷♭5 of V), V¹³ of v, V¹³ of V, Ger. 6th,	vii⁷ of V, V of V or v, V⁷ of V or v, V M⁷
5 New in Ex. 20-18 N6th, ♭vii, ii° of iv, IV⁷ of ♭VI, ii⁷ of ♭VI			**1 New in Ex. 20-18** III+ of ♭vii		
				31	
28	7	5	10	40	

182 • *Dodecaphonic Tonality*

Our next task is to write out the scales and key signatures for all 12 stations on the dodecaphonic quintcircle. The scales are fairly easy to do. In each case, we just write the chromatic scale, beginning on the tonic. The letter names of the tonic and the dominant are used only once; the other five letter names are used twice each, and accidentals are filled in as necessary. That way, we have that extra sharpened (or raised) note needed for the dominant key. As examples, the scales of C#/c#/F#/f#/G#/g# and A♭/a♭/D♭/d♭/E♭/e♭ appear as shown in Example 20-19 below.

Ex. 20-19 Two Dodecaphonic, Bi-Modal scales

The key signatures pose somewhat of a problem. There are no excluded tones now, and the appearance of three key signatures showing three bi-modalities is ridiculous, extremely confusing, and almost meaningless. We must resort, *albeit reluctantly*, to a different method. Each of our triple bi-modalities can be re-written as the sum of two major keys whose roots lay a semitone apart. In the case of C/c/F/f/G/g, there is one sharp and four flats, so the two keys are G+ and A♭+, or G/A♭. This indication is extremely misleading, so it is an absolute *must* to write out the three bi-modalities in each case. Example 20-20 on the next page shows all twelve "sandwiches" (triple-Decas), their corresponding bi-tonalities of the form I/♭II, and the accidentals that will be used in their key signatures.

Ex. 20-20 All 12 Triple-Deca sets

Triple-Deca Set	I/♭II	Accidentals for Key Signatures
C / c / F / f / G / g	G / A♭	f# / b♭, e♭, a♭, d♭
G / g / C / c / D / d	D / E♭	f#, c# / b♭, e♭, a♭
D / d / G / g / A / a	A / B♭	f#, c#, g# / b♭, e♭
A / a / D / d / E / e	E / F	f#, c#, g#, d# / b♭
E / e / A / a / B / b	B / C	f#, c#, g#, d#, a# / ( )
B / b / E / e / F# / f#	F# / G	f#, c#, g#, d#, a#, e# / f#
F# / f# / B / b / C# / c#	C# / D	f#, c#, g#, d#, a#, e#, b# / f#, c#
C# / c# / F# / f# / G# / g#	G# / A	fx, c#, g#, d#, a#, e#, b# / f#, c#, g#
A♭ / a♭ / D♭ / d♭ / E♭ / e♭	E♭ / F♭	b♭, e♭, a♭ / b♭♭, e♭, a♭, d♭, g♭, c♭, f♭
E♭ / e♭ / A♭ / a♭ / B♭ / b♭♭	B♭ / C♭	b♭, e♭ / b♭, e♭, a♭, d♭, g♭, c♭, f♭
B♭ / b♭ / E♭ / e♭ / F / f	F / G♭	b♭ / b♭, e♭, a♭, d♭, g♭, c♭
F / f / B♭ / b♭ / C / c	C / D♭	( ) / b♭, e♭, a♭, d♭, g♭

NOTE: G#+ and F♭+ are theoretical keys, having 8 sharps and 8 flats, respectively, but we have to use them, because it is necessary to choose either all sharps or all flats.

The key signatures for all 12 dodecaphonic bi-modalities are written out in Example 20-21 on the following page.

184 • *Dodecaphonic Tonality*

Ex. 20-21 Key Signatures for all 12 Dodecaphonic Bi-Modalities

NOTE: Here again, the key signature should be stated only once, at the beginning of the composition (as we always do with the time signature). We could also start a new trend here, and state the key signature only in print, and forget about the accidentals entirely.

We can now write out the Triple-Decaphonic, or Dodecaphonic, Bi-modal Quintcircle; this is done in Example 20-22 on the next page.

Ex. 20-22

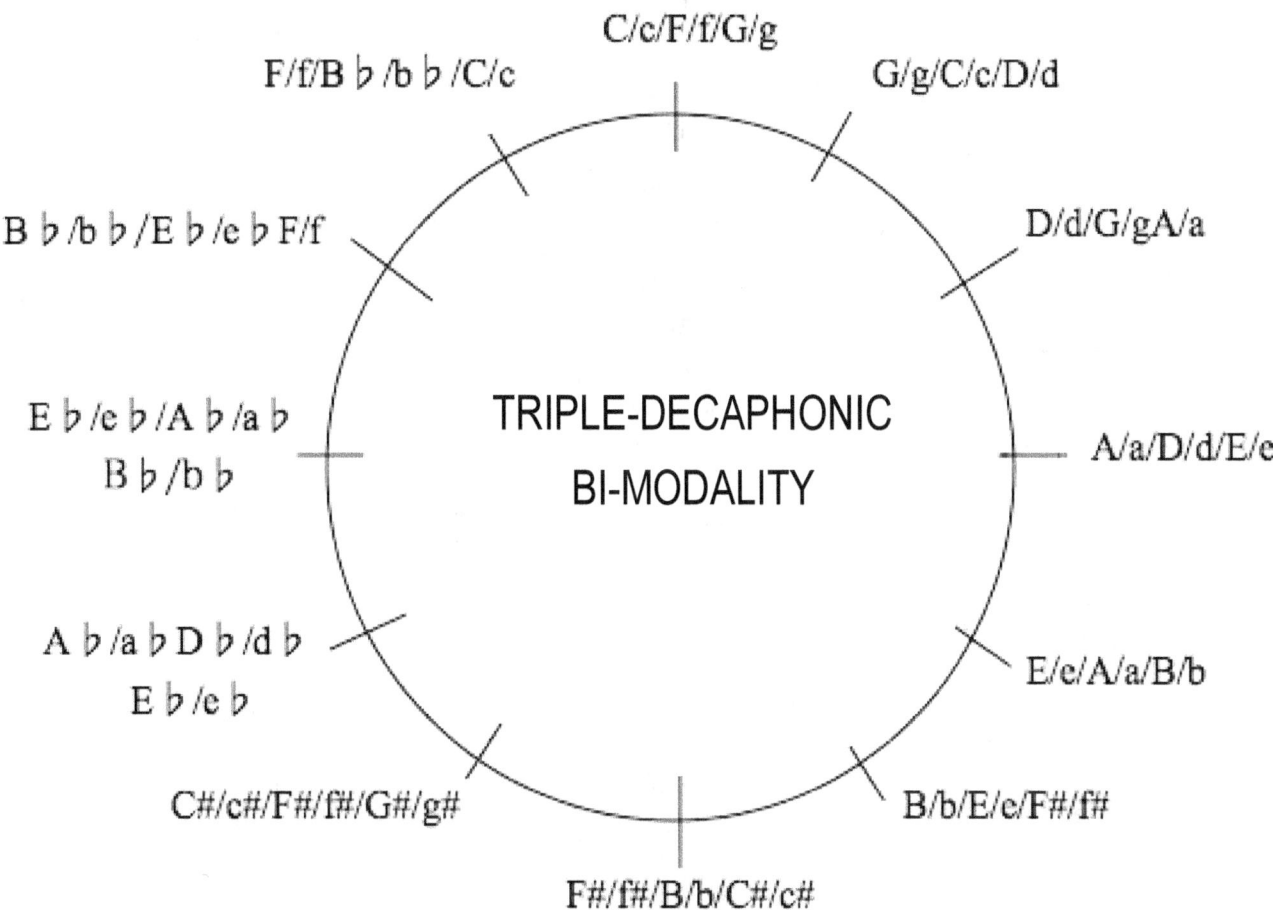

Our last task in this chapter is to calculate the chromatic clashes of SATs for our dodecaphonic sets, and to compare the totals. Chart 20-1 on the next page shows the calculations and totals for our "jigsaw puzzle set," where C = I. Next, Chart 20-2 shows the same for the traditional set I/vi/IV/ii/V/iii, where C = I. Finally, Chart 20-3 shows the data for our Triple-Deca sets, I/i/IV/iv/V/v, I/i/II/ii/V/v, and I/i/IV/iv/♭VII/♭vii. These all have the same chromatic clashes, because all three are comprised of C/c plus F/f plus G/g.

Chart 20-1

PAIRS OF KEYS	SATS	CHROMATIC CLASHES	SAT CLASH POINT VALUE	CLASH STRENGTH
C/c	c e g b c eb g b	e (third) eb (third)	3 + 3	6
C/D	c e g b d f# a c#	c (root) c# (l. n.)	4 + 2	+ 6
C/b	c e g b b d f# a#	c (root) b (root)	4 + 4	+ 8
	c e g b b d f# a#	g (fifth) f# (fifth)	1 + 1	+ 2
	c e g b b d f# a#	b (l. n.) a# (l. n.)	2 + 2	+ 4
C/G	c e g b g b d f#	——— ———	0 + 0	+ 0
c/D	c eb g b d f# a c#	c (root) c# (l. n.)	Duplicate	+ 0
c/b	c eb g b b d f# a#	c (root) b (root)	Duplicate	+ 0
	c eb g b b d f# a#	eb (third) d (third)	3 + 3	+ 6
	c eb g b b d f# a#	g (fifth) f# (fifth)	Duplicate	+ 0
	c eb g b b d f# a#	b (l. n.) a# (l.n.)	2 + 2	+ 4
c/G	c eb g b g b d f#	——— ———	0 + 0	+ 0
D/b	d f# a c# b d f# a#	a (fifth) a# (l.n.)	1 + 2	+ 3
D/G	d f# a c# g b d f#	——— ———	0 + 0	+ 0
b/G	b d f# a# g b d f#	——— ———	0 + 0	+ 0
				39

Chart 20-2

PAIRS OF KEYS	SATS	CHROMATIC CLASHES	SAT CLASH POINT VALUE	CLASH STRENGTH
C/a	c e g b a c e g#	g (fifth) g# (l. n.)	1 + 2	3
C/F	c e g b f a c e	——— ———	0 + 0	+ 0
C/d	c e g b d f a c#	c (root) c# (l.n.)	4 + 2	+ 6
C/G	c e g b g b d f#	——— ———	0 + 0	+ 0
C/e	c e g b e g b d#	——— ———	0 + 0	+ 0
a/F	a c e g# f a c e	——— ———	0 + 0	+ 0
a/d	a c e g# d f a c#	c (third) c# (l.n.)	Duplicate	+ 0
a/G	a c e g# g b d f#	g# (l.n.) g (root)	Duplicate	+ 0
a/e	a c e g# e g b d#	g# (l.n.) g (third)	Duplicate	+ 0
F/d	f a c e d f a c#	c (fifth) c# (l.n.)	Duplicate	+ 0
F/G	f a c e g b d f#	f (root) f# (l.n.)	4 + 2	+ 6
F/e	f a c e e g b d#	f, c, e e, b d#	4 1 2 + 4, + 1, + 2	+ 14
d/G	d f a c# g b d f#	f (third) f# (l.n.)	Duplicate	+ 0
d/e	d f a c# e g b d#	d (root) d# (l.n.)	4 + 2	+ 6
G/e	g b d f# e g b d#	d (fifth) d# (l.n.)	Duplicate	+ 0
				35

Chart 20-3

PAIRS OF KEYS	SATS	CHROMATIC CLASHES	SAT CLASH POINT VALUE	CLASH STRENGTH
C/c	c e g b c e♭ g b	e (third) e♭ (third)	3 + 3	6
C/F	c e g b f a c e	——— ———	0 + 0	+ 0
C/f	c e g b f a♭ c e	——— ———	0 + 0	+ 0
C/G	c e g b g b d f#	——— ———	0 + 0	+ 0
C/g	c e g b g b♭ d f#	b (l.n.) b♭ (third)	2 + 3	+ 5
c/F	c e♭ g b f a c e	e♭ (third) e (l.n.)	Duplicate	+ 0
c/f	c e♭ g b f a♭ c e	e♭ (third) e (l.n.)	Duplicate	+ 0
c/G	c e♭ g b g b d f#	——— ———	0 + 0	+ 0
c/g	c e♭ g b g b♭ d f#	b (l.n.) b♭ (third)	Duplicate	+ 0
F/f	f a c e f a♭ c e	a (third) a♭ (third)	3 + 3	+ 6
F/G	f a c e g b d f#	f (root) f# (l.n.)	4 + 2	+ 6
F/g	f a c e g b♭ d f#	f (root) f# (l.n.)	Duplicate	+ 0
f/G	f a♭ c e g b d f#	f (root) f# (l.n.)	Duplicate	+ 0
f/g	f a c e g b♭ d f#	f (root) f# (l.n.)	Duplicate	+ 0
G/g	g b d f# g b♭ d f#	b (third) b♭ (third)	3 + 3 = 6 - 5 duplicated	+ 1
				24

Example 20-23 below summarizes our results. It is actually a continuation of Example 19-11.

Ex. 20-23 Continuation of Ex. 19-11

SET	KEYS	TONAL CENTRES	CARDINALITY	CLASH INTENSITY
I/i/II/vii/V	5	4	12	39
I/vi/IV/ii/V/iii	6	6	12	35
I/i/IV/iv/V/v and I/i/II/ii/V/v and I/i/IV/iv/♭VII/♭vii	6	3	12	24

Clearly, our Triple-Deca set has the lowest clash intensity rating. But we can lower it even more by performing some "explainable magic." In the Triple-Deca system, duplications occur even more often than in the Double-Deca case of the previous chapter. The set I/i/II/ii/V/v can be regarded as I/i/II/ii with subset V/v (because of the "in between" rule). And in the set I/i/II/ii, the six combinations are I/i + I/II + I/ii + i/II + i/ii + II/ii. Since each combination involves 6 point values, if we just added them up, the total would be 36. But in Chart 20-3, if we let F = I, G = II, and C = V, then there are actually only three different chromatic clashes: a/a♭ in I/i, b♭/b in II/ii, and f/f# in the other four combinations. So the total is only (3+3) + (3+3) + (4+2) = 18, and the last line above now appears as follows:

I/i/II/ii and IV/iv/V/v and I/i/♭VII/♭vii	4	2	12	18

It should be noted that these are *not* Double-Deca sets (because those are two *consecutive* bi-modalities on the dodecaphonic quintcircle). These are still Triple-Deca sets, having a cardinality of 12, but the set that lays in between the other two (on the Dodecaphonic quintcircle) is treated as a subset. This means that the composer has a choice of raising or lowering the clash intensity rating by using it, or by refraining from doing so.

* * *

At this point, we have all but reached the end of our long journey in quest of dodecaphonic tonal sets. We have some more analysis to do, in the next chapter, with regard to functionality in 12-tone tonality. But we can end this chapter with the following conclusion, which readers should memorize.

THE WORLD'S BEST DODECAPHONIC TONAL SYSTEM IS COMPRISED OF THE SUM OF THE THREE UNI-TONAL BI-MODALITIES I/i, IV/iv, AND V/v, OR ITS EQUIVALENT SETS, I/i/II/ii/V/v, OR I/i/IV/iv/♭VII/♭vii, WHICH CAN BE REDUCED TO THE SETS IV/iv/V/v, OR I/i/II/ii, OR I/i/♭VII/♭vii, RESPECTIVELY. AMEN.

CHAPTER TWENTY-ONE:

Dodecaphonic Tonality and Functionality

We now have our precious model of dodecaphonic tonality. In this chapter, we take a closer look at it, and see how we can make it work. Since traditional tonality, unless otherwise stated, naturally implies functionality of chords, this will be the focus of our study.

Just before we start, a paragraph is in order regarding non-functionality, in case any readers were bothered by how many times they saw "NF" in the preceding chapter (where 16/30 chords were labeled as such). When we repeatedly pick one note from here, one from there, a third one from "over there," and perhaps a fourth one from "way over there," and combine them, inevitably, we will end up with "nonsense chords," which people would normally never write. For example, the "seventh" chord consisting of the notes "b-d♭-f#-a" makes no sense from the structural standpoint, because it includes a diminished third and an augmented third. And the spelling of the triad "b♭-d♭-f#" is senseless, because one can write "b♭-d♭-g♭" instead. The reason that so many of these types of chords appeared is that we considered every possible triad and seventh chord that it was possible to construct using the 12 notes which comprise C/c/F/f/G/g. And the only reason we did that was to make sure that we did not miss out on any useful chords. So, the appropriate expression here is: "Not to worry." We simply ignore the junk, and work with the good stuff.

The great German music theorist, Hugo Riemann (born on the same day as this author, but 105 years earlier), declared, in 1893, that in functional harmony, there are three and only three functions, and that every chord can be categorized as belonging to at least one of these. Today, rather than playing "true or false" with this statement, we will focus on the "at least" portion of it.

If, in traditional tonality, some chords can be shown to be bi-functional, or even tri-functional, then does it not make perfect sense that in our 12-tone, 6-key, 3-tonal-centre system, even more chords have more than one function? This is what we have to explore.

To begin, let us re-write Example 20-11, which illustrates the set I/i/II/ii/V/v, and this time use F/f = I/i (because we are now working with C/c, F/f, and G/g only). This is done in Example 21-1 on the following page.

Dodecaphonic Tonality and Functionality • 191

Ex. 21-1 Venn Diagram of I/i/II/ii/V/v, where F/f = I/i

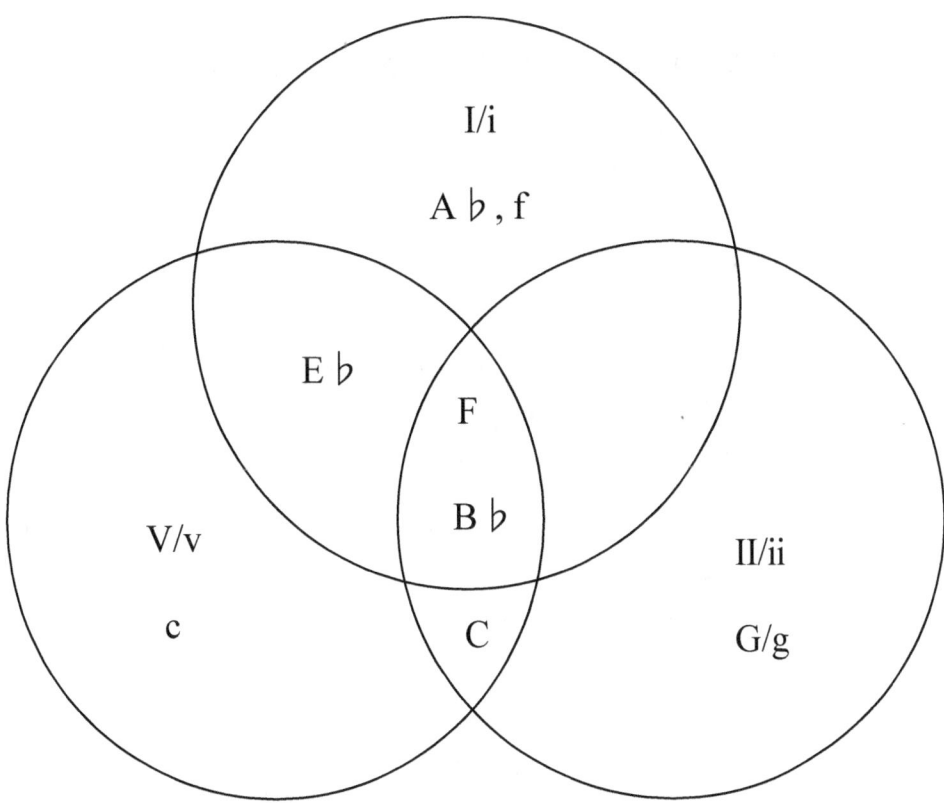

Example 20-13 illustrates the set I/i/IV/iv/V/v; it is reproduced below for ease of reference.

Copy of Ex. 20-13 Venn Diagram illustrating I/i/IV/iv/V/v, where C/c = I/i

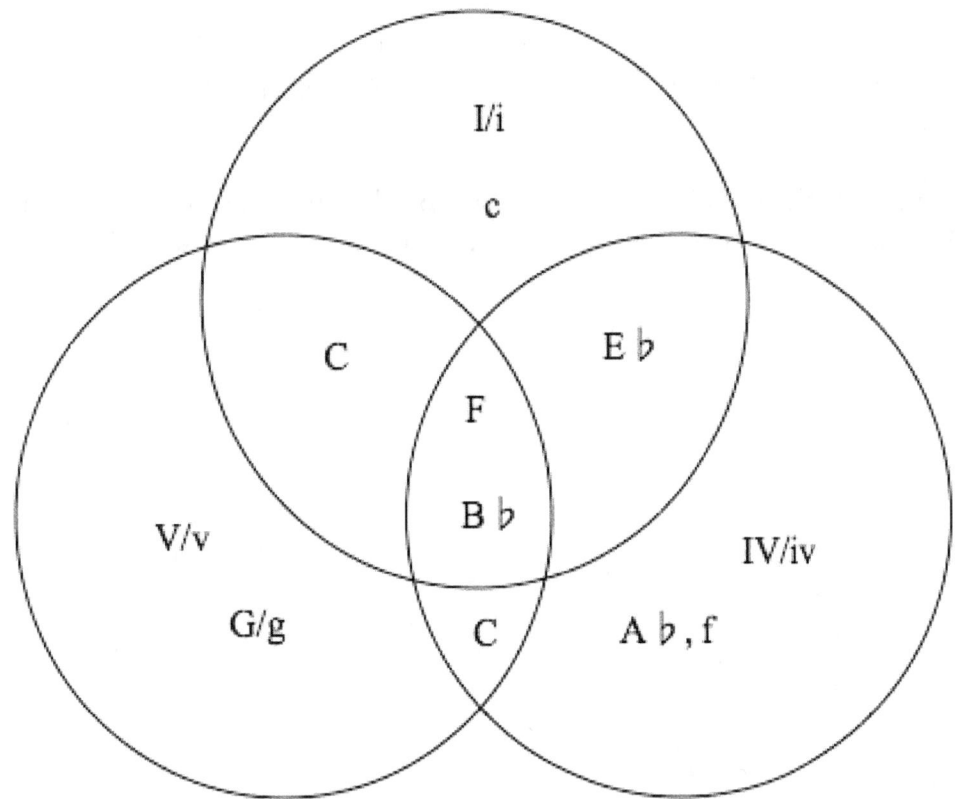

Now we still have to illustrate I/i/IV/iv/♭VII/♭vii; this is done in Example 21-2 below.

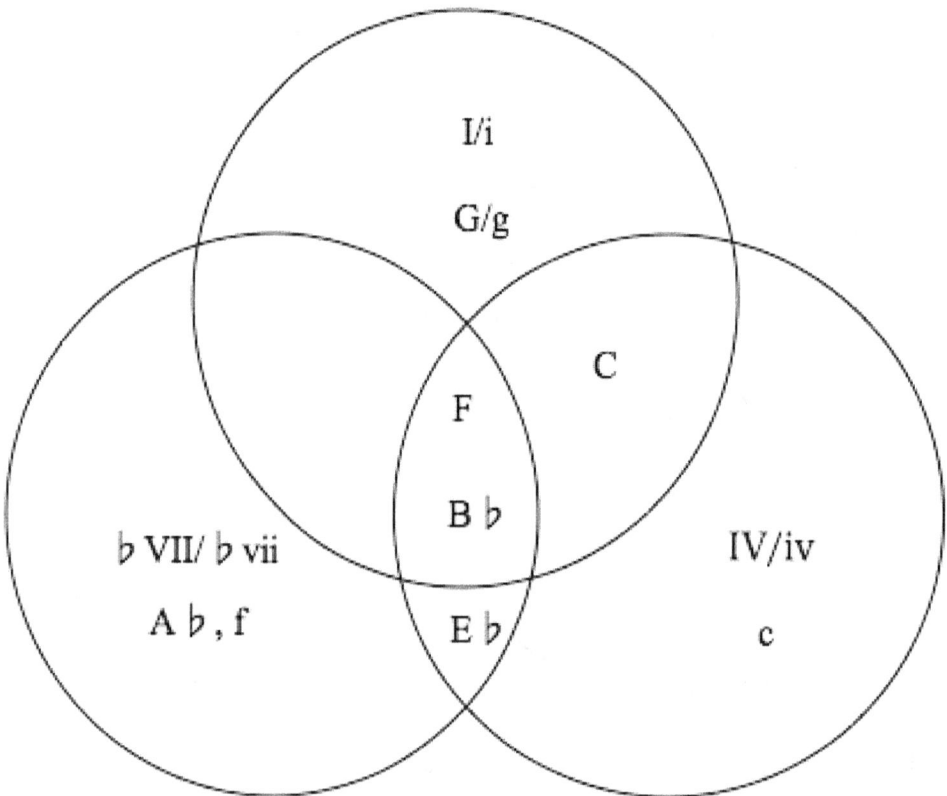

Ex. 21-2 Venn Diagram of I/i/IV/iv/♭VII/♭vii, where G/g = I/i

We can see in these three diagrams that F and B♭ remain in the central ("white") zone, while the remaining seven keys rotate around them, from one diagram to the next, from one peripheral zone to the next ("red" to "blue" to "green").

We now summarize all of this (and more) in two charts of all 26 triads found in our system. The first chart, 21-1, shows all 18 triads, and their harmonic symbols, that are found in all three keys when C/c = I/i, or F/f = I/i, or G/g = I/i.

Chart 21-1

Triad:	C	c	D♭	D♭+	D	d	d°	E♭	E♭+	e	e°	F	f
I/i													
C/c	I	i	*	*	*	ii	ii	♭III	♭III	iii	iii	IV	iv
G/g	IV	iv	NF	NF	V	v	*	♭VI	♭VI	vi	vi	♭VII	*
F/f	V	v	♭VI	♭VI	NF	vi	vi	♭VII	*	*	vii	I	i

Triad:	f#°	G	g	g°	A♭	A♭+	a	a°	B♭	B♭+	b♭	b	b°
I/i													
C/c	*	V	v	*	♭VI	♭VI	vi	vi	♭VII	*	*	*	vii
G/g	vii	I	i	NF	*	*	ii	ii	♭III	♭III	NF	iii	iii
F/f	NF	*	ii	ii	♭III	♭III	iii	iii	IV	NF	iv	NF	*

These 18 triads also include the following chords that are present in two of the three keys, but absent in the third key. Their locations are marked with 16 asterisks * in the chart.

CHORD	PRESENT IN	ABSENT IN	REASON
N6	C/c, G/g	F/f	note g♭ is missing
♭II+	C/c, G/g	F/f	note g♭ is missing
V of V	C/c, F/f	G/g	note c# is missing
vii° of V	C/c, F/f	G/g	note c# is missing
v°	C/c, G/g	F/f	note g♭ is missing
♭VII+	C/c, F/f	G/g	note c# is missing
♭vii	C/c, G/g	F/f	note g♭ is missing
vii	C/c, F/f	G/g	note g♭ is missing

The total number of functional chords is (18 x 3) + (8 x 2) = 70. This leaves us with eight triads that are non-functional (marked NF in the chart). Four are in G/g: D♭, D♭+, g°, b♭, and four are in F/f: D, f#°, B♭+, b. That accounts for all 26 x 3 = 78 chords.

Next, we draw up Chart 21-2, which shows the functions of the 70 functional chords found in Chart 21-1. The number of different functions that each triad can have is shown at the bottom of each column.

Chart 21-2

I/i	C	c	D♭	D♭+	D	d	d°	E♭	E♭+	e	e°	F	f
C/c	T	T	S	D	D	S	S	M	M	M	M	S	S
G/g	S	S	NF	NF	D	-D	S	SM	SM	SM	SM	S	S
F/f	D	D	SM	SM	NF	SM	SM	S	M	M	D	T	T
Total	3	3	2	2	1	3	2	3	2	2	3	2	2

I/i	f#°	G	g	g°	A♭	A♭+	a	a°	B♭	B♭+	b♭	b	b°
C/c	D	D	-D	S	SM	SM	SM	SM	S	M	S	M	D
G/g	D	T	T	NF	S	D	S	S	M	M	NF	M	M
F/f	NF	D	S	S	M	M	M	M	S	NF	S	NF	D
Total	1	2	3	1	3	3	3	3	2	1	1	1	2

Out of the 26 triads, 6 have only one function. 10 are bi-functional, and 10 are tri-functional. From the horizontal viewpoint, each bi-modality has 2 Tonic functions. C/c has 6 Dominant functions; G/g has 4, and F/f has 5. C/c and G/g have 8 Subdominant functions each; F/f has 5. C/c and F/f have 6 Mediant functions each; G/g has 4. Each bi-modality has 4 Submediant functions. The –D in each bi-modality is the minor dominant. So the totals are as follows: T: 6, D: 15, S: 21, M: 16, SM: 12, NF: 8, for a total of 3 x 26 = 78 chords. With regard to the non-functional chords, some authors would label some of these as chromatic mediant or doubly chromatic mediant relationships. But in terms of functionality, just how far do we want to push the concept of "relationship," anyway? Maybe they should be called "unrelationships." It is too much like calling a relative your tenth cousin, four times removed. So we leave them marked NF.

* * *

Throughout this study, we have been constructing our house (or library) of chords, categorized by functions, in a cumulative manner. Since this was done progressively, using C = I, the only logical thing to do in Examples 19-16 and 20-18 was to stay the course, and to continue to regard chords as they relate to C/c = I/i, and so we did. However, in Example 19-17 (the Double-Deca quintcircle) and in Example 20-22 (the Triple-Deca quintcircle), there are two and three bi-modalities (respectively) occupying each station. Does this not imply that two and three tonic keys (respectively) are present in these systems? It certainly does. Since Charts 21-1 and 21-2 reflect this, they actually serve as more accurate models of the Triple-Deca Tonality I/i/IV/iv/V/v than does Example 20-18. Missing from the charts, of course, are the seventh chords and augmented sixth chords. Readers can add these themselves, and then the two models will look very similar.

Back in Chapter Fourteen, in Example 14-8, we already got a taste of what equivalent sets are like, when we saw that the sets I/V/vi and I/IV/ii are interchangeable. Now, we are again dealing with equivalent sets, but this time, there are three of them, consisting of three bi-modalities each. (Incidentally, "equivalent" (symbolized by ~) means "capable of being placed into one-to-one correspondence," while "equal" means "identical").

All of these observations, taken together, lead to the conclusion that C/c, G/g, and F/f, as well as every set of three bi-modalities found at every other station in Example 20-22, are not just any three disjoint bi-modalities; they are "One for all and all for one" sets; they are…The Three Musketeers! (C/c is MiC/c-key, G/g is G/goofy, and F/f is DaF/fy).* Chart 21-1 is their house, a very long, three-bedroom bungalow (with a flat roof).

This is one of two key concepts required to have an understanding of how the Triple-Deca system works. The other is to think of each bi-modality as *one* key, rather than two, because there is only one tonal centre, a common dominant, and two common subdominants. Taken individually, each bi-modality can be regarded as Nonaphonic, having no subsets. However, in each case, the tenth tone is found in each of the other two bi-modalities, so taken all together, they all end up being Decaphonic sets.

We began with the bi-modality C/c. However, when combined with G/g plus F/f, C/c can actually be regarded as a subset of the other two (because of the "in-between" rule). But then again, when Mickey, Goofy, and Daffy stand in a circle and hold hands, which one of them is in the middle?

The rest of this chapter is about what could have been done, but was not done, and why. There is another way to combine the bi-modal sets I/i/IV/iv/V/v, I/i/II/ii/V/v, and I/i/IV/iv/♭VII/♭vii, and that is by letting C = I, and leaving it that way. If we were to do that, then II/ii would be D/d, and ♭VII/♭vii would be B♭/b♭. That would mean that we would have to add to our set the note c# (the leading note of D/d), and the note g♭ (the sixth scale degree of b♭-). So we would have a 12-tone, 14-note set, with two enharmonics. Also, we would be adding not just D/d, but the key of D♭+, which would give us five bi-modalities, and thus sabotage our tightly knit set. At this point, the more enharmonics, the bigger the mess; that is why we avoid adding them.

Example 21-3 below illustrates what this situation would look like.

Ex. 21-3

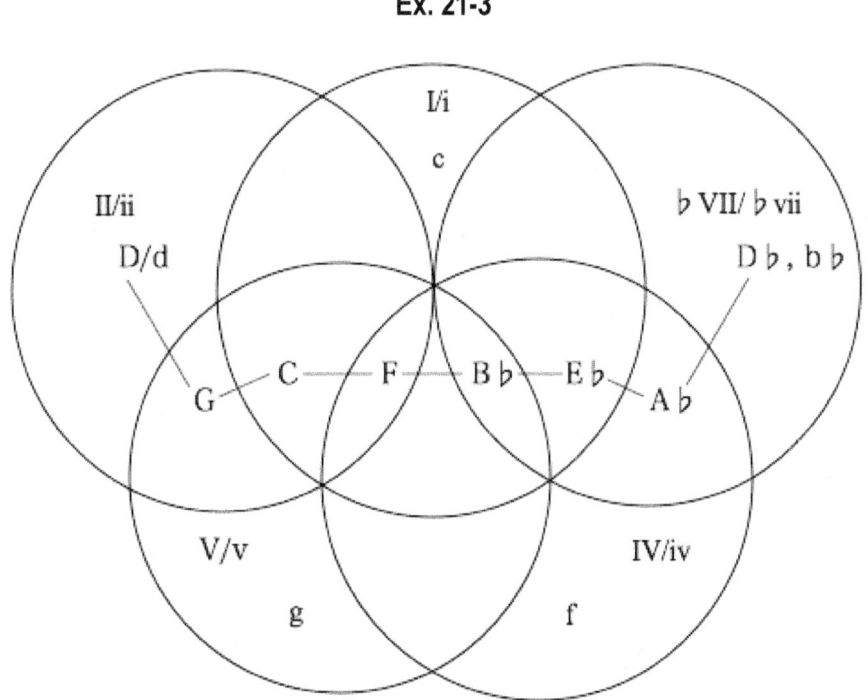

---

*Memorization techniques work for people of all ages, not just children.

As we can see, *this* I/i/II/ii/V/v, and *this* I/i/IV/iv/♭VII/♭vii, when superimposed on the same I/i/IV/iv/V/v that is shown in Example 20-13, is very much different. When C = I in all three cases, we no longer have "One for all and all for one." We have a string of eight major keys, as shown by the lines in Example 21-3. If we added D/d and B♭/b♭ to Chart 21-2, many columns would have a functional symbol in one of these two rows, and an NF symbol in the other. That is what happens when the given sets are not equivalent or interchangeable. The result is not good. Let us stick with "The Three Musketeers."

CHAPTER TWENTY-TWO

"Tonality, Atonality, Pantonality" by Rudolph Réti

This chapter, and the next two, can be considered as "optional chapters." Nevertheless, all three have their own special contribution to make to this study. It is easy enough to find writings in the literature on the topics of "bi-tonality" and "polytonality," but on the topic of "bi-modality," there is little more than a basic dictionary definition to be found. There is, however, a book entitled "Tonality, Atonality, Pantonality" by Rudolph Réti (1885 — 1957), and it contains some material that relates to some aspects of our study of bi-modality. In this chapter, we paraphrase some of Réti's ideas, and examine how they relate to our system.

In Part One (Tonality), Réti explains that the "tonical" effect in classical tonality is rooted in harmony and harmonic progressions, so this type of tonality can justifiably be called *harmonic tonality*. (p. 13) He adds, though, that there is another type of tonality that is manifested through melody only, and this type of tonality is what he calls *melodic tonality*. (p. 17) In addition, he claims that some of the works of Mahler and Strauss are examples of a tonal style that could be called *expanded tonality*. (p. 21). Furthermore, he claims that in Debussy's melodic lines, *melodic tonality plus modulation is modern tonality*. (p. 23) He says that Debussy's successions of parallel chords are in essence not harmonies at all, but rather 'chordal melodies,' enriched unisons. (p. 27)

"Melodic tonality" and "expanded tonality" are fitting descriptions of our bi-modal system as well. The more tones or notes we add, the more expanded the tonality becomes, simply because at every stage, the diatonic family grows. That is obvious when we compare each "house" example to the previous one. But the concept of melodic tonality matches that of bi-modality even better, because if we write a melody in which we constantly, repeatedly alternate between the major and minor thirds and sixths, then the result is already bi-modal, even if we never harmonize our melody. From that point of view, perhaps not enough emphasis was placed throughout this study on counterpoint. Maybe we should have started writing a fugue back in Part One, and kept adding and adding voices to it as we studied 10- and 11- and 12-tone sets. At this point, this is an appropriate homework assignment for interested "fuguealists" (writers of fugues).

Part Two of Réti's book, on Atonality, contains at least three passages which are relevant to our study. The first of these states that there is no scale of gradation set up in musical theory for dissonances. Réti says that theoretically, there is no difference in degree of dissonance between, for example, an augmented fourth and a major seventh, because both must be prepared and resolved according to specific rules. (p. 38)

In writing this, Mr. Réti certainly has identified an area in which music theorists have fallen behind. But the reason for this has been that the topic of consonance and dissonance belongs just as much to the field of musical acoustics as it does to that of music theory. Over half a century has passed since Mr. Réti wrote this, and during that time, much has been done in the field of musical acoustics.* Let us look back again at Example 13-4, which shows intervals in order from most consonant to most dissonant. Does this solve the problem, and answer the question? Only partly, because the just scale is older than equal temperament; people have known of these ratios

---

*Even this author made a small contribution in 1978, when he wrote his master's thesis entitled "The Fundamental Mathematical and Acoustical Properties of Woodwind and Brass Instruments," University of British Columbia, Vancouver, Canada.

for centuries. Example 13-4 shows the *relative order of proximity* of the other 11 tones to the fundamental. We cannot automatically conclude from this order, for example, that the major third c-e is more consonant than the minor sixth c-ab, or the major third ab-c. Also, it matters a great deal whether we are speaking of melodic (horizontal) or harmonic (vertical) intervals. However, Example 13-4 does provide the best answer that we have to the problem outlined by Mr. Réti.

And now, what about our chromatic clashes of SATs and their various point values that we have been using? Well, these are, in fact, a scale of gradation for one dissonance (the semitone), but on a different plane. We are not comparing intervals, but we are speaking of *relative* degrees of dissonances between a specific pair (or set) of keys as compared to others.

The second passage found in the section on Atonality that is relevant to our study is Réti's statement that the atonal, 12-tone concept makes no distinction between consonance and dissonance, and, in fact, declares the whole phenomenon of harmony non-existent. He argues that whether this concept is maintainable at all remains doubtful, and adds that the entire history of 12-tone technique seems to point to the contrary. (p. 47)

This passage is thought-provoking, because it implies that even if one deliberately sets out to write an atonal composition, elements of tonality are still present in the final result, even if it be in small proportion.

When one has been reading or playing or analyzing music for 10, 20, 30, 40, or (in this author's case) 50 years, or even longer, it is almost impossible to look at a 12-tone row and see it the same way that one sees a dozen eggs or 12 cans of Coke! One automatically, instinctively, relates each note to the preceding and following one(s). In fact, unless you do exactly that, how are you to go about memorizing atonal music?

A blatant example of this is the tone row of the famous Berg Violin Concerto, shown in Example 22-1 below.

Ex. 22-1

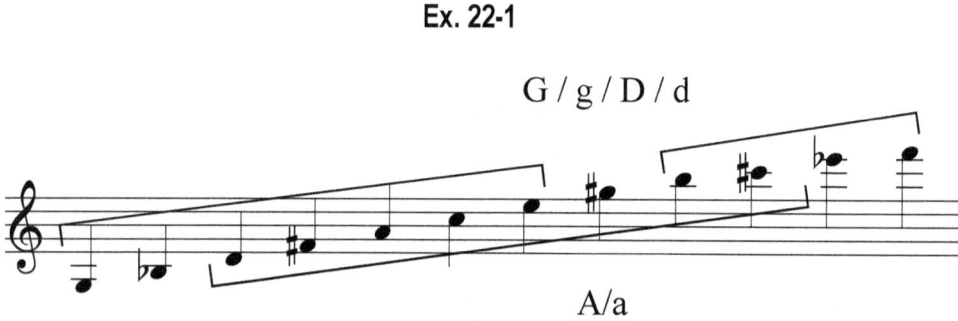

It is obvious that what we have here is the g- triad, followed by its V^7 (with the note d in common), followed by the a- triad (with the notes a and c overlapping), followed by its V (with the note e in common), followed by the three leftover notes. But there is more to it than that, as shown in the example. This tone row, minus the note g#, is our 11-note set G/g/D/d, and tones 3 to 10 inclusive are 8 of the 9 notes of our nonatonic set, A/a. So altogether, we have here our triple-deca set D/d/G/g/A/a, which occupies the 2 o'clock station on our quintcircle.

There is even more. Rudolph Réti mentions (in Part Three of his book, on p. 140) that in his Violin Concerto, Berg makes a clear attempt to blend the 12-tone technique, that is, atonality, and tonal ideas into one unified style. Towards the end of the work, he uses the key signature of two flats. And what is our key signature for D/d/G/g/A/a? Just exactly what you see in this tone row: 3 sharps and 2 flats.

People say that in atonal music, enharmonics are interchangeable. If that were the case, then we could re-write Berg's tone row as shown in Example 22-2 on page 199, could we not?

Ex. 22-2

Which keys would be present in this case? The "default key," (C major), and no others. The point of doing all this is that it relates back to something that was said way back at the beginning of Part One: The notes that a composer chooses to use are his raw materials. Berg deliberately constructed a "tonal atonal" row. So even in atonal music, enharmonics have an effect on the result. But in tonal music, the set of notes chosen, with its specific cardinality, and its specific components, is of paramount importance in the final outcome.

The third point that Réti makes in this part, that is relevant to our study, is that it is astounding that a stylistic bridge, a gradual, organic expansion and loosening of tonality as we see in the works of Reger and Strauss, is almost missing in [Schoenberg's] music. Réti claims that Schoenberg shunned any intermediary state and, instead, turned from outright tonality to outright atonality. (p. 33)

This is precisely what has been referred to in this study as "the gap" between the "premature end" of tonality and the advent of atonality. What remains to be done is an investigation into the works of composers such as Reger and Strauss (and Mahler, and Sibelius, and others) to ascertain to what extent these composers used bi-modality and 12-tone tonality in those of their works which partially filled in "the gap." This is a good homework assignment for interested "tonalists" (scholars of tonal music).

Part Three is the last and longest part of Réti's book, and it is entitled "Pantonality." There is no section on bitonality, or polytonality, or bi-modality, but references are made to various types of tonalities. For example, he speaks of "indirect tonality," about which he says that on the surface, it seems to be atonality, but, in fact, tonality is created in it by the ear singling out hidden relationships of tones. (p. 65) He goes further, and states that in two successive chordal groups, the tonic within the first group can be shifted; it can move to another note. He claims that this concept of movable tonics is the point of departure for the understanding of the phenomenon of 'pantonality.' (p. 66) He calls this a structural state in which several tonics exert their gravitational pull simultaneously. (p. 67)

These statements are very important for us, because by them, Reti is actually describing how our process of semi-modulation would work! Not only that, he is describing how our "Three Musketeers" would work together by taking turns at playing the role of I/i.

One word, however, is questionable, and that word is "several." We can hope to be able to hear two or three tonics, and that only if the keys are chosen strategically. But to expect listeners to really, honestly, truly hear, and distinguish between, more than three tonics is pushing it. In a way, he says something similar to this on the next page, where he speaks of "undefined tonality." He states that even in the music of Strauss, Mahler, Sibelius, and others, there are often sections which are decidedly tonal, although their actual key relationships cannot be determined. They float in the realm of several keys. (p. 68)

In this regard, when we consider that in our system there are 22 possible semi-modulations, in addition to the 12 original uni-tonal bi-modalities, then yes, if the changes of keys occur in rapid succession, and keys sometimes overlap each other, then it is indeed possible that within less than one minute, several different tones can claim to be the tonic note.

Some of Réti's English is difficult to understand, because it sounds like a translation from German (Serbian?), which it probably is. So he uses terminology which English writers almost never use. However, his terms "moving tonics" and "fluctuating harmonies" are actually excellent ones to describe a rapid succession of semi-modulations, or the simultaneous use of C/c and G/g and F/f, during which any one of these bi-modalities can be I/i at any time.

After all, because of the overlaps that are present in our system, C/c or F/f can be made to sound like I/i *or* IV/iv, and C/c or G/g can be made to sound like I/i *or* V/v.

Réti summarizes this segment of his discussion by saying that with phenomena such as atonal tonality, fluctuating harmonies, movable tonics, tonics of different types — a new compositional category, pantonality, is in the making. (p. 69) If so, then it is still in the making, because our system actually can be described as "pantonal."

The last few pages of Réti's book are a combination of his analysis of the musical trends of his day (the first half of the twentieth century), and his "crystal ball" predictions of where everything that he was observing was heading. After reading this, we can understand why Part Three is on "Pantonality," and not on "Polytonality."

Réti's concept of pantonality does not exclude atonality. He states that pantonality can embrace any atonal expression, and can make it a part of its own system of multiple tonalities. (p. 111) He actually envisions pantonality as a trend that parts equally from unconditional tonality and unconditional atonality, endeavouring to create something new, a third concept. He visualizes pantonality's highest and final function to be the great synthesis within the musical tendencies of the age. He says that when tonality and atonality may wondrously interpenetrate and pantonality becomes the great unifier, it may even combine all three — tonality, atonality, and itself, into one universal style of organic freedom. (p. 118)

Now there is an idea that was never mentioned in this study, because … this author never thought of it! This entire book is written from a tonal perspective *only*. But if we think about it, there is no better way to put music temporarily into neutral territory than to insert an atonal passage between modulations or semi-modulations which lay within the framework of dodecaphonic tonality. This would also be an excellent way for a composer to try to drive a future music theorist out of his mind …

CHAPTER TWENTY-THREE

"Twelve-Tone Tonality" by George Perle

Our next optional chapter is about a book by George Perle (1915–2009) whose title, Twelve-Tone Tonality, could well be the title of our study. And the title of Perle's book could easily have been "Tonality in Atonal Music," or at least aspects thereof. George Perle was one of America's greatest, and most prolific, composers of atonal music. He published this book towards the end of his life (23 years after Allen Forte's "The Structure of Atonal Music"), largely to explain the structure of many of his own compositions. One is reminded here also of Paul Hindemith's "The Craft of Musical Composition," written for the same reason.

This book is extremely difficult to digest, even if one holds a degree in mathematics. It contains 119 examples and 86 tables; you have to see it to believe it. Even though Perle is writing exclusively about atonal music, and our study is exclusively about tonal music, there are still many concepts and ideas in his book that relate to what we are doing. Only these will be discussed in this chapter.

Ironically, one of Perle's most alarming statements comes on page xiv of his Preface to the Second Edition. Here is a paraphrase of it.

The composers of diatonic music had a harmonic system, and, as a composer of 12-tone music, he wanted one, too. It was this need of his that led him to the discovery of the cyclic set as the basis of a harmonic system of twelve-tone tonality.

Now here is something for us to think about for a couple of years: A composer of atonal music went on a quest for tonality, and found it. He wanted to use all 12 tones, he wanted atonality, but he did not want 12-tone music without a harmonic system. So why did he not use all 12 tones, and use a tonal harmonic system to begin with? He never answers such questions per se, but it does come out in the wash that he became most successful when he discovered a way to incorporate his own type of tonality into his fundamentally atonal music.

Perle writes much about Alban Berg's music (especially "Lulu") and his writings. He even quotes Berg's "Master Array of the Interval Cycles" from a letter that Berg sent to Schoenberg on July 27, 1920. But, as was shown in the previous chapter, Berg's most famous tone row is "tonal atonal." On this subject, Perle tells us that out of all possible tone rows (of which there are 479,001,600), very few are inherently suitable for use as the basis for a composition. He speaks a lot of "precompositional" elements, by which he means about the same thing that we mean when we speak of careful and strategic selection of tones as raw materials to be used in a composition. His message is that what "makes or breaks" a tone row is the relationship of each tone to its two closest neighbors (cyclic dyads, cyclic chords).

Many, many chapters, which include numerous charts, tables, and examples, are devoted to elaboration on this fundamental principle. Here is a partial list of the large number of terms that Perle uses to explain it all.

Cyclic Sets, Cyclic Chords, Cyclic Keys
Cognate Sets
Adjacency Sums
Axis Notes, Axis Keys
Twelve-Tone Modes
Key of an Array, Triadic Arrays
Sum Tetrachords
Tonic Set Forms
Derived Sets
Master Modes, Master Keys, Master Arrays
Semi-Transpositions, Semi-Inversions
Transpositional and Symmetrical Equivalence
Modulation Through: 1) Tonic Chords, 2) Substitution, 3) Reinterpretation
The Three Tonalities (Tonality 0, Tonality 1, Tonality 2)

Any readers who wish to know what these terms mean will have to read Perle's book for themselves to find out; that is by no means the purpose of this chapter. We just have to keep in mind that all these terms refer to atonal music.

The main purpose of this chapter is to make analogies, and to show how and where we could have used many of these terms to describe features of our tonal dodecaphonic system. So let us look back at Example 20-11 (although we could equally well use Example 20-13). Example 20-11 is reproduced below for ease of reference.

Copy of Ex. 20-11 Venn Diagram illustrating Ex. 20-10

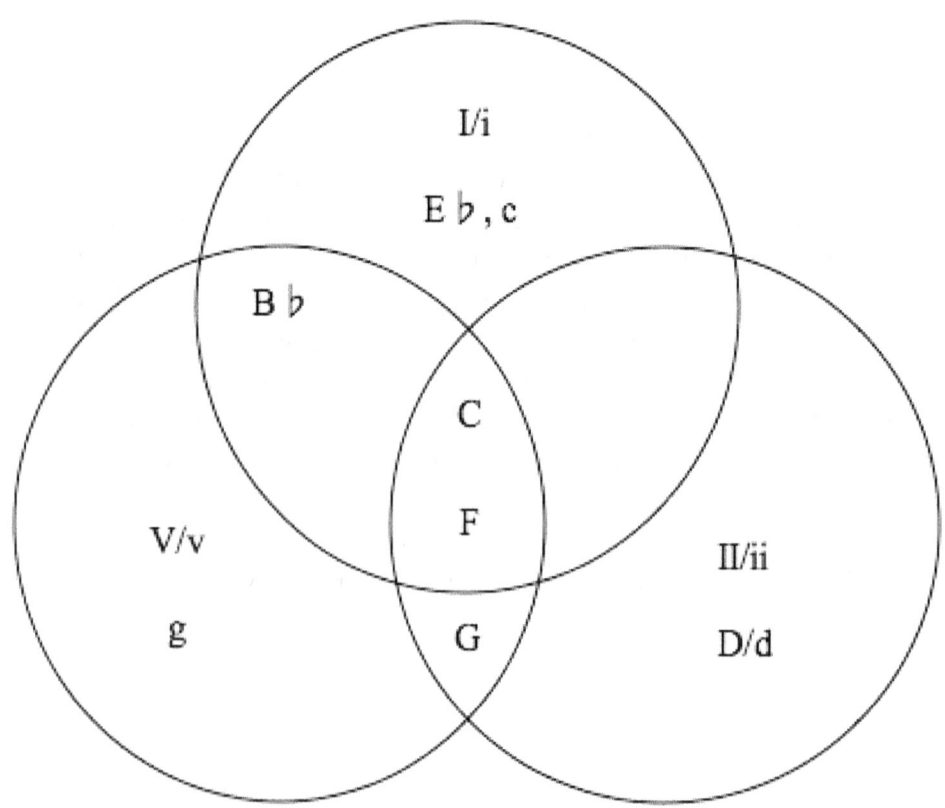

Because we use Set Theory to explain our structures, we speak in terms of sets, subsets, and intersections of sets. But in this example we could consider I/i, II/ii, and V/v to be cyclic sets, or cyclic keys, or cognate sets. We could also consider C and F to be axis keys, since they remain constant, while the other keys rotate, or alternate, around them.

Our basic nonaphonic and decaphonic scales could be considered twelve-tone modes, because, when used together, they create our basic dodecaphonic system.

Our basic dodecaphonic set comes in three forms (I/i/II/ii/V/v, I/i/IV/iv/V/v, and I/i/IV/iv/♭VII/♭vii), so these could be called tonic set forms. We have, in fact, called many of our sets "derived," especially by addition and/or subtraction. With regard to Master Keys,* in our case, we could call our Three Musketeers the Master Keys. Similarly, Perle speaks of three basic tonalities (0, 1, and 2) inherent in a tone row. We could also speak of the three bi-modalities as our three basic tonalities.

But for us, the most fascinating and most pleasant surprise is to see Perle writing about phenomena such as semi-transpositions, semi-inversions, transpositional and symmetrical equivalence, and modulations through tonic chords, substitution, or reinterpretation. He comes so close to using our term, "semi-modulation," that it was a thrill for this author to read about these terms after coining the term "semi-modulation." And the transformation of I/i/II/ii/ V/v into I/i/IV/iv/V/v or into I/i/IV/iv/♭VII/♭vii (or vice-versa) can certainly be described as modulation through reinterpretation, since a key change takes place whenever a given key is interpreted as being I or II or IV or V or ♭VII.

* * *

People generally do not like to get bogged down with terminology, and meanings and uses of terms. However, we are stuck with terms, because they are the names of concepts and ideas. One has only to look at the Latin language to see that there is a precise term in it for almost every imaginable thing. To this day, when someone gets a new idea, or even makes a new observation, he/she often coins a new term for it. For example, Nicolas Slonimsky introduced the term "pandiatonicism,"** a term that refers to the use of the diatonic scale without the limitations of functional tonality.

Now that we are near the end of our study, and have also looked briefly at the contents of books by Réti and Perle, and the terms that they use, we could come up with some terms of our own. It is better to refrain from using vague terms such as "tonal atonality" or "atonal tonality," because such terms just leave people guessing as to what is really meant by them. Instead, I propose two counterparts to the term "functional tonality."

"Multi-functional Tonality" would be a good term to use to describe our system, for obvious reasons. For one thing, we have shown how certain mediant and submediant chords are multi-functional. But most importantly, each of our Three Musketeers takes turns at playing the role of I/i, and, when he does, the other two change their functional configuration as well. On the other hand, after reading Réti's and Perle's books, we could refer to the types of tonalities that they describe as "Non-functional Tonalities."

---

*These are not the same keys that give the janitorial staff access to every room in the music building.
**See The Harvard Dictionary of Music for a more complete definition and description of "pandiatonicism."

CHAPTER TWENTY-FOUR

Composers of Bi-Modal Music and Psychology of Music

During my research for this project, I searched for a long time to find anything and everything that I could about bi-modal writing in the entire History of Music. Under "bi-modality," I never did find a thing. However, I did find "bimodalism." There is a composer by the name of Enrique Ubieta, who has developed his own method of bi-modal writing. Readers should now take a "time out" and read about bimodalism on that composer's own website, www.Ubieta.com, because that information will not be reproduced here.

All sorts of things could be said about Enrique Ubieta's bimodalism. But for us, the single most important observation to be made is that his system is based on the homophonic use of the chord that Allen Forte labels as [0, 3, 4, 7], namely root plus minor third plus major third plus perfect fifth.

On his website, composer Ubieta makes reference to the experimental works of an Italian composer by the name of Pietro Raimondi (1786–1853). He mentions that in 1849, Raimondi wrote a work entitled "Due Fughe In Una," of which "Esempio No. 4," for two mixed choruses and organ, has one chorus singing in D+, while the other sings in d-. However, not once do the D+ and d- triads sound together. So, if we use Forte's language, [0, 3, 7] and [0, 4, 7] are heard all the time, but [0, 3, 4, 7] is never heard. This, of course, means that this work is an anticipatory example of our bi-modality. We can just imagine what the score for the organ accompaniment must look like!

The point is that we have here two different composers, both of whom engage in bi-modal writing, but they do so in very different ways. Also, it is fortunate that Mr. Ubieta calls his system "bimodalism," and we call ours "bi-modality."

Ashamed and embarrassed that I had never heard of Raimondi, not to mention his experimental works, I immediately began to read more about this ingenious master of counterpoint. It turns out that Raimondi also wrote other fugues in several simultaneous keys and modes, for multiple groups of different instruments. He caused a sensation with his Triple Oratorio, a set of three oratorios to be performed first consecutively, and then together. At the time of his death, he was working on a double opera, which was also to be performed either consecutively or simultaneously.

Raimondi considered these types of works to be experimental. It is indeed unfortunate that this specific trend was never followed up by anyone else. So now, it is up to us to carry on his experiments! In fact, towards the end of the twentieth century, Raimondi's music did catch the attention of a young American scholar by the name of Jesse Rosenberg, who, in 1996, wrote his doctoral dissertation entitled "The Experimental Music of Pietro Raimondi."

If there ever is a Part Three to this project, it will very likely be about Raimondi's experimental works, and how closely they do, or do not, resemble the types of bi-modalities presented in this book. If I — or someone else — did this, we would find out which tonalities Raimondi combined (when he did so), and how his combinations compare to ours. So far, it is good to see that the one composer that we know of who practiced our type of bi-modality was a genius of counterpoint, because it was counterpoint that came to mind first and foremost during our study.

Until we study Raimondi's scores, we can only speculate on how closely his bi-modalities resemble ours. But just finding out about him is exciting news for us, because we already know that the above-mentioned example is in what we call the key of D/d; it hardly matters whether he uses 9 or 10 tones for his basic set. But it would be most interesting to learn which key combinations and which key signatures he uses in his other experimental works, and how he carries out modulations, and what we call semi-modulations (if any).

* * *

It is hardly surprising that composers would wish to combine the major and minor tonic triads in their music, in one way or another. However, this is a rather complex matter, so let us shed some light on this subject.

The major key/minor key (or major mode vs. minor mode) debate has gone on for centuries. To start, readers should see the entry in the Harvard Dictionary of Music under "Dualism, dualistic theory." There, we read that music theorists from Zarlino (1517–1590) to Riemann (1849–1919) have had one thing or another to say about this subject. Also, it seems that no matter what one scholar claims, another scholar contradicts.

Here is the problem. The major/minor issue is one that lies within the realms of music theory, and physics of music (acoustics), and psychology of music. When this type of overlap exists, the learning curve is almost always very slow, and very long. In this study, we have dealt primarily with music theory, and secondarily with musical acoustics, but not a word has yet been said from the standpoint of psychology of music.

Some 30 years ago, I was fortunate enough to study this subject, and would have loved to study it more, but no more courses in it were offered at the time. Today's music students are highly encouraged to take at least one course in this subject, as it is most fascinating, and quite unlike any other course that they may ever take. Whenever two disciplines overlap, extraordinary learning takes place. *

Anyway, here is a story that I remember on the subject of major/minor triads. Psychologists love to perform experiments. So a group of them decided to combine the root and the perfect fifth with the "average" of the major and minor thirds, hoping to reconcile the two modes once and for all. (They did it by tuning their third a quarter tone above the minor third = a quarter tone below the major third).

They were most disappointed with what they heard when playing the resulting triad. They reported that it sounded neither here nor there, neither major nor minor, just out of tune.

There is a very big difference between the nature of the arsenal of raw materials of the musician (pitches) and that of the painter (colors). This is because frequencies of sound waves do not behave in the same way as do frequencies of light waves. If a painter combines red with green, then both of these colors disappear, and yellow appears in their place — it is the "average" of red and green. And the color yellow is just as "usable" (so to speak) as is any other color, primary or not. However, if a musician wishes to "average out" the two triads containing a perfect fifth, it doesn't work. Major is major, and minor is minor; there is no in-between. To call them male and female would make just as much sense as anything.

I recently took a good, long look at the literature available today in the discipline of the Psychology of Music, and found that scholars are now studying anything and everything that connects music to the mind. One question that has puzzled many musicians/psychologists for a very long time, and still puzzles them, is: "How do we hear music?" For us, in this study, this is a very important question, one which we must address. Hundreds of pages can

---

*At one point, I wished to write my Ph. D. dissertation in one area of Psychology of Music, but was not allowed do so, because the topic had too much to do with psychology, and not enough to do with Music Theory. But today, degrees in the Psychology of Music are more common, so graduate students who are looking for a thesis or dissertation topic would do well to explore this field, because it is full of unanswered questions, and potential areas of research.

be (and have been) written on this subject, so what is presented here is only a minute fraction of everything that there is to know about this matter.

At first sight, it appears that there are only two possible answers: We hear music either vertically or horizontally (or both). That is fundamentally true. There is no doubt that the ever-present time-line reigns supreme, and this fact supports the argument that, no matter how many instruments or voices are used, we hear sounds successively, as shown in Example 24-1 below.

Ex. 24-1

| | | | | | | | | | | | | | | | | | | | | | | | | | | | | | | | | | | | | | | | | | ...

Here, the lines are, time-wise, only a fraction of a second apart. This example resembles the structure of homophonic music.

On the other hand, when we listen to polyphonic music, for example, a four-voice setting such as a typical SATB choir or a string quartet, we are inclined to argue that we hear sounds simultaneously, in layers, as shown in Example 24-2 below.

Ex. 24-2

_____...
_____...
_____...
_____...

Readers can rest assured that this debate — and often, this heated argument — could go on to infinity, and universal agreement would never be reached. Some say that it depends on the composition; others, that it depends on the listener, or else on the type of listening that takes place at any given time. Some say that our hearing alternates between the two. Some say that it varies with the nature of the texture of a composition. It seems that where there are 10 musicians, there are 11 opinions, as one of them changes his mind … Just for the record, I believe that it does depend on the specific composition, (homophonic vs. polyphonic, where applicable). But most importantly, generally speaking, I believe that successive hearing is the easy, effortless, lazy way of listening (because we do little more than follow the time-line), but to be able to hear simultaneously, in layers, requires concentration and practice, in other words, effort. Experience in ensemble performance helps a great deal, because, even if a composition is homophonic, every individual performs a horizontal melodic line.

Now let us focus on the importance of this issue in our situation. If we are to compose in bi-modality, especially in bi-tonal, tri-tonal, or polytonal bi-modality, the serious question arises: Can listeners hear two or more tonal centres at once? After studying twentieth-century History of Music, we know what happened. Composers wrote bi-tonal and polytonal music, in which, sure enough, one voice was in one key, while another was in a different key, and perhaps a third voice was in a third key. On paper, it was so, indeed. But, before long, critics and opponents blasted these composers, saying that what we hear in these compositions is not bi-tonality or polytonality, but atonality. The ear does not hear two or three tonal centres; it hears none.

So, knowing this, where do we go from here? Well, there is a solution, and we can call it "imitation to the rescue." Have any readers ever wondered why imitation has been used by composers for almost five centuries, and is still being used to this day? It is because imitation affords us with the opportunity to exploit a third dimension of music, which is neither vertical nor horizontal, but diagonal. For example, in a four-voice fugue, what we hear can be illustrated as shown in Example 24-3 on the next page.

Ex. 24-3

The diagonal dimension comes to life at the entrance points of the voices. Here, the vertical lines are, time-wise, several seconds apart, and, in the interim, we cannot help but hear horizontally, even if we are "lazy listeners!" Imitation possesses a simple, but very powerful property. It sends a clear message to the brain, which says: "Hey! Listener! You just heard this melody a few seconds ago, and now you are hearing an extremely similar melody again!"

And that is precisely the point. Except in cases of real answers in fugues, the imitating voices do not duplicate the original voice exactly, just similarly. This is just what we need in order to introduce a change of mode, and, subsequently, a semi-modulation, or bi-tonal or tri-tonal or polytonal bi-modality. Through the strategic use of imitation, we can get listeners to hear more than one tonal centre simultaneously.

This is, of course, an over-simplification, for we know that there are many other factors involved, some of which will work for us, while others will work against us. The choice of key combinations is always of paramount importance, and that is why so much of this book has been devoted to the study of key relationships and compatibility of keys.

It would not surprise me one bit if someone composed a piece of music in two extremely compatible keys (such as C/d), performed it for a group of listeners, and found that a large percentage of them could identify the two keys as X-major and (X plus a whole tone)-minor. Nor would it surprise me if someone else composed a piece in two extremely incompatible keys (such as C/e♭) and found that nobody could identify the relationship of the two tonal centres involved, no matter how well-written the composition was.

So here is a proposal to those interested in Psychology of Music experiments. Compose short pieces in various different bi-modalities, and perform them for a group of musicians. Ask them to identify the relationships of the keys involved, and record your findings. And, by all means, feel free to send me your results to:

<u>Nonaphonic_Bi-Modality@shaw.ca</u>

CHAPTER TWENTY-FIVE

Recapitulation and Coda

If we care to think of this entire project as a "Visual Sonata," then all of Part One could justifiably be called its Exposition. The two themes presented there were the standardized octatonic minor scale, and the basic nonaphonic, bi-modal scale and key, with its own original key signature. Chapters 12 and 13 (of Part Two) were a transition, and the Development took place in Chapters 14 to 21. There, we literally did develop more nonaphonic bi-modalities, and then, progressively, decaphonic, hendecaphonic, and dodecaphonic bi-modalities as well. Finally, this chapter is the Recapitulation, in which we summarize the results that were obtained in Chapters 14 to 21, and then make some concluding remarks in the Coda.

Our first noteworthy discovery was in Chapter 14, where we showed that
> **I/V/vi is equivalent to I/IV/ii.**

Next, in Chapter 17, we found a similar
> **equivalency relationship between I/V/iii and I/IV/vi.**

In Chapter 18, we briefly introduced the set
> **I, plus its tonic minor, plus its relative minor = I/i/vi.**

But the main focus of that chapter was the fundamental decaphonic, bi-modal set,
> **I/i Deca with subsets ♭III, IV, and ♭VII.**

This came about because we formed the sum of
> **i plus its tonic major plus its relative major = I/i/♭III**
with subsets IV and ♭VII.

Our "Visual Sonata" could have ended there. However, since we had seen that it was possible to create other nonaphonic bi-modalities besides the basic set I/i, it only made sense to explore the possibilities of creating other decaphonic bi-modalities besides the basic I/i Deca.

The first thing that we discovered in Chapter 18 was that if we combine the two sets of Chapter 17, we get a ten-tone, but an eleven-note set, which we called:
> **The "Mega-Set" = I/i/vi/♭III**

While "mega-set" is a good name for it, we could have called this set the "Hot Water Set," because if we place vi and ♭III in close proximity of each other, we are asking for trouble. (Just recall the chromatic clashes of SATs involved).

The most delightful set of this chapter was
> **I/IV/iv, which is equivalent to I/i/V = "Reversible Coat" Set.**

In addition, we discovered that
> **I/ii/IV leads directly to I/vi/IV/ii, and indirectly to I/vi/V/iii.**

These two sets were the winners of our Deca Set Beauty Contest. The whole goal here was to balance the modes equally.

In Chapter 18, we also had our first encounter with the lopsided set
> **I/vii/II/v,** which can be doctored into **the "Jigsaw Puzzle" Set** of Chapter 20.

Our "crazy" Chapter 19 turned out to be not so crazy, after all. We found the set
> **I/i/V/vi, consisting of 10 tones plus one enharmonic.**

While trying other such combinations, we hit the jackpot when we discovered the
> **Bingo Set = I/i/V/iii.**

Our first truly hendecaphonic set was
> **I/i/IV/ii.**

In these three cases, the goal was, again, to balance the modes equally. Also, these sets make wonderful companions for the winners of our Deca Beauty Contest.

When we looked back to the bi-modality
> **I/♭vii and its equivalent II/i,**

we found that, together with their subsets, these lead to
> **the equivalent sets I/IV/♭VII/♭vii and I/i/II/V and I/IV/iv/V.**

Finally, in that chapter, we developed our
> **Fundamental Double-Deca sets I/i/IV/iv and I/i/V/v.**

In Chapter 20, we encountered the twelve-tone set which occupies the 12 o'clock plus 11 o'clock plus 1 o'clock positions on the traditional quintcircle:
> **I/vi/IV/ii/V/iii.**

We also formulated the set that is unlike any other, because it contains a ♭, a ♮, and a # (when C = I),
> **the "Jigsaw Puzzle" Set, I/i/II/vii/V,**

in which the member keys complement each other, because each one contributes tones that the other two do not have. This turned out to be a rare workable set which combines keys whose roots lay a semitone apart, as such sets are very difficult to find.

Finally, we reached the fortissimo climax of our study by defining the Triple-Deca (or Triple-Nona)
> **equivalent sets I/i/II/ii/V/v and I/i/IV/iv/V/v and I/i/IV/iv/♭VII/♭vii.**

We determined that this is the world's best Dodecaphonic Tonal System, and showed that it can be reduced to
> **I/i/II/ii or IV/iv/V/v or I/i/♭VII/♭vii.**

In Chapter 21, we observed that the Triple-Deca sets have the characteristic of being "one for all and all for one," so we dubbed them "The Three Musketeers."

The complete list of our so-called "good" sets appears in Example 25-1 below.

Ex. 25-1 Complete List of Good Sets

I/V/vi ~ I/IV/ii

I/V/iii ~ I/IV/vi

I/i/vi and I/i Deca = I/i/♭III with subsets IV and ♭VII

I/i/vi/♭III (Mega-Set)

I/IV/iv ~ I/i/V (Reversible Coat)

I/ii/IV

I/vi/IV/ii

I/vi/V/iii

I/vii/II/V

I/i/V/vi

I/i/V/iii (Bingo)

I/i/IV/ii

I/♭vii ~ II/i leads to: I/IV/♭VII/♭vii ~ I/i/II/V ~ I/IV/iv/V

I/i/IV/iv ~ I/i/V/v (Double-Deca)

I/vi/IV/ii/V/iii

I/i/vii with subsets II and V (Jigsaw Puzzle)

I/i/II/ii/V/v ~ I/i/IV/iv/V/v ~ I/i/IV/iv/♭VII/♭vii (Triple-Deca), which can be reduced to: I/i/II/ii ~ IV/iv/V/v ~ I/i/♭VII/♭vii

Readers should take a good, long look at Example 25-1, because it comprises a full summary of what we call "good" sets. (Time out).

Let us look together at something that you, the reader, may not have considered, and that is, which keys are not present in our list of "good" sets. There are 14 keys present, but the following 10 are absent: ♭II, ♭ii, ♭iii, III,

♭V, ♭v, ♭VI, ♭vi, VI, and VII. For various reasons that were explained throughout this book, it is not surprising that ♭II, ♭ii, ♭iii, ♭V, ♭v, ♭vi, VI, and VII are missing. However, we should look at the remaining two keys (III and ♭VI). Very many pages have already been devoted to Mediants and Submediants. For these two keys, we need to recall that we must regard them not as they relate to I or to i, but to I/i. Now, we go back to our charts, and look up the intensity of the chromatic clashes of SATs involved between III and i (and its relative major, ♭III) and then between ♭VI and I (and its relative minor, vi), and we have our answer.

When describing sets, the adjective "good" is actually not a good one, because it is much too vague. Looking at the keys that are present (and their combinations), and those that are absent, helps us somewhat. But we have, in fact, done much more than that. In Part One, we studied tones and chords in common between keys, and we assigned proximity points for all possible key combinations. In Part Two, we devoted an entire chapter to Musical Acoustics, and studied how tones and keys relate to each other from that standpoint. Then we devoted another chapter to Compatibility of Keys, and we introduced a type of system of measurement of the degree of their compatibility, performed through calculations and comparisons of chromatic clashes of SATs. This is a new concept, and it could take a while to sink in, so, as the saying goes, "not to worry." Once again, we do not think of these as demerit points, unless their total is high. If their total is very low, then the keys are not compatible, either (although, in bi-modalities, we rarely encounter that problem). *The totals are <u>relative</u>, and should always be so regarded. They also enable us to predict in advance how dissonant certain key combinations will sound, as compared to other combinations of keys.* Perhaps this fact was not emphasized enough in that chapter.

"Good" sets are those that have desirable characteristics, of which there are several. The component keys complement each other; they are not too similar, and not too dissimilar. They do not fight each other for supremacy, and they do not get in each other's way. Ideally, the modes are equally balanced, but they do not have to be. For example, I/i/V should be regarded as I/i with its dominant, so I/i/V is not really inferior to the set I/i/V/v. When you use a closed set (one having no subsets), you can't lose! When a set has an automatic (default) subset, that you find is an undesirable, uninvited guest, then your only way out is to suppress the undesirable set, that is, avoid using it. Throughout this study, we have seen that many sets contain more major keys than minor keys, and that the opposite never happens. So if a set contains one more major key than minor key, we must still consider it to be a good set; otherwise, we would end up "set-challenged"!

In the chapter on Rotating Quintcircles and Semi-Modulations, we formulated the family of 21 closely related bi-modalities and, by the same token, we identified the semi-modulations and modulations that are closely related to I/i. This formed a point of departure for exploration of larger, more complex, sets.

From the standpoint of harmony, in Part One, we discussed the European System of Harmonic Analysis, as well as Mediants, Submediants, and Functionality, and The Fundamental Theory of Harmony, which applies universally, in any tonal system, including our Dodecaphonic Tonality. All the way along, we kept building our vocabulary, or library, of chords, and kept them classified in our Houses of Bi-Modalities, beginning with Nonaphonic and Decaphonic, moving on to Hendecaphonic, and ending with Dodecaphonic, and the House of "The Three Musketeers."

Finally, the culminating point of our study was to define the best Dodecaphonic Tonal set possible. All the way along, we had examined dozens and dozens of possible 9-, 10-, 11-, and 12-tone sets, and it was this progressive, systematic approach which led us to the logical, and therefore inevitable, conclusion that it is the Triple-Deca, or Triple-Nona, Bi-Modal set that surpasses all others as the best model of Dodecaphonic Tonality.

Coda

Part One of this project was originally written in 2007, using the Deca set, and was entitled "Decaphonic Bi-Modality." However, that system was not uni-tonal, and the author soon discovered that it could be made so by subtracting one tone, and using the basic nonatonic set. That is how the basic system of Uni-Tonal Nonaphonic Bi-Modality was born. This original, modest objective, which was merely to define and create a basic bi-modal key, had already been accomplished.

At the same time, though, the Deca system was already in existence, so Part Two was already taking shape. Readers know at this point what evolved since then. The overall title "Dodecaphonic Tonality" is appropriate for Parts One and Two together, because, of all things, most readers will probably be more interested in that than in anything else. However, everything that precedes it should not be regarded merely as anticipatory. You can have a happy life using only 9-tone, or 10-tone, or 11-tone sets. Furthermore, since the Dodecaphonic Tonal system is rather complex, some readers may not take to it readily. To those readers I say: Use Part One only at first. **Part One can stand alone.** After that, you may move on to using 10-, 11-, and 12-note sets at your own pace.

Here is the overall picture. In traditional tonality, before starting to compose, you have only two choices to make (excluding the meter). You decide on the mode (major or minor), and you determine the tonal centre by picking one of the 12 available keys.

Now, in our system, more pre-compositional choices must be made, because the basic diatonic system is expanded; very much expanded. Ironically, in most cases, you do not have to choose the number of tones that you will use, because that decision will automatically be made for you, and because the cardinality of your set is not really that important, as compared to other factors. You do have to put some thought into deciding how many tonal centres you wish to have. We know that the basic nonaphonic set I/i has only one tonal centre. And looking at Example 25-1, we can see that the number of tonal centres can be as high as six (in the set I/vi/IV/ii/V/iii). When you are first starting out, if you want to make your work easier, then choose a closed set, that is, one without subsets. For example, use I/i Nona before trying I/i Deca. Next time, you might choose a set with subsets, but take care not to use the subsets in your composition. Later on, you can choose a set that contains subsets, and use the subsets as well. In any event, you must always be aware of the existence of all subsets. Otherwise, your music could end up sounding as if it was written in a key that is one of the subsets, and you will wonder what is going on.

How dissonant do you want your piece to sound? With regard to this, read through the chapter on Compatibility of Keys, examine the tables which show the clash intensity ratings for various key combinations, and choose your keys according to your wishes.

After you have chosen your set, decide which of the 12 tonal centres will be equal to I. Then, go to the chapter that covers your chosen set, where you will find the cardinality of your set, its key signature, as well as the triads and seventh chords that are diatonic in that set. And away you go!

One more point: Even if your set contains five or six tonal centres, that is *not* a scary thing. Chances are that you might never use all of the keys at once, but you will go through all of them, using a chain of semi-modulations.

With regard to Dodecaphonic Tonality itself, I would like to stress that, had I initially set out to create a 12-tone tonal system, I would have never found the ultimate Triple-Deca set! It had to happen progressively, one step at a time, just as it did. I would have never proposed combining two major keys whose roots lay a semitone apart (for example, C+ plus B+). Nor would I have suggested combining three consecutive stations on the traditional quintcircle (for example I/vi/IV/ii/V/iii), because I cannot imagine composers wanting to use six tonal centres all at once. However, if one employs the technique of semi-modulation, then this becomes a real, viable possibility, by using one bi-modality at a time.

The main purpose of building the library of chords, compiled and classified by functions in the Houses, was to keep a written record of how many more, and which, additional triads and seventh chords are gained when we add one more tone to a previously defined set. But along the way, we got a pleasant surprise, when a truly new, previously undefined, chord appeared, which we dubbed the "Polish Sixth." (See Example 19-15). The derivation of this chord was shown to be very logical, indeed.

Those who have read Hindemith's "The Craft of Musical Composition" will know that his six chord groups are quite different from the classifications that make up our Houses. Three of his groups contain chords without tritones, and three are comprised of chords with tritones.

I fully realize that some composers do not care about functions of chords, and just compose without thinking about functions much, if at all (example C. H. Kitson). That is fine, because such composers are either very experienced, or they instinctively write correct progressions all the time, just as some pianists can instinctively play "anything" by ear, without even being able to read music. However, as music theorists, one of the things that we do is we analyze the structure of music, and explain it. That is a large part of our job. Similarly, conductors must do score study, because that is a large part of their job, and we help them to do their work by doing ours.

It is understood that we have Allen Forte to thank for showing us how to use set theory in analyzing the structure of music. Those readers who have read Forte's book (or George Perle's book, for that matter) will realize that the way we use set theory to explain our *tonal* dodecaphonic system must necessarily be different from the way that set theory is used to explain *atonal* music. With regard to this, one important point was perhaps not emphasized enough throughout this book. It was **never** stated, or even implied, that if you use a 9-, 10-, or 11-tone set, you are not allowed to use any of the remaining tones or enharmonics. I truly hope that this statement does not come as a surprise to anybody, because to impose such a condition would make no more sense than to state that if you write in C+, you are not allowed to use any sharps or flats.

There is a quote by Paul Hindemith which reads as follows: "There are only twelve tones. You must treat them carefully." Indeed, we must. In the background to this study lays the question: "How have we treated our twelve tones over the centuries?" Well, to recap, see Example 12-1 (of Part Two). But, in addition, another question haunts us: "How have we *not* treated our twelve tones over the centuries? And one answer is that we have never before defined or constructed specific 9-, 10-, 11-, and 12-tone *tonal* systems, with their own unique scales and key signatures. In this study, we have done so.

Once again, I would like to encourage everyone who is teaching or taking courses in historical musicology or ethnomusicology: From now on, devote at least 5% of your course time to pondering over what did *not* happen in history. You might be surprised at what you think up, if you set your mind to it.

When I say this, I am not thinking of some minor, trivial non-events, or about guesswork about anything at random. Rather, I am thinking about major events that could have, or would have, had a major impact on the direction that the evolution of music was to take. For example, what would have happened if Schoenberg, or some of his followers, would have decided to write twelve-tone *tonal* music instead? Would they have invented only blatantly tonal tone rows, and used them in tonal ways, melodically, harmonically, or contrapuntally? This *is* something to think about.

As musicians and scholars of music, we should be telling the world — literally — that the 24-key major-minor system is one of man's most ingenious creations, ranking right up there with, for example, calculus and chess. In all three cases, there seems to be no limit to what can be done using the particular invention. One of the purposes of this book is to show what more can be done with our tonal system that has not yet been done. And I am absolutely certain that there remains still more to be discovered, and here is one reason why.

Let us look back at Example 18-2, reproduced below for ease of reference.

Copy of Ex. 18-2 Comparison of eight Deca sets

We see that of the eight Deca sets shown there, in six cases, the excluded tones lay a perfect fifth apart. However, in set 3, and in its counterpart, set 14, the excluded tones lay a minor third apart. We called these two our "Reversible Coat" sets, which makes them well-named. But I still cannot explain completely why their excluded tones lay a minor third apart, and why no other such sets were found. This is a mystery to me. To me, these two sets just do not look much different from the other Deca sets, although they evidently are. So if any reader ever figures out how we can explain this exception, please let me know (at the e-mail address given at the end of this chapter), and I will surely think of a valuable prize to give you. I would just love to see an article entitled: "Krush's 'Reversible Coat' Sets Explained!"

Readers have probably noticed that, in this book, there is almost a total lack of exercises in composition, so I would like to explain briefly why this is the case. To begin with, this is not really a textbook; rather, it is an exposé of a bi-modal system, through which dodecaphonic tonality can be achieved. But besides that, it is because of my background. My primary areas of specialization are music theory, music theory, and music theory (in that order)! My secondary areas are piano, organ, mathematics, and historical musicology, but not composition per se. So I am quite certain that professors or students of composition can easily dream up better compositional exercises, using my system, than I can myself!

Instead of compositional exercises, I have included some of what I know best, namely the odd harmony lesson that I have not seen in any textbook. One example of this is my pair of "magic" triangles of harmonic progressions, shown in Example 5-7 (of Part One). And now, here is one final harmony lesson to my readers.

Although most musicians are aware that in music, a healthy balance between unity and variety is of the utmost importance, this point is not emphasized enough, or strongly enough. Let us take, for example, a typical 16-bar melody of the form A-A-B-A, where the identical melody appears three times. The last thing that one should do is to harmonize it in exactly the same way all three times, yet that is exactly what many people do! (They make the organist, or orchestrator, or arranger, do the work by changing something the second and third time). My idea of an exercise in harmony is to harmonize the same melody in four or five different ways.

Our bi-modal system is most conducive to achievement of maintenance of unity and variety. I honestly hope that nobody ever yields to the above-mentioned temptation of identical repetition. You have two thirds, two sixths, and two sevenths at your fingertips, so … alternate them, and use them all, please!

Now let us briefly consider the issue of people not having a steady flow of genuine compositional ideas. This truly is a serious problem for many. It has been said that virtually any sound can be considered to be music, or at least a raw material for music. This statement has been bothering me ever since I first read it some 40 years ago. Even if it is true, do you really want to hear somebody's "Concerto for Nose and Kleenex?" I think that it is most shameful for our beloved profession that people have done things such as tune radios to different stations, play them simultaneously, and present the result as a musical composition. Any moron can do that. To me, it just means that people who do things like that have either run out of decent musical ideas, or never had any in the first place. If you do that, then you would be farther ahead producing a telephone with ring tones that play "When I'm Calling You"…

Be that as it may, in an attempt to please those who are looking for something from that category, there is some "augenmusik," just for you, on the next page.

* * *

216 • *Dodecaphonic Tonality*

Ex. 25-2

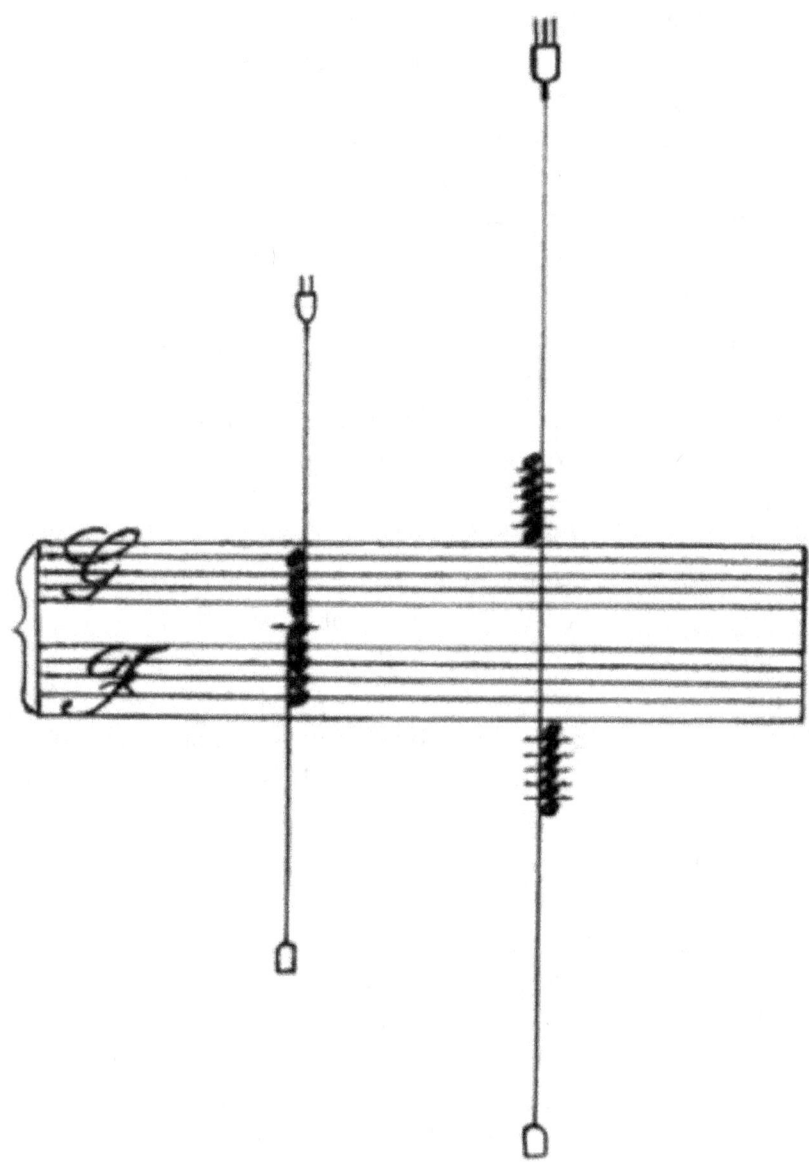

These of course are extension chords, the former, indoor, and the latter, outdoor.

Béla Bartók stated that composition cannot be taught. In one way, it is a shame that he said that, because, not only does music history provide much evidence to the contrary, but hundreds of contemporary professors of composition, and their successful students, are living proof that this statement is not true. But in another way, if we don't just dismiss his claim as false, then we are inspired to do self-study of composition, and this is a most desirable thing. In self-study, teaching and learning become one and the same activity, because the teacher is also the student. The system outlined in this book can either be taught formally or used for self-study. Either way, a blueprint is provided, and thereby, I truly hope that seeds which will grow into authentic musical ideas have been sown.

When I was about ten years old, for some reason, I wanted to hear what "God Save the Queen" would sound like in the minor mode. That was my very first fake composition. Today, of course, I play it in X/x bi-modal. (Neither version sounds too bad; try playing it). I bring this up because it is exactly what I intend to do with this system, and suggest that readers do as well. In ordinary English (or another language), you learn to write by reading, and by reading a lot. The same holds true in musical composition. Mozart claimed that nobody else studied the works of the great masters more than he did. So we too can do the same. We can study the experimental music of Raimondi in detail. But even before that, we can revive the Neo-Baroque spirit. We can take, for example, the Two- and Three-Part Inventions of J. S. Bach, and do some fake composing by re-writing them in X/x bi-modal, just to get practice, and to hear how they sound. Some will sound just fine; others will not. As soon as you have figured out what works, and what does not, go ahead and try writing an original, real composition of your own, no matter what your age, and no matter if you have never tried composing before. Eventually, perhaps we can collectively compose 12 Preludes and Fugues in the 12 bi-modal keys, and call that "The Extremely Well-Tempered Clavier." Those who wish to do so are invited to e-mail their compositions to me at: Nonaphonic_Bi-Modality@shaw.ca

For the final cadence of this Visual Sonata, I leave readers with a mission:

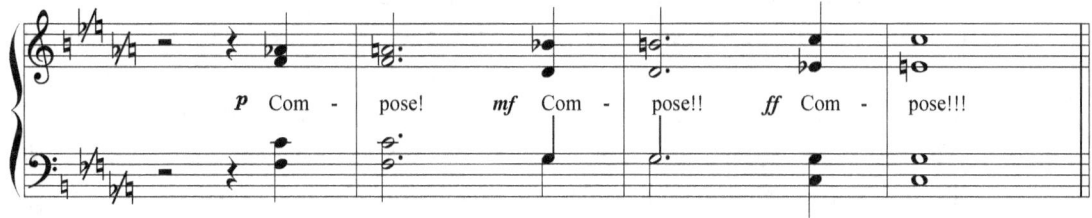

Surrey, British Columbia, Canada,
January 1, 2013

APPENDIX ONE

Theme and Variations — An exercise in Dodecaphonic Tonality

To begin, let us look back at the first page of Appendix One of Part One, reproduced here.

> **Appendix One: Theme and Variations — An Exercise in Nonaphonic Bi-Modality**
>
> The Nonaphonic Bi-modal system was dreamed up fairly recently, on August 27, 2007 (at 4:00 a.m., Pacific time, to be exact!), so not too much music has yet been written using it. But now that we have worked our way through eleven chapters of text, we should have some fun, and compose a nonaphonic, bi-modal piece of music together. The "Theme and Variations" form is a good one to choose for our first composition, because it is an ideal one for combining unity with variety, and that is just what we need here.
>
> The key for this exercise is G+/g-, and the theme consists of six notes: The B-A-C-H notes (b-flat, a, c, and b-natural) plus g as the tonic and f# as its leading note, which altogether comprise a bi-modal set. There are plenty of thirds, but no sixths. Since the predominant features of the nonatonic scale are the two thirds and the two sixths, for Variation One (starting in measure 10), we can introduce the two sixths by transposing the theme into the Subdominant. This works out perfectly, because the thirds of the Subdominant are the sixths of the Tonic. We can employ two-voice counterpoint, because this theme is most conducive to imitation. (The f can be sharp or natural). For Variation Two (starting in measure 17), we can combine the theme with Variation One, and add a third voice in Renaissance fauxbourdon style. The theme, plus the first two variations, are given below.
>
> A countless number of further variations can be written. Readers can feel free to try writing a few of their own. The primary goal, of course, is to make everything sound bi-modal. Persons who wish to do so are invited to send their variations by e-mail to the author at:
>
> Nonaphonic_Bi-Modality@shaw.ca

We began in G/g, used it, and C/c, and stopped on the downbeat of measure 24. Up to that point, it was decaphonic, with no c# or g#. Now, we continue on, and use, in addition, F/f and D/d. F/f is used in measures 25 to 32. Measures 33 to 48 are in D/d. However, from measures 42 to 49, the alto remains in D/d, but the tenor is in G/g. This, of course, illustrates a type of semi-modulation. The score appears on the pages that follow.

Clearly, this is a very simple, elementary example, and is only the beginning of the piece. It sounds bimodal, alright, and a bit like a chorale prelude, sounding better on organ than on piano. It also sounds extremely conservative, and very consonant. However, readers can build on this, increase the texture by adding more and more (and more) voices, and employ more bi-modalities and more semi-modulations. In the process, the dissonance level can rise.

There is practically no limit to what you can do with this. Have fun!

Theme and Variations

Theme and Variations — page two

APPENDIX TWO

List of Examples and Charts in Part Two

EX. 12-1	Time line of the history of music theory		88
EX. 13-1	All a's on the piano and their corresponding Hz		90
EX. 13-2	Frequency ratios in the equal-tempered chromatic scale		91
EX. 13-3	Frequency ratios in the just chromatic scale		92
EX. 13-4	Intervals in order form most consonant to most dissonant		92
EX. 13-5	Comparison of frequency ratios in scales		93
EX. 13-6	The square root of 2		94
EX. 13-7	The vertical tritone		94
EX. 13-8	Cardinalities of various sets		95
EX. 14-1	Rotating quintcircles; majors and octatonic minors		98
EX. 14-2	Semi-modulations of the form I/x where C+ = I		99
EX. 14-3	Semi-modulations of the form X/i where c- = i		100
EX. 14-4	Semi-modulations and modulations closely related to I/i where C/c = I/i		101
EX. 14-5	Family of bi-modalities closely related to I/i		102
EX. 14-6	Blueprint of a series of semi-modulations		102
EX. 14-7	Two nonatonic sets, I/vi and I/ii		103
EX. 14-8	Interchangeability of I/V/vi and I/IV/ii		104
EX. 14-9	Three decatonic sets, I/v, I/iii, and I/iv		104
EX. 14-10	Sets I/vii and I/♭iii (C+ = I)		105
EX. 14-11	Set I/♭vi (C+ = I)		106
EX. 14-12	Set I/#i (C+ = I)		106
EX. 14-13	Set I/#iv (C+ = I)		106
EX. 14-14	Five corresponding closely related bi-modalities of the form X/i		107
EX. 15-1	Order of proximity of keys		108
Ex. 15-2	Tones in common between C/c and the other 11 uni-tonal bi-modalities		109
EX. 15-3	The 22 possible bi-modalities resulting from semi-modulations		109
CHART 15-1	Chromatic clashes of SATs and their intensities		110
CHART 15-2	Chromatic clashes of SATs and their intensities for the 22 possible bi-modalities		112-114
CHART 15-3	Chart 15-2 re-written in ascending order		115
CHART 15-4	Chromatic clashes of SATs in pairings of two major keys or two minor keys		117-119
CHART 15-5	Compatibility of keys comparison chart		121

EX. 16-1	Common tones and chromatic clashes of SATs in nonatonic, tri-tonal sets		123-124
EX. 16-2	Triads and seventh chords in I/V/vi and I/V/iii		124-125
EX. 16-3	Diagram of black-key notes numbered		126
EX. 16-4	40 cases of pairs of black-key notes added to C+		127
EX. 16-5	Key signatures for five nonaphonic, bi-modal systems		128
EX. 17-1	I/i/vi scale		129
EX. 17-2	E+ and f- chords		129
EX. 17-3	Linear relationship of vi ← I → i		130
EX. 17-4	Triads and seventh chords containing g#		130
EX. 17-5	Diminished triad and seventh chord		130
EX. 17-6	Key signatures for C/c/a and A/a/f#		130
EX. 17-7	The C/c Deca scale		131
EX. 17-8	I/i Deca illustrated as two overlapping hexachords		131
EX. 17-9	Tones 1, 3, 5, 7, 9 of C/c Deca (pentatonic)		132
EX. 17-10	Tones 2, 4, 6, 8, 10 of C/c Deca (pentatonic)		132
EX. 17-11	I/i Deca in 2/4, 3/4, 4/4, and 5/4 meters		133
EX. 17-12	Harmonic derivation of the I/i Deca set		133
EX. 17-13	Key signature for C/c/E♭ Deca		134
EX. 17-14	Hypothetical key signature for C/c/F/B♭/E♭		134
EX. 17-15	Key signature for C/c Deca, showing excluded tones		134
EX. 17-16	Key signatures for all 12 uni-tonal Deca keys, showing excluded tones		135
EX. 17-17	Scales of 14 uni-tonal Deca keys		136-137
EX. 17-18	Triads contained in C/c Deca		138
EX. 17-19	Seventh chords contained in C/c Deca		139
EX. 17-20	Eleven chords of C/c Deca containing the note b-flat		140
EX. 17-21	House of Decaphonic Bi-Modality		141
EX. 17-22	Bi-functional and tri-functional chords		142
EX. 17-23	Decaphonic quintcircle with 6 "secret tunnels"		143
EX. 17-24	Decaphonic quintcircle with 36 "secret tunnels"		144
EX. 18-1	Cardinalities of sets resulting from 22 semi-modulations		146-147
EX. 18-2	Deca scales of C/f, C/g, C/b, C/f#, G/c, F/c, D♭/c, G♭/c, indicating excluded tones		148
EX. 18-3	80 cases of triples of black-key notes added to C+		150-151
EX. 18-4	Summary of sets belonging to category (2)		152
EX. 18-5	Summary of sets belonging to category (1)		153
EX. 18-6	Clash Intensities of SATs in Category (1) Sets		153
EX. 19-1	Scale of F/f/C/d		155
EX. 19-2	Scale of G/g/e/B♭		156
EX. 19-3	Scale of B♭/e with subsets G/g		156
EX. 19-4	Linear relationship of vi ← I ←→ i → ♭III		156
EX. 19-5	The scale of C/b♭		157

EX. 19-6	The 11-note sets {c, c#, d, eb, e, f, g, ab, a bb, b} and {c, db, d, eb, e, f, g, ab, a, bb, b}	157
EX. 19-7	The 11-note set {c, d, eb, e, f, f#, g, ab, a, bb, b}	158
EX. 19-8	The 11-note sets {c, db, d, eb, e, f, f#, g, ab, a, b} and {c, c#, d, eb, e, f, f#, g, ab, a, b} and {c, c#, d, eb, e, f, f#, g, g# = ab, a, b}	158
EX. 19-9	The 11-note sets {c, c#, d, e, f, f#, g, g#, a, a#, b} and {c, c#, d, e, f, f#, g, g#, a, bb, b}	159
EX. 19-10	Six different 11-note sets	159
EX. 19-11	Chromatic clashes of SATs in six 11-note sets	161
EX. 19-12	Key signatures for all 12 Double-Deca keys	162
EX. 19-13	List of triads and seventh chords containing f#	163
EX. 19-14	Six triads containing f# and their analysis	163
EX. 19-15	Twelve seventh chords containing f# and their analysis	164
EX. 19-16	House of Double-Decaphonic Bi-Modality	165
EX. 19-17	Double-Decaphonic quintcircle	167
EX. 20-1	Illustration of jigsaw puzzle	170
EX. 20-2	Chain of semi-modulations in I/i/II/vii/V	170
EX. 20-3	Subsets contained in C/B, C/Db, c/b, and c/c#	171
EX. 20-4	32 possible dodecaphonic sets	172
EX. 20-5	Six dodecaphonic sets of the form I/bII	173
EX. 20-6	Sets 4), 13), and 21) from Ex. 20-4	173
EX. 20-7	Sets 2), 11), 16), and 24) from Ex. 20-4	174
EX. 20-8	Sets 10), 17), 23), and 31) from Ex. 20-4	174
EX. 20-9	Sets 15), 18), 20), 26) from Ex. 20-4	174
EX. 20-10	Set I/i/V/v plus the note c#	175
EX. 20-11	Venn Diagram illustrating C/c/D/d/G/g	176
EX. 20-12	Set I/i/V/v plus the note db	176
EX. 20-13	Venn Diagram illustrating C/c/F/f/G/g	177
EX. 20-14	List of triads and seventh chords including c#	178
EX. 20-15	List of triads and seventh chords including db	178
EX. 20-16	Ten triads containing db and their analysis	179
EX. 20-17	Twenty seventh chords containing db and their Analysis	179
EX. 20-18	House of Dodecaphonic Bi-Modality	181
EX. 20-19	Two Dodecaphonic, Bi-Modal Scales	182
EX. 20-20	List of 12 Triple-Deca sets and their accidentals	183
EX. 20-21	Key signatures for all 12 dodecaphonic bi-modalities	184
EX. 20-22	Dodecaphonic Quintcircle	185
CHART 20-1	Chromatic clashes of SATs in I/i/II/vii/V	186
CHART 20-2	Chromatic clashes of SATs in I/vi/IV/ii/V/iii	187
CHART 20-3	Chromatic clashes of SATs in Triple-Deca sets	188
EX. 20-23	Summary or results shown in Chapter 20 Charts	189
EX. 21-1	Venn Diagram illustrating F/f/G/g/C/c	191

EX. 21-2	Venn Diagram illustrating G/g/C/c/F/f	192
CHART 21-1	18 triads in C = I, G = I, and F = I	193
CHART 21-2	Functions of all chords found in Chart 21-1	194
EX. 21-3	Venn Diagram illustrating C/c/D/d/F/f/G/g/B♭/b♭	195
EX. 22-1	Tone row of Berg's Violin Concerto	198
EX. 22-2	Tone row of Berg's Violin Concerto re-written, using enharmonics	199
EX. 24-1	Illustration of vertical hearing	206
EX. 24-2	Illustration of horizontal hearing	206
EX. 24-3	Illustration of diagonal hearing	207
EX. 25-1	Complete List of Good Sets	210
EX. 25-2	Extension Chords	216

APPENDIX THREE

References Cited

Chapter Thirteen: Harvard Dictionary of Music, Tone: A Study in Musical Acoustics, Second Edition, by Siegmund Levarie and Ernst Levy, Kent State University Press, 1968, p. 201.

The Structure of Atonal Music, by Allen Forte, New Haven: Yale University Press, 1973.

Chapter Twenty-two: Tonality, Atonality, Pantonality, by Rudolph Réti, Greenwood Press, Westport, CT, USA, 1958, reprinted 1978.

Chapter Twenty-three: Twelve-Tone Tonality by George Perle, The Regents of the University of California, University of California Press, Berkeley and Los Angeles, California; London, England, 1996.Harvard Dictionary of Music

Chapter Twenty-four: Wikipedia: Pietro Raimondi, Harvard Dictionary of Music

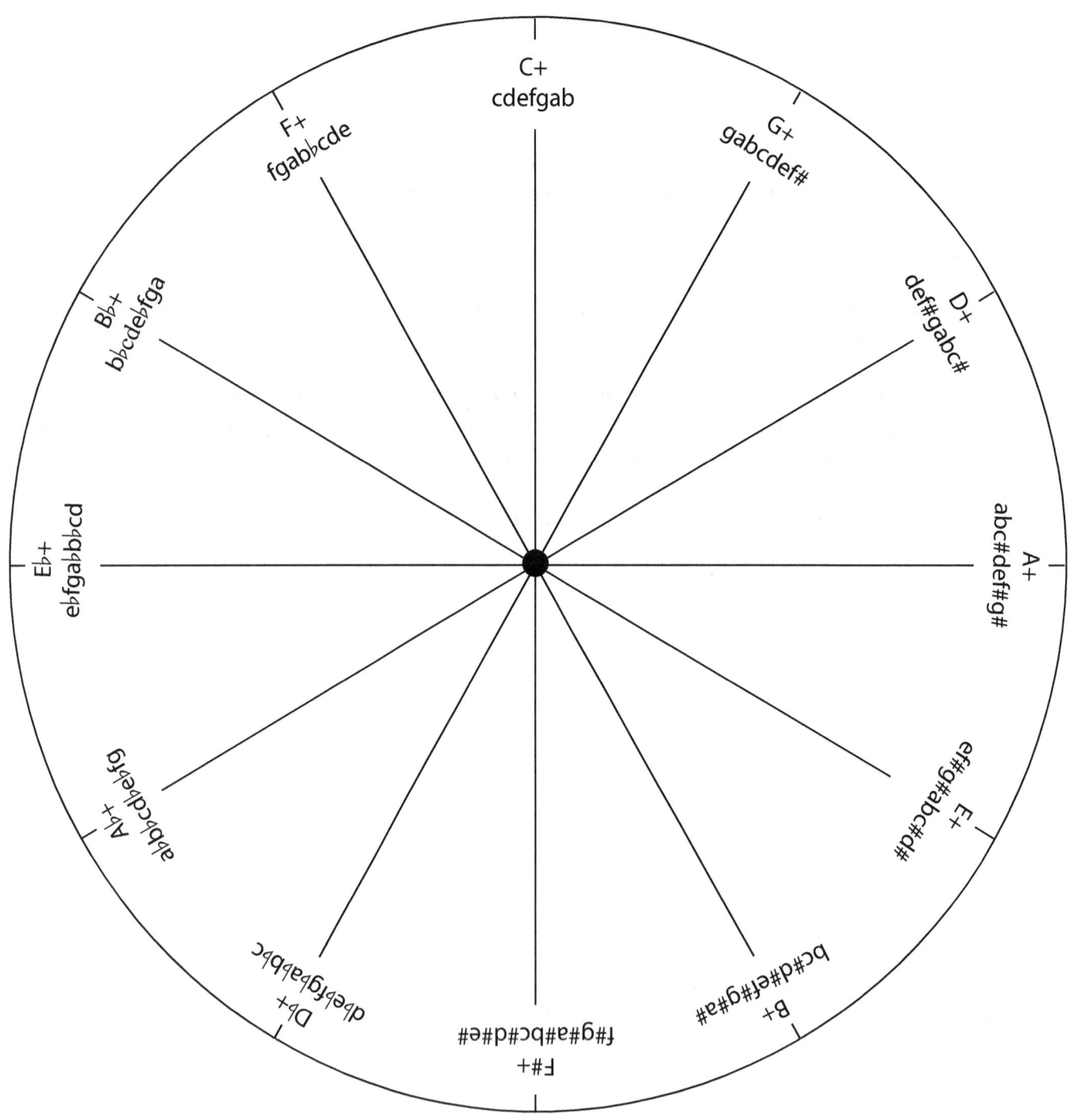

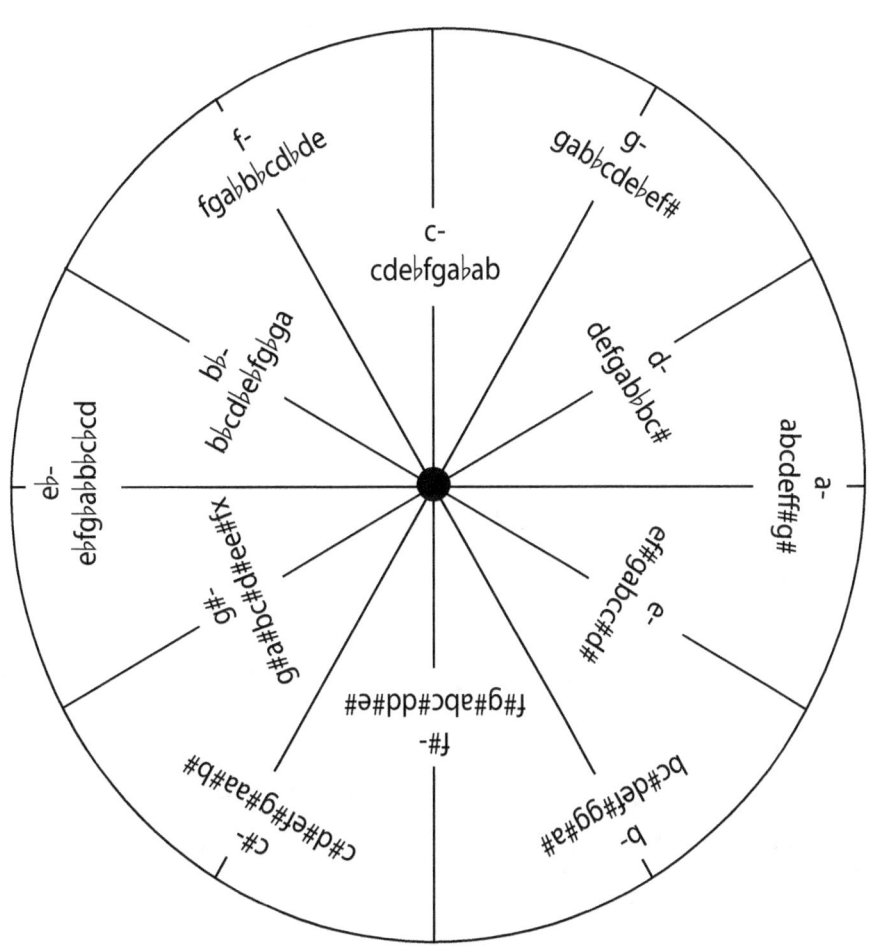

www.ingramcontent.com/pod-product-compliance
Lightning Source LLC
Chambersburg PA
CBHW051403070526
44584CB00023B/3275